P9-AQQ-873

The Long Afterlife
of Nikkei Wartime Incarceration

ASIAN AMERICA
A series edited by Gordon H. Chang

The increasing size and diversity of the Asian American population, its growing significance in American society and culture, and the expanded appreciation, both popular and scholarly, of the importance of Asian Americans in the country's present and past—all these developments have converged to stimulate wide interest in scholarly work on topics related to the Asian American experience. The general recognition of the pivotal role that race and ethnicity have played in American life, and in relations between the United States and other countries, has also fostered the heightened attention.

Although Asian Americans were a subject of serious inquiry in the late nineteenth and early twentieth centuries, they were subsequently ignored by the mainstream scholarly community for several decades. In recent years, however, this neglect has ended, with an increasing number of writers examining a good many aspects of Asian American life and culture. Moreover, many students of American society are recognizing that the study of issues related to Asian America speak to, and may be essential for, many current discussions on the part of the informed public and various scholarly communities.

The Stanford series on Asian America seeks to address these interests. The series will include works from the humanities and social sciences, including history, anthropology, political science, American studies, law, literary criticism, sociology and interdisciplinary and policy studies.

A full list of titles in the Asian America series can be found online at www.sup.org/asianamerica

The Long Afterlife
of Nikkei Wartime
Incarceration

Karen M. Inouye

STANFORD UNIVERSITY PRESS

STANFORD, CALIFORNIA

Stanford University Press
Stanford, California

©2016 by the Board of Trustees of the Leland Stanford Junior University.
All rights reserved.

No part of this book may be reproduced or transmitted in any form or
by any means, electronic or mechanical, including photocopying and
recording, or in any information storage or retrieval system without the
prior written permission of Stanford University Press.

Printed in the United States of America on acid-free,
archival-quality paper

Library of Congress Cataloging-in-Publication Data

Names: Inouye, Karen M., author.
Title: The long afterlife of Nikkei wartime incarceration / Karen M. Inouye.
Other titles: Asian America.
Description: Stanford, California : Stanford University Press, 2016. |
   Series: Asian America | Includes bibliographical references and index.
Identifiers: LCCN 2016027700 (print) | LCCN 2016028417 (ebook) | ISBN
   9780804795746 (cloth : alk. paper) | ISBN 9781503600560
Subjects: LCSH: Japanese Americans--Evacuation and relocation, 1942-1945. |
   Political prisoners--Effect of imprisonment on--United States. | World
   War, 1939-1945--Concentration camps--United States. | Japanese
   Americans--Political activity--History. | Collective memory--United States.
Classification: LCC D769.8.A6 I55 2016 (print) | LCC D769.8.A6 (ebook) | DDC
   940.53/1708956073--dc23
LC record available at https://lccn.loc.gov/2016027700

Typeset by Bruce Lundquist in 11/14 Adobe Garamond

Contents

Acknowledgments

This is a book of second chances. For many of these second chances, I am grateful to a number of people.

In California, Shirley Geok-lin Lim introduced me to Asian American studies, and at Brown University Bob Lee, Daniel Kim, Naoko Shibusawa, and Evelyn Hu-Dehart helped me learn more. I will always have wonderful memories of Bob's Asian American studies seminar and continue to appreciate our discussions about the field and my work. I was also fortunate to have worked with the indefatigable Jim Campbell, who often stayed up all night to get his own writing done after working all day with his students. From my first graduate seminar through the final draft of my dissertation and then first published article, Mari Jo Buhle provided the perfect combination of rigor, encouragement, and sound advice.

The Center for Race and Ethnicity at Brown was a wonderful space in which to write my dissertation, the ghost of which haunts Chapter One. For that space, I owe a special thanks to Evelyn Hu-Dehart, Matt Garcia, and Ralph Rodriguez. During those magical years at Brown, many others provided encouragement and support as well, including Dake Ackley, Jim Gatewood, Morgan Grefe, Christi Hancock, Shiho Imai, Carl Kaestle, Tom Rinehart, Judith Rosenbaum, Christi Ruffo, Josefina Saldaña, Susan Smulyan, Carla Tengan, and Susanne Wiedemann. The Women of Color Dissertation Collective—a smart and fun group from Yale, Brown, and Harvard—reminded me of the importance of the shared (and social) endeavor in what is otherwise often solitary work; special thanks go to my fun officemate Stéphanie Larrieux and to Régine Jean-Charles for bringing us together.

Indiana University provided the space and resources to research and write this book. I am grateful for research support from the College of Arts and Sciences and from the New Frontiers in the Arts and Humanities Program. In Ballantine Hall, Paula Cotner and Carol Glaze helped with the logistics for research trips and other day-to-day tasks too numerous to name. Matt Guterl and Deb Cohn provided support as chairs of IU's Department of American Studies. Others at IU provided myriad help, ranging from friendly encouragement and interest to teaching and research support: Marlon Bailey, Purnima Bose, Fritz Breithaupt, Cara Caddoo, Alex Chambers, Melanie and Nick Cullather, Ellen Dwyer, Wendy Gamber, Illana Gershon, Vivian Halloran, Scott Herring, LaMonda Horton-Stallings, Bob Ivie, Pam Jackson, Giles Knox, Jed Kuhn, Alex Lichtenstein, Sylvia Martinez, Courtney Mitchell, Marissa Moorman, Khalil Muhammad, Amrita Myers, Ashlyn Aiko Nelson, John Nieto-Phillips, Dina Okamoto, Diane Reilly, Steve Selka, Christina Snyder, and Shane Vogel. Special thanks to Lessie Jo Frazier, Jennifer Lee, Susan Lepselter, Jason McGraw, Michelle Moyd, Micol Seigel, and Ellen Wu for reading parts of early drafts. During an especially critical moment, Pam Walters and Stephanie Li cleared a path; also at a critical juncture, Jean Robinson helped change my career trajectory and provided unwavering support. Jennifer Lee and Denise Cruz continue to quiet the self-doubt this type of work engenders. They have made this long journey far less lonely.

I also want to thank those scholars who have reached out at certain moments with encouraging words and/or useful advice: Art Hansen, Sarika Chandra, Kandice Chuh, Matt Delmont, Josephine Lee, Karen Leong, Mary Liu, Martin Manalansan, Susette Min, Eric Mueller, Asha Nadkarni, Ricardo Ortiz, Paul Spickard, Amy Sueyoshi, and Elaine Tyler May. Multiple conversations with Chris Lee sparked an important expansion of the project to Canada and then helped shape my thinking about the challenges of the transnational frame. Subsequent conversations and feedback from Denise Cruz, Bob Lee, Shelley Lee, Brian Niiya, and Greg Robinson led to new and important ways of reenvisioning aspects of the project. Their enthusiasm made all the difference. I am especially grateful to Chris and Denise for eleventh-hour readings and suggestions.

The staff of the Special Collections and Archives in the Dr. Martin Luther King, Jr. Library at San Jose State University moved heaven and earth to help me find my way through the seemingly infinite number of boxes that comprise the Norman Mineta Papers. Similarly, the staff at the California State Library and in the Division of Rare and Manuscript Collections at the Kroch Library of Cornell University did more than make crucial primary sources available to me. They also provided me with excellent working environments—much more than just accessible archives. In addition, I relied on the invaluable Denshō digital archives.

At Stanford University Press, Eric Brandt and Friederike Sundaram met the project with enthusiasm as well as lightning-quick responses and updates. They chose readers who provided detailed suggestions and insightful queries, equal parts challenging and encouraging—precisely the sort that make a writer eager to roll up her sleeves and get back to work. Special thanks to Kate Wahl, Margo Irvin, Mariana Raykov, and Nora Spiegel for getting me across the finish line. I am particularly grateful to Gordon Chang, series editor for Asian America, for his feedback, encouragement, and faith in the project. Parts of Chapter One appeared in the *Journal of the History of the Behavioral Sciences* in 2012, and a shorter version of Chapter Five appeared in the *Journal of Asian American Studies* in 2014. I thank the editors of both journals, Ian Nicholson and Min Hyoung Song, respectively, as well as multiple reviewers for their rigor and generosity.

For their perspectives and friendship through the years, and for their check-in calls and reminders of the more carefree times in Santa Barbara, I am grateful to Almeria, Christie, and Mary. I also thank Jill, Scott, Jackie, Wendy, Lesli, Tom, and Susan for getting me to leave my laptop and venture out into the fresh air, if only for a short walk or to sit in the park. My sisterly friends, Nancy and Stefanie, have provided the kind of support that only comes with almost thirty years of friendship. As brilliant intellectuals and fierce political activists, they remain inspirational.

This book would not exist without the hard emotional and political work of those who survived wartime incarceration and who advanced the afterlife of it, whether or not they lived behind barbed wire. For their willingness to sit for interviews and to fill in the many gaps in my understanding, I am eternally grateful to Warren Furutani, Tetsu Kashima, Mary Kitagawa, Art Miki, Vivian Nelson, Roy Oshiro, Richard Shiozaki, Grace Eiko Thomson, Teiso Edward Uyeno, and the many others whose stories have yet to be told.

In many ways, this book is also my own family's story—especially that of my grandparents and parents, who had fewer chances to begin with. I also want to thank the many other Inouyes, as well as the Uchidas, Chinns, and Rothsteins who have supported this project in its many forms throughout so many years and in so many locations. Special thanks to my sister, Susan, and her family for opening up their home again and again; to my brother John for our early conversations about Asian American literature; to my brother Peter for his sometimes outrageous but always informative humor; to my aunts Marian and Ellen for their news clippings and care packages, and for their willingness to let me publish a childhood photo of them; thanks for permission to reproduce that photo also are due to uncles Richard and George, and to my cousin Prentiss, who joined them on that bench in Tule Lake. (My uncle Dennis, who always figured prominently in my grandmother's stories about incarceration, is unfortunately not in the photograph.) To my in-laws Ginny and Gerry, I am grateful for many generous forms of support along the way including trips to Providence soon after Claire was born; and to my mom, I am thankful for understanding that I may not move back to California after all. (As I hope this project shows, in some sense I never left.)

My greatest debt is to Bret and Claire. From the moment she could speak, Claire has had a knack for saying just the right thing. Her good humor, endless quest for fun, and insights on the world have provided necessary reality checks along the way. Bret provided different but equally important reality checks, helping me untangle both the intellectual and the emotional webs of this kind of work. He has read every page of every draft of this book—and my life—with patience, love, and generosity.

Finally, I dedicate this book to the memory of my father, Tom Inouye, and my grandmother, Fumiko Uchida. Although neither was alive when I started writing this book, they are present throughout it.

Abbreviations

ACLU	American Civil Liberties Union
BSR	Bureau of Sociological Research
CWRIC	Commission on Wartime Relocation and Internment of Civilians
JACL	Japanese American Citizens League
JCCP	Japanese Canadian Centennial Project
JERS	Japanese American Evacuation and Resettlement Study
NAJC	National Association of Japanese Canadians
NCJAR	National Council for Japanese American Redress
NJASRC	National Japanese American Student Relocation Council
SI	Symbolic Interactionism
UBC	University of British Columbia
USC	University of Southern California
UW	University of Washington
WRA	War Relocation Authority

The Long Afterlife
of Nikkei Wartime Incarceration

FIGURE 1 Charles Kadota, former president of the Japanese Canadian Citizens'
Association, at the University of British Columbia's May 2012 Honorary Degree
Ceremony for Japanese Canadian Students of 1942. University of British Columbia
Archives, Photo by Martin Dee (UBC 35.1/948).

Introduction

Unearthing the Past in the Present

The history of wartime incarceration for North Americans of Japanese ancestry holds untold surprises.[1] Consider the story of how Karen Korematsu-Haigh learned the history of her father, Fred Korematsu. Korematsu was one of a handful of Japanese Americans who challenged Executive Order 9066 at the time it was issued, and his case contributed to legal precedent twice over: first, when the Supreme Court affirmed the validity of Executive Order 9066; second, in 1983 when the United States District Court for the Northern District of California reversed that 1944 decision.[2] This story is remarkable enough, but so is that of how Korematsu-Haigh heard it in the first place:

> It was in a social studies class when my friend Maya got up in front of all of us to give a book report, an oral book report, about the Japanese-American internment. Her book was called "Concentration Camps USA" [by Roger Daniels]. And when she was talking about the Japanese-American internment, it was a subject I had not heard of before. No one spoke about it in my family. And then she went on to say that someone had resisted the exclusion order and resulted in a famous Supreme Court case, *Korematsu v. the United States*. Well, I sat there and said that's my name. And the only thing I knew is that Korematsu is a very unusual Japanese name.[3]

Korematsu-Haigh's experience was common. As both Harry Kitano and Yasuko Takezawa have documented, mid-century Issei (immigrants) and Nisei (the children of immigrants) could be reticent about their wartime history, partly because of traditional Japanese values and partly the shame associated with imprisonment, even when it was so flagrantly baseless.[4]

When Korematsu-Haigh quizzed her father, her questions had as much to do with the intervening years of silence as with the legal challenge. His response was simple: "My father said, you know, we're always very busy with our lives being Americans. I mean, that's what my father believed, was he wanted to get on and be an American and do all the activities that are privileged to us." And yet, she recalled, "I could see . . . the pain in his eyes." As a result, despite this extraordinary revelation, the contact between past and present remained fragmentary. Recognizing the depth of her father's suffering, Korematsu-Haigh stopped asking questions, and in the wake of their conversation a renewed silence fell over the household: "The irony to this story is that my brother, Ken, who is four years younger than I am, found out the same way in high school."[5]

This pattern—of a story told and then disremembered, a past recovered and then reburied—raises three issues. First, it indicates that wartime incarceration continues to shape the lives of Nikkei (people of Japanese ancestry) in North America, even decades after their wartime experiences. The customary view is that former inmates tend to be largely silent about their wartime experience, a view reinforced in the popular and scholarly literature.[6] This view is to some extent accurate: until recently, Nikkei North Americans have tended not to speak loudly or at length about the indignities and injustices they endured after the bombing of Pearl Harbor. But that view ignores important exceptions. Some, such as the artist and author Miné Okubo, began to voice their thoughts early on; a growing number have found that voice more recently, particularly after the 1988 achievement of redress in Canada and in the United States.[7] It also leaves out the fact that the targets of wartime incarceration have hardly left behind that injustice. In Korematsu-Haigh's telling, for instance, her father was initially silent, then reticent, then silent again, but he became increasingly vocal after his 1983 court victory, and at no point was the topic ever far from his mind. Nor could it be: both Korematsu and his daughter remarked on multiple occasions that the 1944 Supreme Court verdict against him had very real and durable negative consequences that persisted for decades afterward.[8] The delays and lacunae in this account are important, but less so than an underlying persistence of memory, for while wartime incarceration came to an end shortly after the surrender of Japan in 1945, its effects continue to play out in both Canada and the United States.

Second, Korematsu-Haigh's anecdote demonstrates that wartime incarceration not only transformed former inmates but also continues to do so. As this book will demonstrate, it also continues to transform their children, grandchildren, and great-grandchildren. That abortive conversation she had with her father, for instance, prompted questions and concerns that eventually drove Korematsu-Haigh to help establish a foundation in his name, to ensure that that foundation would work to perpetuate the memory of his legal fight and, thereby, to help prevent future violations of civil liberties. That conversation also belonged to a sequence of postwar events that ultimately led Korematsu to rekindle his court battle. (The conversation with his daughter was of a piece with his later contact with the historian Peter Irons, which was the immediate prompt to reinitiate legal proceedings.[9]) Interactions such as these, which stemmed from a history he had felt he could no longer broach on his own, led Korematsu to recognize the enormous social and political importance of his personal history. In response, he eventually became a willing public speaker, discussing his particular case as well as contemporary analogs, such as the increased inclination toward racial and religious profiling after 9/11.[10] Korematsu underwent several profound transformations, from reluctant political activist to low-profile citizen to wholehearted political activist, all beginning with Executive Order 9066 and its economic and political aftereffects.

He did not change entirely on his own. Like others discussed in this book, he changed in large part because of those around him whose own readiness to address the legacy of wartime incarceration did more than just stir the memory of injustice. That readiness also allowed what had long dogged Korematsu to take shape as conscious political engagement. (Contrariwise, continued unwillingness to face the history of wartime incarceration can, as we often see, slow or even prevent such engagement.) Reactivated by changes in the people around him, the legal, economic, and even cultural losses that had once isolated him both from American society and from his fellow Nikkei eventually sharpened his sense of a larger social and political obligation. Wartime incarceration ultimately held surprises for Korematsu himself because it reverberates, persisting in the present. It possesses what Saidiya Hartman has called an afterlife in her work on slavery.[11]

Third, Korematsu-Haigh's anecdote reveals perhaps the biggest surprise about wartime incarceration as a historical subject: that Nikkei North Americans have increasingly seized on that subject as a means to transform those who come into contact with it. As a result, this book is ultimately a study of transformation within and between individuals, among generations, and across perceived racial, religious, and cultural boundaries. The transformation at stake was a long time in coming; it really only became recognizable in the late 1960s and 1970s. But it has accelerated rapidly since, with more and more Nikkei North Americans adding their voices to a growing chorus. This increasing involvement indicates that the political and social engagement by Japanese Americans and Japanese Canadians comes from a couple of causes. One is that, following almost total economic and political disenfranchisement, former inmates and their family members only eventually regained enough stability within their respective nation-states to begin exercising the rights that had been taken from them. Another comes through in Korematsu-Haigh's story: with each surprising revelation, people who learn of wartime incarceration and its human cost have been shaken out of their complacency. And, of course, the civil rights movement also helped create a receptive audience for the cultural work of Nikkei North American activists, in addition to providing some of their more activist constituencies with a venue for engagement.[12] This book addresses the three main issues raised by that story: the persistence of memory, the evolution it has spurred and spurs within Nikkei North Americans, and the ways those people have then turned around and tried to promote the same kind of evolution in others. It is designed both to recount that transformation and to participate in it as well. In order to do so, *The Long Afterlife of Nikkei Wartime Incarceration* draws on a range of sources, from academic studies of unjust imprisonment to newspaper accounts and new interviews conducted both in Canada and in the United States.

Background

To begin with, it is important to lay out the basic facts of wartime incarceration in North America. In the United States, the course was as follows. In February 1942, after the bombing of Pearl Harbor, President Franklin D. Roosevelt issued Executive Order 9066, which directed state and local authorities to locate and detain Japanese American citizens and their family members in the Western United States at several prison sites.[13] In addition to being given only days to prepare for their imprisonment, Japanese Americans received little information about their destinations, the proposed length of their stay, or the conditions they would face. They were told to pack what they could carry and then were abruptly forced from their homes. Of the roughly 120,000 people who were subjected to this treatment (primarily in the West Coast states of California, Oregon, and Washington, as well as Arizona) most spent the next three years in one of the prisons.[14] Those who escaped this fate by moving east before the eviction began were nonetheless barred from the West Coast for the duration of the war.

Before being formally incarcerated, Japanese Americans were first detained in so-called assembly centers—thirteen in California, two in Arizona, and one each in Oregon and Washington. The majority of these temporary jails were makeshift arrangements located in former fairgrounds, racetracks, or camps for migrant workers; three were the site of an old mill, an abandoned Civilian Conservation Corps camp, and a livestock exposition hall.[15] Following this interim period, inmates were sent to their longer-term prisons. Called "relocation centers" in most official correspondence (but also concentration camps on occasion), these prisons were created and administered by the War Relocation Authority (WRA). A total of ten such camps, as Nikkei came to call them, held the resulting influx of inmates: Gila River and Poston in Arizona; Granada in Colorado; Heart Mountain in Wyoming; Jerome and Rohwer in Arkansas; Manzanar and Tule Lake in California; Topaz in Utah; and Minidoka in Idaho.

In both the short-term way stations and longer-term prisons, Nikkei inmates endured repeated violations of their civil and human rights, as well as a host of related indignities. These left them in a constant state of distress and uncertainty about their safety and future, particularly given the clear link between wartime incarceration and the years of anti-Asian prejudice that preceded it. That prejudice had been growing from the 1850s onward, with people of Chinese ancestry initially bearing the brunt of the xenophobic sentiment. Over time, though, Japanese immigrants also began to figure prominently in white fantasies of physiological, cultural, and moral degradation. Passage of the 1924 Immigration Act, with its emphasis on preservation of the "Nordic race," compounded the situation by effectively curtailing Japanese immigration. Although a 1932 study declared that the Immigration Act was having a positive effect on the lives of Nikkei, in truth there remained significant obstacles to full participation in American cultural, political, and social life.[16] This situation was especially pressing for the second generation, or Nisei. These children of first-generation immigrants felt little or no kinship with their elders, whose language skills and cultural patterns seemed increasingly isolated after 1924. Caught between attempts to maintain cultural traditions in the home and the desire to participate in rituals associated with American life, they became doubly displaced: first from their parents' country of origin, and second from the country of their birth. At the same time, they and their parents continued to endure the same economic, legal, and political disadvantages as they had before the Immigration Act. Aggression by Japan thus fed an already high degree of mistrust among non-Nikkei. In the months between the bombing of Pearl Harbor and the issuing of Executive Order 9066, suspicion of Japanese Americans was so acute that government policy allowed their homes to be subjected to warrantless searches; their bank accounts frozen; curfews imposed; men questioned and held; and property confiscated and destroyed. Shortly after Pearl Harbor was bombed, Nikkei on the West Coast were told to pack "only what they could carry" and report to designated sites where they were tagged with large identifying numbers that hung from strings around their necks and transported to interior states, far from the coast where they supposedly might help with any Japanese military ventures. Despite the lack of evidence of any traitorous activities, growing anti-Japanese sentiment on the West Coast was enough to tip the balance in favor of their wholesale removal.[17]

Other countries also engaged in the forced wartime migration and confinement of Nikkei citizens and their family members. The creation of racially motivated policies involving Nikkei was in fact an international phenomenon, running from Peru northward. Because of the close postwar links among Nikkei North Americans, this study will concentrate on Canada and the United States. Like Japanese Americans, Japanese Canadians along the West Coast were also subject to exclusion orders.[18] The impact of these orders (called Orders-in-Council) was profound. As of fall 1941, 23,000 Japanese Canadians were working primarily as fisherman, miners, and foresters. They lived mostly in coastal towns in British Columbia. As in the United States, white residents had long viewed them as both an economic threat and a political menace, and local papers were more than happy to capitalize on the resulting tensions. In fact, Canada seems to have been especially vigorous in its persecution of Nikkei residents.

Though he had long been suspicious of people of Japanese ancestry, it was only after the bombing of Pearl Harbor that William Lyon Mackenzie

King, the prime minister of Canada, decided to forcibly remove them from the coast to the interior.[19] In January 1941 he received a special report recommending that Nikkei be exempted from military service due to pervasive racism among whites in the Canadian armed forces. Unconvinced by the report's finding that there were no subversive elements in the community, he argued in favor of special identification cards for Japanese and Japanese Canadians north of the 49th parallel. Some ambivalence persisted, such as when King reprimanded members of Parliament who had issued blanket condemnations of all Nikkei in Canada. Events of the following December, however, made such a position untenable. King's government responded with a partial evacuation of the West Coast, with an emphasis on Japanese immigrants. By the following February, however, all Nikkei were formally evicted from the area and sent inland.

After the issuing of formal exclusionary orders, Nikkei in Canada first were held in livestock barns in Hastings Park, on Vancouver's Pacific National Exhibition grounds. Wealthier Japanese Canadians who could see how the wind was blowing were able to relocate more or less voluntarily to points east, such as Toronto. Later, families lacking the means to leave Vancouver were moved to remote sites further inland. For them, circumstances resembled those south of the border (though General John DeWitt, head of the Western Defense Comand, halted all voluntary Japanese American relocation in March 1941). There were, however, several major differences in how the Canadian government removed Nikkei from the coast. In the United States, most families were kept together. By contrast, a number of Nikkei men in Canada were separated from their families and assigned to road-building crews in Ontario and near the border with Alberta.[20] Others were sent to work on sugar beet farms on the prairies, while still others were sent to a prisoner of war camp in Ontario. Women and children were moved to towns in the interior, which were often referred to as "ghost towns" due to their remoteness, generally poor condition, and minimal populations, which either could not (and in some cases would not) vigorously oppose the influx of supposedly undesirable people.[21]

After the end of the war, the Canadian government attempted to return over 4,000 Nikkei to Japan under the guise of "repatriation," even though many had never set foot on Japanese soil before.[22] After this policy failed to deliver the desired results, the provincial government of British Columbia passed a number of laws extending the exclusion of Nikkei from parts of the region for years after the war ended. Indeed, Japanese Canadians were unable to return legally to Vancouver, among other places, until the spring of 1949, by which time most had already established themselves elsewhere in Canada. Thus, Prime Minister King had largely achieved what he set out to do: "to settle the Japanese more or less evenly throughout Canada . . . where they will not create feelings of racial hostility"—and, he added, where they would no longer be able to concentrate in any kind of demographically significant way.[23] Moreover, those who did return to British Columbia did so under difficult economic circumstances, for representatives of the Canadian government had sold off, usually at fire-sale prices, Nikkei businesses and property; the proceeds were then applied to the cost of imprisonment.

Afterlife

Despite the initial reticence of many Nikkei North Americans, aspects of the emotional as well as cultural and social impact of wartime incarceration were recognized even at the time, most notably in the Japanese American Evacuation and Resettlement Study (JERS), a sociological assessment of wartime incarceration and its immediate fallout undertaken by social scientists at the University of California, Berkeley. Those effects were even more clearly analyzed in an often-overlooked study by the psychiatrist Alexander Leighton under the aegis of what he called the Bureau of Sociological Research.[24] But documentation of the cultural, emotional, and political traumas that Nikkei North Americans suffered has built up only slowly and fragmentarily. Publications related to JERS, for instance, dealt almost exclusively with large-scale phenomena, while Leighton's book went down in history as merely a study of administrative dynamics. And virtually all studies of wartime incarceration published in the 1950s and 1960s either documented the basic political history or debated questions of constitutional validity and military necessity. However, the lingering effects of wartime injustice—its afterlife—tended to defy expression for a very long time.

Perhaps it goes without saying, but every historical event could conceivably have an afterlife. Nonetheless, as Korematsu-Haigh's story shows, it is precisely the complexity of afterlife, the myriad ways it shapes personal, cultural, and political investments, that necessitates study. The burden of history rests heavily both on Nikkei North Americans who endured wartime incarceration and on their families. That burden is especially familiar to Japanese Americans and Japanese Canadians, who continue to experience it as a persistent intrusion of the memory of imprisonment on the present. And while that persistence tends to make itself felt intermittently, it is both forceful and complex. Consider the following two examples. The first, which shows the extended force of wartime incarceration, was my father's lifelong insistence that he would only buy cars produced by American-owned companies. To do otherwise, he felt, might lead people to question his patriotism, even after the achievement of redress. Decades after the fact, even years after an official government apology, the memory of being a teenage target of officially sanctioned bigotry continued to have a remarkable impact on him. The second example demonstrates the complexity of how the memory of Executive Order 9066 and its effects continue to play out. In the mid-1990s members of my extended family and I took a trip, for which we mistakenly booked our stay in a dilapidated hotel that also doubled as a youth hostel. The rooms were dirty, the neighbors were loud and the roaches were bold, so my siblings and I spent much of the trip joking about our situation. The jokes continued as we waited for our flight home. During a brief pause, my grandmother quietly remarked that she had seen worse. Asked where, she smiled slyly and said, "in camp." More than fifty years after Executive Order 9066, wartime incarceration was so woven into the fabric of our family life that it could even crop up in surprising moments of humor.

Wartime incarceration of Nikkei North Americans constituted a very real and important trauma, as the anecdotes about both Fred Korematsu and my father suggest. But as the story of my grandmother also suggests, to speak of trauma is not necessarily to speak of passive victims. It is simply to note the intangible damage done to a group. What happens to that group later, what members of it do afterward, is another story altogether, one that shows the richness of political and cultural agency. For that reason, this book is concerned with moments when the emotional and cultural circumstances produced by wartime incarceration erupted or were redirected into concrete action. It is concerned with moments that drove people to revisit the injustices they suffered as injustices, moments when trauma activated people rather than incapacitated them, to draw them into proactive engagements rather than force them into defensive postures.

In other words, this book maps where a lingering feeling crystallizes into both individual and collective action. It charts the afterlife of wartime incarceration. In so doing, I take as my point of inspiration the work of Avery F. Gordon on haunting, which comprises a wide range of phenomena that enable scholars to interrogate the complexities of power and personhood. One of those phenomena in particular stands out: a continuing, though not necessarily continual, presence of the "over-and-done-with." As Gordon has noted, "haunting is one way in which abusive systems of power make themselves known and their impacts felt in everyday life, especially when they are supposedly over and done with . . . or when their oppressive nature is denied. . . . Haunting is not the same as being exploited, traumatized or oppressed, although it usually involves these experiences or is produced by them." Like exploitation, trauma, and oppression, "haunting raises specters, and it alters the experience of being in time, the way we separate the past, the present, and the future." But the uncanny effect of haunting differs in its potential for provoking activist kinds of reflection. As Gordon goes on to point out, "haunting, unlike trauma, is distinctive for producing a something-to-be-done. . . . [It is] that moment (of however long duration) when things are not in their assigned places, when the cracks and rigging are exposed, when the people who are meant to be invisible show up without any sign of leaving, when disturbed feelings cannot be put away, when something else, something different from before, seems like it must be done."[25]

At times—not always—haunting provides an opportunity for one to "imagine otherwise," that is, to envision a different present and future. And in imagining otherwise, one gets the chance to *do* otherwise.[26] Therein lies the inspiration for this study: in that transition from injustice to agency through personal experience.

However, this book is not a study in haunting per se, though much could still be gained by viewing wartime incarceration through that methodological lens. Gordon's term designates a range of phenomena, many of which are evanescent—if even perceptible in the first place—and which do not necessarily result in concrete action. By contrast, although afterlife as conceived of in this study begins with lingering, complex feelings, it also encompasses actions and statements that are purposefully detectable. These actions and statements are the result of people bringing their lingering experience into view in order to perpetuate that experience rather than achieve closure. Those people are breathing life back into an experience others might consider, or simply wish, over and done with in order to make it immediate and recognizable to other people. And they do this in order to avert complacency in the face of continuing injustice.

Afterlife manifests itself idiosyncratically, but one can trace it across temporal, generational, and geographical lines. Sometimes it disappears for a while—the missing person in a photograph, the absent presence in family conversations,[27] the silence in a Nisei scholar's pre-1960s work—but it resurfaces time and again in this long and continuing narrative. In short, this book traces what a lingering feeling can achieve across generations, across cultures, and across different systems of oppression.

This is not to imply that Nikkei North Americans all thought and acted alike. On the contrary, the pursuit of redress both north and south of the 49th parallel generated significant disagreement, at times open conflict, among people of Japanese ancestry. Furthermore, political and cultural engagement by people of Japanese ancestry in Canada and the United States took a range of forms.[28] They also addressed histories that diverged at key moments. Though the populations of both countries share a legacy of injustice, the ways they do so differ enormously, depending on where, when, and how their paths intersected with that of wartime racism and economic malfeasance. The Japanese Canadian whose recent move to Chicago saved him from incarceration might be inclined to approach that history in ways that differ substantially from those of a woman who was forced from her Vancouver home and sent inland as a child.[29]

There is ample evidence of both trauma and associated coping mechanisms, some of it documented formally, much of it anecdotal, like the examples I cited above.[30] As discussed in this book, afterlife differs from such phenomena in two important ways. First, it constitutes a self-conscious engagement with that slippage between past, present, and future.[31] Second, it also engages those not immediately subject to that slippage by extending the experience of injustice beyond people it impacts directly or obviously. Sometimes those differences show up on a large scale, as in the cases of redress, of organizational work on pilgrimages and retroactive diplomas, or of attempts to build the history of Executive Order 9066 into the K-12 curriculum. Other instances are smaller in scale, such as inviting someone to join in a pilgrimage. In all cases, though, the goal is to preserve civil society in the future not just by pointing out its violation in the past but also by modeling its protection in the present.[32] Cases such as these are examples of the afterlife of wartime incarceration in their emphasis on what can still be done, rather than what should have been done.

This investment in the afterlife of wartime incarceration does more than demonstrate a profound change in Japanese American and Japanese Canadian agency and identity. The increasing refusal of many Nikkei to treat racism as the cost of doing business in North America is important. But so is their recognition that others must undergo a similar change. For this reason, the secondary goal of recent Nikkei North American activism in its diverse forms has been to relay the afterlife of wartime imprisonment, to impart it even to others who see themselves as having no direct connection to its history (and, as a result, the present and future). Both the lingering feelings one might have and the afterlife to which they might give rise can vary tremendously. The chapters in this book address just a few examples in order to shed light on a mechanism that produces afterlife: empathetic agency, which is the second key concept in this study.

Empathetic Agency and First-Person Experience

The advancement of an afterlife is more than a matter of recording historical facts or even measuring their human toll. The latter two activities are meant to frame the past as a discrete object of study. However, for many Nikkei North Americans the emotional and cultural toll of unjust imprisonment became not only something to which they were subject, but also something with which others might empathize. Conveyed in insistently personal terms, their lingering feelings defied being put away by becoming the disturbance of others. The goal of doing this, I argue, was to produce analogous feelings in onlookers as well as fellow Japanese Americans and Japanese Canadians, not just an abstract acknowledgment of a past injustice. Externalizing their experience and their continued engagement with history, Nikkei North Americans have tried to inspire other people to work—albeit in complex and often differing ways—against repetition of what happened to them.

The first-person character of such work is especially important. It can take a verbal form, such as personal testimony provided during the fight for redress and in the wake of 9/11.[33] It also can take a nonverbal form, such as the decision of many Nikkei to participate physically in retroactive diploma ceremonies. It involves the explicit discussion of moods and mental states, topics that are rarely associated with postwar Nikkei cultures. It involves reenactment, such as that performed by participants in the Manzanar pilgrimages (the subject of Chapter Four). As a result, even when someone is no longer able to speak in that first person, such as the late Fred Korematsu, the main mode of address remains the same. Empathy comes to the fore as a force for political engagement.

Given this last point, Nikkei North American agency—activated in part by empathy—can be thought of as potentially contagious. The adjective has a strong negative association with disease—an association that has also linked it at critical moments with discourses of race[34]—but it may be particularly apt here, because the goal of Japanese American and Japanese Canadian political engagements discussed in this book has been to produce new behavior in other people, behavior those people had been capable of but not necessarily predisposed to. In other words, the goal has been to share the afterlife of injustice in order to provoke stronger and more egalitarian participation in civil society by modeling it, providing physical and emotional experiences associated with that society and its failures, experiences that can create an empathetic connection to the past. To share incarceration's afterlife presumes that productive political engagement can, like a mood that drives it, be infectious. The actions of the people described in this book are like an inoculation that operates case by case and person to person. Its mechanism is, above all else, empathy, and the vector is *contact*: physical interaction, or seeing and hearing someone at a graduation ceremony or in congressional testimony.[35] Whether Korematsu-Haigh speaking with her father, Nikkei legislators and activists testifying before Congress, or former students retroactively receiving their diplomas at the University of British Columbia in 2012, all of these people promote change through human interaction that is simultaneously physical, interpersonal, historical, emotional, and intellectual. With the afterlife of Nikkei wartime incarceration, and unlike disease, the contagion disrupts an *unhealthy* state: that of historical and political complacency. It does so by relaying itself from person to person, and primarily as a result of empathetic identification.

It has become a truism that the past is a foreign country, but experiences such as Korematsu-Haigh's show how such a truism nonetheless often remains accurate. Such experiences also demonstrate that we live and interact with that foreign country on a daily basis. And that interaction has the potential to transform us, especially when it takes the form of afterlife. With that in mind, this book tells a story of Nikkei North American empathetic agency, a story of people who have worked not simply to change the people around them, but to change the way those people might change in the first place: the way Korematsu's historical example accidentally provoked questions in his daughter, for instance, or the way her questions helped provoke renewed reflection and, eventually, purposeful activism on his part.[36] This book also tells the story of how the past lingered among Nikkei in Canada and the United States, despite their wish to simply get on with postwar life, and of how that lingering eventually compelled a significant number of people to take action. From Korematsu's visible pain to his daughter's astonishment at her hidden family history, the wartime injustices visited upon people of Japanese ancestry in North America continued to play out decades after the initial injury. *The Long Afterlife of Nikkei Wartime Incarceration* thus also tells the story of a past that continues to defy resolution. That defiance holds not only for those evicted from the West Coasts of Canada and the United States, but also for their children and grandchildren, the Sansei (third-generation), Yonsei (fourth), and even Gosei (fifth), who continue to feel the effects of their parents', grandparents', and even great-grandparents' experiences. Living and interacting with the past, they continue to change, and strive to change others, in response to its continuing presence. Like the category of "Asian America" as described by Kandice Chuh, the force of that past lies in its indeterminacy, rather than in its supposedly stable, identifiable, and identifying over-and-doneness.[37]

The afterlife of Nikkei North American incarceration and its empathetic foundation also extends beyond a specific historical moment. This is perhaps one of the biggest surprises we meet when we turn our attention to Executive Order 9066 and its aftermath. Most of the discourse surrounding post-incarceration life for Nikkei North Americans has revolved around righting past wrongs, as if in some definitive way. However, Americans and Canadians of Japanese ancestry have long recognized that what happened to them and to their predecessors could easily happen to others, that civil liberties are contingent, particularly in times of crisis. For many of them, revivifying, and not just recalling, the history of wartime incarceration has become an ethical and even moral obligation that compels Nikkei citizens to address contemporary threats similar to what they and their family members faced. Ever mindful of their own past, they call attention to how easily a society may violate the rights of its marginal constituents. Rather than seeking to lay a shameful episode to rest, they have tried to keep that episode in view as a cautionary tale. It is a task of increasing historical and cultural importance as former inmates age, others seek to gloss over that history, and North American societies continue to trumpet what they consider a post-racial era. In her pioneering study of the fight for redress, Alice Yang Murray recently remarked that, "one could have devoted an entire book to a more detailed examination of how one individual's memories and representations of internment evolved over time."[38] This book takes up that challenge, charting the evolution of key individuals (Tamotsu Shibutani, Norman Mineta, and Warren Furutani), and examining how such evolution can initiate the same kinds of change in others (retroactive diploma ceremonies and the Manzanar pilgrimages). This phenomenon is not limited to Nikkei North American political and cultural engagement. Renee C. Romano, Patricia Hill Collins, and others have documented similar sorts of dynamics among blacks and their interlocutors.[39]

As this last point might suggest, *The Long Afterlife of Nikkei Wartime Incarceration* also addresses the way Nikkei North Americans have repeatedly demonstrated the larger applicability of personal experience. Shibutani writing sociological studies of rumor and demoralization in the wake of Executive Order 9066, Mineta testifying in the 1980s before Congress, Furutani walking with fellow pilgrims to Manzanar in the 1960s and 1970s, retroactive diploma recipients participating in the 2012 graduation ceremony at University of British Columbia, Mary Kitagawa leading the fight for those diplomas in Canada, and of course Fred Korematsu speaking about his legal battles: all have done more than reclaim their or their loved ones' rightful place in North American societies; all have done more than repeat a narrative in the hopes of demonstrating its continued significance for them. Performing crucial parts of Nikkei North American experience, these Japanese Americans and Japanese Canadians have chosen self-consciously to demonstrate in the first person the contingency of belonging as well as its relationship to power and the social construction of race.

As a result, this book tells a story of perpetuation rather than closure, of self-conscious haunting. Taking history out of books and into the lives of others, these Nikkei North Americans continually feel the presence of the past. But they also aim to keep the past alive by making it part of the personal experience of those around them. The personal experience of history therefore becomes a means to change the course of society in the future. Making their own past part of the lives of others helps Japanese Americans and Japanese Canadians demonstrate the political potential of those around them and, consequently, the responsibilities that come with membership in a civil society. Having found his way from voice to silence and back again, for instance, Korematsu worked diligently for the rest of his life to help others find that same potential for self-expression. Likewise, Mineta, the Manzanar pilgrims, and advocates of retroactive diplomas have all talked about their work not only as political action, but also as opportunities for people to empathize with each other across differences of generation, ethnicity, race, and class. Continuing to speak of wartime incarceration and to embody its aftermath is a means to fight complacency, the presumption that constitutional protections are transparent and universally applied. Empathy is critical in this respect, as older generations enact a kind of foreign-exchange program in which younger generations and non-Nikkei observers live and interact with the past in a personal way. Embodiment provides those people with the opportunity to identify with a story that often seems both done and, more to the point, dusted, especially after the achievement of redress in 1988. The shared afterlife of wartime incarceration directs them toward the same transformative experience Nikkei North Americans underwent and continue to undergo. All of which is another way of saying that the people who form the basis for this book want their own agency to become contagious, moving well beyond the confines of the Japanese American and Canadian communities.

Afterlife and Empathetic Agency beyond Asian America

This book is a history neither of wartime injustice nor of the pursuit of judicial, legislative, and economic reparations. Excellent work has already been done on those topics. Regarding the United States, the earliest texts were mainly sociological studies, though with emphasis on the basic history of Executive Order 9066 and its many implications. (Chapter One will discuss the most famous of these, which stemmed from JERS.[40]) Several important authors have since revisited wartime incarceration and its circumstances in Canada and in the United States. Ken Adachi, Roger Daniels, Greg Robinson, and Ann Gomer Sunahara, among others, have published groundbreaking work on institutional factors that contributed to the decision to issue exclusionary orders, on life in camp, and on postwar attempts by Nikkei North Americans to reconstruct their lives.[41] Daniels, Stephanie Bangarth, and Peter Irons have written extensively about the history of legal challenges to wartime incarceration.[42] And authors including Mitchell Maki and his colleagues, Roy Miki, Maryka Omatsu, and Alice Yang Murray have produced excellent studies of the fight for redress in Canada and the United States.[43]

Rather than attempt to walk the historical path these scholars have marked out, this book builds on the recognition that wartime incarceration continues to hold many surprises, and that those surprises are a barometer of the lingering presence of injustice in the lives of both Nikkei North Americans and those around them. This book provides an interdisciplinary study of how ideas of political agency changed within an immigrant community over time. It builds not only on historical and sociological publications, but also on new primary sources. The latter include interviews with Nikkei activists and politicians, as well as previously unpublished wartime sources. It also examines public discourses of wartime incarceration, particularly from the past twenty years.

The Long Afterlife of Nikkei Wartime Incarceration examines those discourses from a transnational perspective while also addressing the limitations of such a method. Empathetic agency, the building of bridges between individuals and among groups, does not stop at the border of one nation or another. In order to address that bridging as fully as possible, this book employs a transnational frame that can help us understand more fully both mass incarceration and its aftermath. Approaching wartime incarceration as a transnational phenomenon is particularly important, given how small a place the Japanese Canadian narrative has tended to occupy in the larger history of the topic. But thinking continentally rather than nationally can also help explicate the complexities of Asian American identities.[44] Drawing on the work of Iyko Day, Eleanor Ty and Donald Goellnicht, Christopher Lee, and Roy Miki, who have done much to shed light on the differences between Asian American and Asian Canadian studies (and related activism), this book addresses what Lee has called the "lateness of Asian Canadian Studies"—that is, two kinds of latency that perpetually defer the development of Asian Canadian studies as a recognizable field of study with a recognizable set of subjects.[45] Specifically, *The Long Afterlife of Nikkei Wartime Incarceration* delineates one set of such subjects in order to elucidate the boundaries of Canadian Asian-ness and, along the way, to reframe the concept of Asian America.

The chapters follow a trajectory from individuals to groups, and from Japanese American actions to more broadly Nikkei North American ones. The first two chapters discuss two important former inmates of prison camps in the United States, Tamotsu Shibutani and Norman Mineta, who provide examples of how the afterlife of mass incarceration helped transform some people into resolute agents, whose work might begin in localized ways but extends toward other marginalized groups. Shifting the geographical and cultural scope of the book, Chapter Three looks at Canadian discourses of redress as they developed in tandem with, but also sometimes at a remove from, those that arose in the United States, expressing a complex and sometimes contradictory transnational Nikkei sense of self. Chapter Four expands the temporal scope of the book by looking at how the lingering effects of unjust imprisonment were transmitted from generation to generation, and how younger generations who had not experienced life in camp sought to extend that transmission as well as understand its roots. Chapter Five synthesizes these approaches by talking about key individuals in the international and, in some respects, also transnational pursuit of retroactive diplomas; by highlighting intergenerational engagement; by discussing enlisting non-Nikkei observers; and by shedding light on attempts to establish a kind of afterlife that will extend into the future.

As the historical moments represented in this book show, every iteration of Nikkei North American incarceration, while complex and hard to capture in detail, is a chance to recognize the embodiment of the past in the present: the beginning in the 1960s of pilgrimages to prison sites; the fight for redress during the 1970s and '80s; warnings and reminders about the contingency of civil liberties after 2001; and ongoing diploma ceremonies for formerly evicted students. Across decades, diverse communities, and borders, the business of wartime incarceration remains unfinished, not only because former inmates, their children, and their grandchildren continue to feel the effects of that injustice, but also because they also recognize the need to perpetuate the personal as well as political memory of that injustice, particularly during times of crisis. By directing people outward, the goal of producing empathetic agency has made Nikkei North Americans increasingly vocal about their experience, or that of their parents or grandparents.

That they have done so and how they have done so are historically important; so, too, is *why* they have done so. Having given voice to the persistence of history they have long felt, they now work to extend that persistence to others through stimulating empathy and action based on that empathy. *The Long Afterlife of Nikkei Wartime Incarceration* hence examines but one link in a chain that binds people together, allowing them to exist and coexist in groups. This book is an effort to help others live and interact with that past in order to become more fully human.

Knowledge Production as Recasting Experience

Tamotsu Shibutani was not a combative man, but he encountered far more than his share of trouble. Having endured racism and other sorts of bigotry throughout his childhood and early adult life in California, he eventually secured a place for himself as a student at the University of California, Berkeley. Forced from campus by Executive Order 9066, he went to work for the Japanese American Evacuation and Resettlement Study (JERS), a contemporaneous survey of the sociological impact of mass incarceration. And, with work that might keep him intellectually active, he eventually clashed with the director of JERS, Dorothy Swaine Thomas. In a letter dated October 30, 1943, Shibutani wrote: "I don't know if we should get so excited about this thing, but it seems that this is the prelude to the storm to break in December."[1] The "storm" to which he referred had to do with a major conflict over questions of both the methodology and the purpose of JERS. As a bright, aspiring scholar and, perhaps more importantly for Thomas, an insider with access to information within the prison camp at Tule Lake, Shibutani was one of several Japanese American students hired to collect data about life in the camps. Yet, difficulties arose soon after he began his JERS work. And while he and Thomas generally got along, significant differences of opinion would set them at odds in the years to come.[2]

The initial phase of those differences, like Shibutani's measured assessment of it, came at a time when Shibutani was reliant on Thomas for intellectual and logistical support.[3] And yet, despite the inequality of their relationship, he continued to express his concerns. Like other Nikkei who participated in JERS, Shibutani disagreed with Thomas about how the study should be conducted, what sort of data should be collected, and how they should be used. As Thomas herself knew, the motivations behind the project were complex and not always clear.[4] JERS had undergone tremendous changes after its initial conceptualization, resulting in a project that bore little resemblance to how it was originally designed. But the methodological differences those younger scholars had with their supervisor were more than academic. They derived from the direct experience of mass imprisonment. Life within the camps proved fraught, not only because of the forced displacement and unjust incarceration but also because of conflicts within the Japanese American community itself.[5] Scholars of Asian American history have documented the problems associated with this kind of work, including with respect to imprisonment.[6] Less familiar are the ways that wartime incarceration continued to inform the work of many JERS researchers long after the end of the Second World War. And yet, the afterlife of injustice ultimately drove these researchers to give form to their experience, thus lending emotional immediacy and urgency to the political claims that experience necessitated.

For Japanese American JERS researchers, life behind barbed wire stood at odds with aspects of quantitative analysis, which was Thomas's preferred method. It exposed them to daily complexities and countless insults, to contradictions and innumerable tragedies that seemed to defy measurement even as they demanded consideration. The resulting dissonance produced in those researchers a sense that mass imprisonment had yet to be understood properly—let alone fully, even after the JERS work ran its course. And that sense, surfacing time and again over the years following incarceration, eventually led some of those researchers to revisit their experiences in order to meet the demand they had first felt while in camp. Direct experience of that life did not make Nikkei researchers somehow smarter than Thomas, but it did provide them with insights so profound that in many cases those insights would become apparent only years later.

On a related note, it must be acknowledged that despite his high academic profile, Shibutani was in many ways typical. Other JERS workers, most famously James Sakoda and S. Frank Miyamoto, also returned to their experience of incarceration in the decades that followed their release from the camps.[7] As this chapter will demonstrate, Shibutani was very much like his colleagues in that he recognized the incompleteness of the record that

Thomas's quantitative work produced, the inability of that method to account for things he sensed were sociologically and psychologically important, even if he could not articulate that importance at the time. And, as someone who experienced those things, Shibutani continued to think about that experience after he was released from camp. He was in good company in that regard. Like Sakoda and Miyamoto, he did not set out to write about incarceration, waiting until he had somehow recovered his equilibrium; incarceration kept at him until he found a theoretical model that allowed him to give voice to it in a manner consistent with his larger intellectual and social investments. Similarly, he did not somehow rise above or redeem his discipline. Rather, he used his discipline to reshape personal experience, refusing or declining to write until his lingering feelings became viable as scholarly, and thus pragmatically political, engagement. In writing, he gave concrete form to ambiguous and conflicted impulses, rendering them new, active, and directed outward—reconstructing them as a scholarly afterlife that, while not wholly bound up with empathy, nonetheless provided points of emotional entry for others.

Treating Shibutani's experience as a case study in how several Nikkei JERS workers responded to mass imprisonment over the years following the end of Executive Order 9066 is important for several reasons. First, it reveals that those workers were not docile, but in fact often expressed strong opinions about the study, its director, and even their own roles both as inmates and as social scientists tasked with studying the lives of their fellow inmates. Second, it makes visible how wartime observers both within the camps and outside them recognized that the damage wrought by Executive Order 9066 was psychological and social, in addition to being economic and legal. Third, it shows how largely unrecognized feelings about wartime incarceration lingered over decades and sometimes unexpectedly intersected with former inmates' professional pursuits. The work of Shibutani demonstrates all three of these points. Focusing on him, this chapter aims to illustrate one of the two main issues at stake in this study: the ways that the afterlife of wartime imprisonment—those decades-old lingering feelings—gave rise to purposeful action.

Shibutani is not customarily discussed in the literature on postwar Nikkei political work. He enjoyed no clear record of strong public activism, for instance, and even as an academic his research at first seems far from that of people more commonly associated with Japanese American political engagement. To this day Shibutani is best known as a sociologist's sociologist, someone who helped advance disciplinary methods associated with the University of Chicago. Yet thinking of him purely in these terms can blind us to the fact that both he and his work were marked indelibly by the experience of unjust imprisonment and its impact on him, his family, and their community. Shibutani made no secret of that impact, either, returning to it on two important occasions in work he published during the 1960s and 1970s. But that work is so resolutely sociological that it all too often slips under the radar, leading us to miss the strong sense of ethical and political obligation that compelled Shibutani to return to wartime incarceration in the first place. In fact, his very disciplinary emphasis was itself driven by that sense of obligation.

Shibutani's work provides two important examples of how wartime incarceration continued to linger in the minds of former inmates. The first is his book *Improvised News: A Sociological Study of Rumor* (1966), which treated rumor as a meditation on powerlessness. In this book, Shibutani provides examples from a range of groups, including but not limited to Japanese Americans responding to the attack on Pearl Harbor and to the circumstances surrounding Executive Order 9066. Published in 1966, *Improvised News* predated virtually all of the legal battles over Nikkei mass incarceration, save those initiated by a handful of Japanese Americans who resisted Executive Order 9066 at the time.[8] It also predates legislative work in pursuit of redress by nearly twenty years. It even predates the self-consciously activist pilgrimages of the late 1960s onward (see Chapter Four). In this light, the inclusion of former camp inmates is notable for its implicit indication that imprisonment—all but forgotten in many quarters at the time—merited discussion alongside other, more familiar upheavals. *Improvised News* built on the afterlife of wartime incarceration, making key scholarly and political claims that would figure even more prominently in Shibutani's later work.

The second example is *The Derelicts of Company K: A Sociological Study of Demoralization*, a 1978 book about social corrosion that Shibutani based on a Japanese American military unit in the late 1940s. This book is roughly contemporaneous with the establishment of the Commission on Wartime Relocation and Internment of Civilians, or CWRIC, which in fact cited *The Derelicts of Company K* several times. In this book, the tacit claims about large-scale injustice in *Improvised News* became much more explicit and detailed as a result of hard intellectual work Shibutani had done during the intervening twelve years. At the same time, Shibutani came to concentrate on those claims and the people to whom they referred. In the conclusion to the book he engages in comparative study, but the vast majority of his text deals exclusively with Japanese American experience. Thus, *The Derelicts of Company K* demonstrates the continuing evolution of Shibutani's thinking about the experience of wartime incarceration and its subsequent impact, the latter now the object of study.

Improvised News and *The Derelicts of Company K* are infrequently associated with Asian American studies not because they declined to treat racism and mass incarceration as profound injustices, but because they declined to treat them in ways consonant with the field. When Shibutani did discuss the injustices and sociopolitical dislocation Nikkei experienced in the United States, he addressed them as examples of something fundamentally sociological. That is to say, he wrote about wartime incarceration as the outcome of failures in governmental policy, driven by corrosive patterns of behavior among privileged groups in American society. For Shibutani, then, Executive Order 9066 and its aftermath were not uniquely tied to people of Japanese ancestry or even to anti-Asian sentiment in the twentieth century. Rather, they were the sort of thing that could happen to any vulnerable group in any society under the right circumstances. He treated them in the manner of a sociologist operating under a strong sense of disciplinary responsibility: as sociological phenomena in need of proper analysis.

Shibutani's work calls to light the dearth of contemporaneous scholarship on the topic in Canada. There are specific historical causes for this. Whereas many college-age Japanese Americans from the West Coast were able to relocate and thus continue their studies, Canadian institutions, which had been unwelcoming to begin with, were largely unwilling to help the few students who had actually managed to gain access to higher education.[9] Furthermore, after the war, Canada continued to implement specifically anti-Japanese policies, which greatly increased the obstacles faced by Nikkei wishing to rebuild their lives. In the United States, by contrast, Japanese American communities reestablished themselves with less difficulty (due in no small part to considerably less government hostility), and their constituents were more able to regain their social and economic footing. The result was a set of circumstances north of the border that irreparably damaged the academic and professional prospects of an entire generation. Consequently, Japanese Canadian academics of that generation were few and far between.[10]

There is another, more important reason for the dearth of postwar Nikkei academics working on mass incarceration and displacement in Canada. As discussed briefly in the Introduction, there was simply no program comparable to JERS or the lesser-known Bureau of Sociological Research (BSR), which the psychiatrist and anthropologist Alexander Leighton oversaw at the prison camp just outside Poston, Arizona.[11] While the experience of wartime incarceration was a catastrophe for those of Japanese ancestry, it represented a windfall for American social and behavioral scientists. Scholars were on the scene soon after the inmates arrived in camp, having been assigned the task of studying the socioeconomic effects of forced mass migration, the dynamics of large groups under stress, and the problems and tasks associated with administering forcibly constituted communities. Many of the questions these scholars grappled with pertained to group solidarity, cultural traditions, and intergenerational and interethnic tensions. Thus, for contemporaneous researchers, the camps served as laboratories, rich with opportunities for data collection. In fact, both academics and government officials alike shared the view that the effects of Executive Order 9066 merited a dedicated social scientific study. This view helped establish wartime incarceration as a viable topic for research.

Such academic work played a vitally important role in postwar scholarship, and not simply for those who read the publications that it generated.[12] The Nikkei who worked for social and behavioral scientists studying the impact of mass imprisonment found themselves in an unusual situation. First, the existence of these studies confirmed the extraordinary nature of their circumstances and framed those circumstances as worth studying. Second, each study gave its participants a framework for conceptualizing those circumstances, even if in some cases that model was as much a counterexample as anything. Third, each study also enabled its participants to think of their experiences as a kind of data set, something that could in theory be organized, analyzed, and interpreted for others, even if not at the time. The effects of these three factors are particularly clear in regard to JERS, which had many Nikkei researchers who went on to produce scholarly work on wartime incarceration. Among these, three figure especially prominently: Shibutani and two of his fellow Tule Lake inmates, Miyamoto and Sakoda. All three went on to careers in the behavioral and/or social sciences. Miyamoto taught at the University of Washington; Sakoda first at the University of Connecticut and then Brown University.[13]

Shibutani, Miyamoto, and Sakoda all wrote dissertations on wartime incarceration, and each approached the topic in ways that differed from Thomas's method. Miyamoto's dissertation (University of Chicago, 1950) was "The Career of Intergroup Tensions: A Study of the Collective Adjustments of Evacuees to Crises at the Tule Lake Relocation Center." Sakoda wrote "Minidoka: An Analysis of Changing Patterns of Social Interaction" (UC Berkeley, 1949), noting in the introduction his debt to W. I. Thomas and Kurt Lewin for discussing precisely those aspects of social formation that Dorothy Swain Thomas had believed immune to analysis. (Sakoda pursued a degree in social psychology rather than sociology.[14]) While at Chicago, Shibutani wrote both his Master's thesis ("Rumors in a Crisis Situation," 1944) and his dissertation ("The Circulation of Rumors as a Form of Collective Behavior," 1948) on rapidly changing social configurations.

All three continued to discuss imprisonment in the years that followed, though in different ways. Sakoda, for instance, returned to the topic relatively late, contributing two watershed essays to Yuji Ichioka's landmark 1989 volume *Views from Within*.[15] Miyamoto wrote several essays specifically about Nikkei on the West Coast of the United States, especially in Washington State. Yet he was interested in Japanese American identity as a whole, and thus the bulk of his writing on the topic treated imprisonment as a critical historical moment rather than the object of his analysis.[16] Shibutani returned to the experience of forced migration and mass imprisonment repeatedly and at length in his published research. These scholars returned to mass incarceration in ways consistent with interests they had had before being imprisoned, addressing underlying psychological or sociological phenomena rather than the historical specifics of a given situation. And yet, where Sakoda and Miyamoto have become known as pioneers in the study of Japanese American wartime imprisonment, Shibutani came to be known narrowly as a sociological innovator rather than an authority on this key aspect of Nikkei North American experience. Consequently, it is easy to overlook the political implications of his work in comparison to that of other former inmates, JERS workers and otherwise, who addressed wartime incarceration in more recognizably activist ways.

Shibutani demonstrates the richness and complexity of the afterlife of Executive Order 9066, both in the material he discussed and in the manner he ultimately chose to discuss it. As with many of the JERS participant observers, consistent intellectual and political interests seem to have propelled him from early on. As Sakoda remarked in an interview with historian Arthur Hansen, "Each person also had his own pet project. Tom Shibutani was interested in rumors. I'm not sure what Frank was interested in. And I was interested in psychological reactions of different groups."[17] However, Shibutani's interests ran deeper, according to Sakoda: "Tom certainly had this academic orientation. He was always making outlines of this or that, what we had gotten on the study."[18] Such was Shibutani's reputation, in fact, that it contributed to a rumor about a "wholesome Nisei girl" he was dating (and later married): "We had heard that he was dating her to get information on the Nisei, and she accused him once of that, that he was only interested in her for the information. We were wondering whether he was going to get in trouble or not. Well, he ended by marrying her, so I guess it was all right."[19] Though enticing, such anecdotes only hint at a situation that Shibutani's later publications bear out: that he had long entertained questions about the intangible, seemingly unmeasurable aspects of social interaction, such as cultural values or intragroup tensions. When answered in large part with data he began gathering in earnest while incarcerated, those questions would ultimately help reshape sociological practice.

Shibutani's Early Life: Race and Questions of Belonging

Shibutani's academic and professional trajectories were governed by a strong sense of social and political obligation. As John Baldwin has noted, Shibutani had exhibited intense interest in the social and political implications of difference since the mid-1930s, when he experienced discrimination as a youth in Stockton, California.[20] A capable student and avid reader, he pursued an interest in race and human relations from the outset of his academic career, first at Stockton Junior College and then at UC Berkeley, where he majored in sociology and philosophy. Though to some extent a product of working with Thomas, this academic emphasis likely owes more to the guidance of Shibutani's Issei father, who was himself academically inclined. By the time Shibutani was in high school he had become keenly aware of racial discrimination, especially against Japanese immigrants in central California. He asked his father what to study to learn about race relations, and his father suggested sociology.[21] As a result, by high school Shibutani was already reading the work of key sociologists as well as that of Freud, who piqued his interest in psychology.[22] While at Stockton, Shibutani read John Steinbeck's *Grapes of Wrath*, and according to Baldwin, "Tom dreamed of writing such a novel that would help the Japanese Americans as Steinbeck had helped the Okies."[23] By 1939, Shibutani had also read John Dewey's *How We Think* (1910), which confirmed in him an affinity for pragmatism.[24] He felt that this philosophical stance was the best for identifying and solving problems, both personal and social. He particularly liked the flexibility of pragmatism, its recognition that "all knowledge is hypothetical and open to challenge, further investigation, and further reconstruction."[25] As would become evident in Shibutani's later writings, most notably *Improvised News* and *Society and Personality* (1961), he embraced the idea that pragmatism is concerned as much with solutions as with problems. From his perspective, sociological pragmatism thus created an opening for intellectuals not only to understand the causes of racial conflict, but also to offer mechanisms for addressing it.[26]

This perspective would ultimately dictate his educational choices. By the time Shibutani transferred to UC Berkeley, he realized he could not write the great Asian American novel, but he was still committed to pragmatism as a foundation for addressing race relations.[27] As a result of the Second World War, however, Shibutani's university education would be interrupted. But, as was the case for several of his fellow Japanese American college students, Shibutani used his status as a participant observer to remain academically engaged. More importantly, like his fellow Nikkei JERS researchers, he also understood that the project was a singular opportunity to advance understanding of what was happening to Japanese Americans and their family members. Unfortunately, he increasingly came to believe that the history and structure of JERS worked at cross-purposes to that aim.

Conflicted Identities and Participant Observation in the Camps

In the wake of Executive Order 9066, three separate groups of social scientists conducted research on Nikkei inmates. JERS, the largest, was initiated by a group of social scientists at the University of California, though unforeseen staffing changes eventually placed it entirely under the control of Dorothy Swaine Thomas, then professor of sociology at Berkeley.[28] With an extensive background in economics and social demography, Thomas conceived of the project as a study of how "enforced mass migration" would impact cultural traits and social patterns common among Japanese Americans.[29] When she applied for funding from the Rockefeller Foundation, she said that UC Berkeley was interested in pursuing such a project because mass imprisonment was "an important sociological event" that would provide insight into the effects of large-scale sociocultural disruption.

Other researchers also undertook contemporaneous studies of wartime incarceration. Another group of social scientists worked officially for the War Relocation Authority (WRA), the federal agency in charge of running the camps. As employees of the WRA, these social scientists were assigned to make recommendations about how to best run the prison camps. Comprising mostly anthropologists, this group did not study wartime incarceration in order to publish academic papers. Instead, they aimed to figure out how government officials should go about the day-to-day running of the camps.[30]

A third group of scholars concentrated on one site, a camp located near Poston, Arizona. This site was noteworthy in that it was one of two located on a Native American reservation and administered by an agency then known as the Office of Indian Affairs, under John Collier.[31] More importantly, Poston was singled out for study because it was the site of widespread political and social unrest in the autumn of 1942.[32] Collier asked Leighton, who was affiliated with Cornell University at the time, to head the study and make recommendations for how to improve administration of the camp in order to prevent further trouble. In response, Leighton established the BSR, which comprised a group of anthropologists, psychiatrics, psychologists, and sociologists. Though he attended to a variety of emotional, cultural, and social dynamics, Leighton ultimately adhered to his charge, publishing a survey of basic and highly visible failures in the administrative dynamic of the camp.[33]

The impact of wartime incarceration was, as one would expect, profound because Executive Order 9066 and its fallout intensified the same questions of social, political, and legal status for Japanese Americans that had occupied Shibutani's attention even before he arrived in camp.[34] In order to understand how the experience of wartime incarceration continued to linger in the mind of Shibutani and helped drive his scholarly intervention, it is necessary first to discuss JERS and the conditions it imposed on him as a researcher.

Those questions of social, political, and legal status for Japanese Americans complicated the job of studying them in the first place. The situation is perhaps exemplified by responses to the February 1943 distribution of the so-called Loyalty Questionnaire, thirty questions designed to assess the suitability of Japanese Americans for placement outside prison camps and, in the case of eligible males, military service. Two of these questions, 27 and 28, were the most disruptive, creating tensions between generations of Nikkei as well as between administrators and inmates. Addressing Nisei males aged 17 or older, the first read, "Are you willing to serve in the armed forces of the United States on combat duty, wherever ordered?" The second read, "Will you swear unqualified allegiance to the United States of America and faithfully defend the United States from any or all attack by foreign or domestic forces, and forswear any form of allegiance or obedience to the Japanese emperor, or any other foreign government, power, or organization?" Answering "no" to one or both questions for any reason meant being categorized as disloyal and potentially moved to segregated camps or even harsher sorts of confinement. Yet, because of factors beyond political discontent, many prisoners either refused to answer these questions or else answered one or more in the negative. For instance, as Thomas and JERS researcher Richard Nishimoto observed in 1946, many prisoners in the camps believed that answering in the affirmative would jeopardize their legal status in the United States, while others simply misunderstood the questions outright.[35]

Even beyond questions 27 and 28 the questionnaire ignited a firestorm. Many inmates felt it was impossible to complete. The questions were particularly difficult for Issei, who could not become legal United States citizens. (The National Immigration Act of 1924 had established national quotas that discriminated against immigrants from Eastern and Southern Europe and essentially excluded Asians altogether.) Other inmates felt they should simply refuse to answer the questionnaire as a protest against wrongful imprisonment. And then there was the basic volatility of life behind barbed wire. Because tensions were running so high, perceived collaboration with white administrators, including on the Loyalty Questionnaire, became a critical concern among many Nikkei.

That concern made it particularly difficult for participant observers who were seen talking to whites.[36] Nikkei who were believed to be selling out their fellow inmates were often called *inu* ("dogs"). Once characterized this way, one could expect treatment that ranged from ostracism to outright violence. And yet, Shibutani and his cohort of incarcerated researchers continued to record their observations for Thomas despite the risks. This is not to say that they did so without a care. Referring to a visit from Dorothy and her husband, W. I. Thomas, Shibutani recorded in his diary on June 24, 1942: "We had supper with the Thomases at our mess hall. The people around were very curious when they saw Caucasians. . . . Jimmy [Sakoda] was still worried about being taken for spies."[37] In a July 21, 1943, report to Thomas, Shibutani elaborated on the seriousness of being considered an *inu*, acknowledging that the term literally meant "dog," but "the Japanese are not referring to canine." Instead, he said, it referred to an inmate who was acting like a "stool-pigeon." He added that this was "one of the most serious charges that could be made."[38]

Nevertheless, in these prison camps participant observation was an important instrument for sociological work. Pioneered by anthropologists such as Bronislaw Malinowski and Edward Evans-Pritchard in the early 1900s, it aimed to obtain the fullest, most detailed map of cultural patterns possible—in effect, a re-creation of culture on paper, exportable to a scholar's home institution and, via publication, to his or her colleagues. Furthermore, researchers hoped this approach would also enable the reader to discern what evidence resulted from direct versus indirect observation. The goal was to generate an account that would allow them to understand a culture as if simultaneously from within and without. The method involved total immersion on the part of the researcher. Well suited to qualitative research, it involved conducting interviews, writing detailed life histories, and attempting direct observation. To conduct such in-depth work, one often had to live within the group under observation, thereby becoming intimately familiar with its cultural patterns. Consequently, participant observation was seen as one of the best ways to obtain intimate knowledge of a culture. Despite the inherent subjectivity of such a method, those who pursued it believed it would yield considerably more detailed information than any other method of data collection.[39] As a result of such research, participant observation became a dominant method used by anthropologists and sociologists to pursue the understanding of cultural groups.

Ironically, the use of participant observers for JERS was largely accidental. Thomas originally wanted to gather information by using formal questionnaires in order to maximize the yield of quantifiable data. Yet, she quickly realized that widespread hostility toward and suspicion of whites would make such an approach unreliable at best. She later wrote, "It was apparent that the main part of the record of what was going on inside the camps could be obtained by 'insiders,' that is by trained observers who were themselves participating in and reacting to the events under observation."[40] These observers made daily records of what she called "the maneuvers and reactions of an insecure, increasingly resentful people to policies imposed by government agencies and to incidents developing from the application of these policies."[41] However, Thomas's understanding of this method was idiosyncratic, and the emphasis on broad and undifferentiated narratives in her published results was frequently at odds with the method's strengths. Most importantly, that inconsistency nagged at many of the Nikkei JERS workers, whose direct experience of incarceration contrasted starkly with Thomas's scholarly grasp.

The majority of Thomas's participant observers were Japanese American. Twelve such observers, all but one of them fluent in Japanese, conducted the bulk of the research. Many of them, including Shibutani, were recruited from among the ranks of Berkeley students. Some had training in the social sciences, though only three had experience as field investigators. One was a graduate student in sociology with some training in political science, and the two others were anthropology students.[42] For Japanese American students (graduate students in particular), employment with the wartime study provided a way to maintain an academic affiliation, if a problematic one. As social scientists, participant observers could also see the potential academic and political benefits of their research. And as individuals they also recognized their importance for advancing that research. Because JERS workers were mostly Nisei (second generation), they were able to draw upon their knowledge of Japanese culture to interpret the feelings of evacuees, while their fluency in English and their familiarity with white academic culture enabled them to transmit those interpretations.[43]

Nonetheless, the strength of participation observation, an insiders' perspective, also created problems for Thomas's participant observers, since they were themselves imprisoned. Although these Japanese American researchers could provide insider information, it was only because they had been deprived of the ability to do virtually anything else. Furthermore, most of them were still students and thus dependent on Thomas and other white researchers for academic opportunities during and immediately after the war. Thomas was influential in her own right, but her husband, W. I. Thomas, was a giant in the field of sociology.[44] And while W. I. Thomas was not employed by the wartime study, he sometimes accompanied his wife when she met with her participant observers. The two thus formed a very visible academic and professional presence at Tule Lake.

"What Are We Looking For?"
Methodological Disagreement and JERS

Like many other JERS participant observers, Shibutani had a complex relationship with Thomas. She was simultaneously academic mentor, friend, director of the study, and wife of an authority in sociology. Both of the Thomases had encouraged Shibutani to pursue study of the discipline. They sent him books and shared meals with him whenever they visited Tule Lake, in part to discuss the study, but also to help with personal matters outside of the prison camp.[45] And yet, as unequal as the power relationship was and despite his appreciation of the personal aspects of their relationship, Shibutani worked hard to advance a practical understanding of the experience of inmates that would build on a more applicable sociological model. As Yuji Ichioka noted, several Japanese American researchers pressed Thomas for clarification of both the objectives and method of study.[46] Shibutani, for instance, did not want to just record every little detail of life at Tule Lake; he wanted to find the theoretical framework best suited for understanding his predicament and subject.

That is why, in lengthy letters to Thomas, Shibutani pressed for clarification about how to best collect and analyze evidence. He wanted specific criteria and a better sense of the methodological framework guiding the study. In his October 30, 1943, letter, for example, he wrote: "The study of the process of group formation is a hell of a tough assignment. We're in a period of flux in a place where you can't easily find people to talk to; we have an enormous field to cover and that is why I'm leaning on some conceptual frameworks that provide some clues as to what I ought to look for."[47] In a memo from earlier that month, Thomas told her workers (including Shibutani) that they were overly preoccupied with what she considered nebulous theories.[48] Suspecting that Thomas would respond with additional criticisms of this sort, he added: "I'll try my darndest to stay clear of ponderous frameworks."[49] And yet, it was clear by the end of Shibutani's October 30 letter that diplomacy had given way to his desire to find a more precise method of study and, perhaps more importantly, a clearer understanding of the problem they were to examine: "It is certainly relatively easy to get data on some things, but what good is all that effort if the results don't have any significance?"[50] For Shibutani, trying to record anything and everything, as Thomas often encouraged her researchers to do, was not just impossible; it was also meaningless. He continued: "This is why I feel that the formulation of problems is so important; because it may lead to a meaningful, purposeful collection of data."[51] Given his pointed criticisms of Thomas's approach, Shibutani anticipated a terse response from his part mentor/part boss. He closed his letter with that line about "the storm to break in December"—when Thomas was due to visit the camp—as a way to mitigate the severity of his criticisms. In an attempt at further diplomacy, he then declared, "My mind is not yet set—thank God—and I am still very susceptible to your influence. I certainly hope we can get this cleared up."[52] Shibutani was not a combative man, but neither was he a pushover. Recognizing the disconnect between what he saw happening around him and what Thomas thought worth publishing, he pressed her to clarify a project the importance of which was as much personal as it was academic and political.[53]

Given the wide range of possible topics to study (e.g., physical structures, food, health care, daily activities, emotional life), the ambiguity of JERS concerning both research questions and method would remain a bone of contention. Ultimately, Thomas said that she simply wanted participant observers to record inmates' "way of life."[54] In hindsight, that statement was tragic. The embeddedness of participant observers was more than a methodological challenge, more than the cause of a complex power dynamic. For scholars tasked with both living and studying unjust imprisonment, the intellectual richness of JERS as a shared endeavor, combined with the ambiguity of its aims and means, seems to have sharpened their sense of injustice even as it provided no clear way to analyze the resulting insights. In some sense, then, Japanese American researchers might be thought of as having requested a theoretical model in part to understand what they were experiencing.

Participant Observation and the Origins of Afterlife

Like haunting, afterlife disrupts the seemingly direct relationship between mind and world, dredging up memories and emotions while begging the question of what might have been.[55] It results from the pressure of the intangible, which so often seems inconsequential for present-tense existence. In this way, both afterlife and the events that provoke it tend to elude methods attuned to phenomena that can be more easily quantified. This was the case with the early study of wartime incarceration. The difference between what JERS workers observed and the analysis Thomas published could hardly be starker. This is all the more important, since *The Spoilage* (1946) and *The Salvage* (1952), two of the first books published after hostilities ended, set the tone for the bulk of future scholarship. Although Thomas's original goal was to measure responses to forced migration, *The Spoilage* became in large part a study of approximately 18,000 so-called disloyal inmates at Tule Lake, many of whom renounced their U.S. citizenship. Explicating political and social circumstances, Thomas concentrated on "repressive measures" and the consequent "impairment" of citizenship for imprisoned Nikkei; she also discussed the "successive protest movements" that arose in response (but neither the individuals who spearheaded them nor the underlying social and cultural shifts). Remarkably, she did so despite being presented with a singular opportunity to discuss the most fragmented and marginalized constituents (the supposedly disloyal) of a group that had already been forced to the margins of American cultural, political, and economic life. Thus, while the unjust wartime treatment of Nikkei in the United States was important in *The Spoilage*, that had more to do with documenting the eviction from the West Coast and with the logistics of imprisonment than with the emotional life of individuals and their families. Thomas did provide smaller-scale detail in some parts of this study, most notably in the passages dealing with the Loyalty Questionnaire. But these tend to be largely descriptive and, consequently, very different from analytical discussions elsewhere in the text. So, as her mention of "government and governed" in the introduction suggests, her JERS work was a survey of large-scale sociopolitical phenomena.[56]

Thomas's second book on wartime incarceration, *The Salvage*, demonstrates this emphasis even more forcefully. Part I documented "patterns of social and demographic change" among Japanese Americans after the war. Thomas dedicated Part II to fifteen life histories meant to account for the circumstances of affected individuals before, during, and after imprisonment. Thus, while the first half of the book was given over to sociocultural texture such as "Immigration and Settlement," "Religious Differentials," "Forced Mass Migration," and "Sociopolitical Orientation," the second half narrowed radically to encompass the individual narratives of a schoolboy, an agricultural student, a journalist, a clerk, a mechanic, a civil servant, and so forth.[57] The individual life histories in Part II of *The Salvage* were meant to provide a detailed account of the patterns discussed in Part I, but they also presented disciplinary challenges for Thomas. As Robert Bannister has observed, she was at a loss for how to analyze the life histories, in particular the data that dealt with values, behavior, and attitudes.[58] Though encouraged by W. I. Thomas to give the life histories a more prominent place in *The Salvage*, she seems to have been unsure of how to do so.[59] Nevertheless, we should view those life histories as an attempt to localize the phenomena discussed in Part I—that is, to generate contexture.

The result was mostly descriptive rather than analytical. As Bannister has suggested, "the publication verbatim of fifteen of [JERS researcher Charles] Kikuchi's life histories in *The Salvage*, with no analysis, left a gap within the book that Dorothy was . . . unable to bridge."[60] This led to raw data coming unmoored from the conceptual framework meant to govern them. Each life history was assigned a reference number, followed by a brief description of the individual.[61] After this cursory introduction, a first-person account of the subject's life history followed, without any further discussion. Thus, where earlier proponents of participant observation used elements of "subjective" life histories to document larger observations, in *The Salvage* Thomas simply grafted the unanalyzed life histories onto the end of the book, juxtaposing them with statistically oriented narratives in a manner analogous to that of *The Spoilage*. Lacking analytical direction, this section of the book left the reader to her or his own devices. What is more, it did little to flesh out the generic narrative Thomas had offered. As Mae Ngai has noted, "the aggregated statistics . . . obscured many subtleties in the internment experience."[62]

In fact Thomas regarded the study of personal matters, emotional states, and the like as methodologically suspect. Following in the footsteps of her mentor, William F. Ogburn, she had even declared earlier in her career, "It is useless and not a little ridiculous to assign numerical values to 'attitudes,' or 'opinions,' and think that thereby we are rendering them fit for statistical treatment."[63] As JERS workers began to question Thomas's approach to camp life, she instructed them to refrain from interpretation as well as undue attention to the mental life of inmates,[64] the better to gather all possible quantitative material without lapsing into what she deemed subjective responses.

In the end, the methodological gap proved too great. As Sakoda once remarked, Thomas "was uncomfortable with field data, which dealt with behavior, attitudes, and values."[65] Combined with the chaos of life in camp and, consequently, the broad net JERS cast to collect data, confusion among the researchers grew. In response, researchers with strong research interests and a clear view of Japanese American life faced a conflict, which Sakoda summed up in an interview with Arthur Hansen: "How did you manage to, at one [and] the same time, serve the leader of your group, Dorothy Thomas, and give her what she wanted, and also serve the nagging conscience that you had as a social historian, really, that there were other things that needed to be taken into account?"[66] That conflict manifested itself first in disagreements within JERS, disagreements in which Thomas, as director of the study, necessarily prevailed. Later, however, Shibutani and his fellow Nikkei academics managed to resolve that conflict differently. Their resolution was more than simply adhering to specific academic interests. As Sakoda's choice of words indicates, the methodological conflicts were both professional and ethical. They arose from a crisis of conscience. Dogged both by the memory of what had happened to him and, perhaps more importantly, what had happened to his fellow Nikkei, Shibutani would go on to produce sociological studies that built on his JERS work, while subjecting its raw data to a method less beholden to statistical analysis and more sensitive to the complexities of human interaction. The method he chose was Symbolic Interactionism (SI), which he studied at Chicago with one of its leading exponents, Herbert Blumer. And over the decades that followed, he used SI to resolve that conflict repeatedly in favor of his lingering sense of the past.

Shibutani, Method, and the Understanding of Experience

In 1943, Shibutani started doctoral work in sociology at the University of Chicago at the urging of W. I. and Dorothy Thomas. He studied with Louis Wirth, Everett Hughes, and Blumer, whose own ideas about sociological method greatly influenced Shibutani's future analysis of Japanese American experience.[67] Working with Blumer in particular, Shibutani found a point of departure from Thomas's approach to sociology, a way to understand the dynamism of meaning, identity, and belonging. As Blumer would later write, "self-interaction puts the human being over and against his world in-stead of merely in it, requires him to meet and handle his world through a defining process instead of merely responding to it, and forces him to construct his action instead of merely releasing it."[68] Meaning, he suggested, neither is inherent in an object nor does it accrete; rather, it is continually made and remade via shifting circumstances of social engagement with that object. For Blumer, society was less a product, a collection of structures that govern human relations, than a process of continual revision that occurred at all levels, most importantly that of the individual, whose engagements with his or her surroundings, fellow individuals, groups and even her- or himself constitute society from moment to moment.[69] Shibutani also continued to study the work of George Herbert Mead, having discussed Mead's work with S. Frank Miyamoto at Tule Lake. Although he was graduate student, Shibu-tani also continued his work for Thomas, shifting his attention to Japanese Americans who had resettled in Chicago during and after the war.

By the fall of 1943, Shibutani was growing excited about new possibili-ties for understanding the experience of wartime incarceration, the effects of which he continued to study for JERS while undertaking his graduate coursework. Suspecting that Thomas would worry about Blumer's influ-ence, Shibutani wrote to her on November 8, 1943. He spoke of topics she might consider "fit for statistical treatment," stating that "the project on pre-evacuation is also coming along. Please don't worry about it in spite of the fact that most of the guidance is coming from Blumer, because Blumer continually insists that I draw my conclusions from my data and not from his theories."[70] Contrary to what he wrote in this note, not only would Shibutani come to embrace Blumer's theories, but later correspondence sug-gests that he also increasingly engaged with SI as a method for interpreting the seemingly random data JERS was accumulating. For example, on Janu-ary 19, 1944, he wrote to Thomas: "I've been taking it for granted that you don't mind my reading now and then since you had always encouraged our studying in the past. We can turn in better reports and do better research when we are even slightly less ignorant."[71] It would seem that studying with Blumer and other faculty at Chicago had presented Shibutani with new ways of seeing the experience of mass incarceration, ways that made visible the complexities of both groups and their constituents.

The resulting changes in Shibutani had less to do with specific interests, since he had long been engaged with race relations, than they did with how best to pursue those interests. It is as if his time at Chicago provided Shibutani with a new lens through which to view the world around him, a lens that gradually cast insistent but inchoate feelings in sharper relief. Blumer in particular helped provide the kind of methodological framework that Shibutani had unsuccessfully sought from Thomas, one that allowed for a fuller understanding of the emotional and social dimensions of exclusion and belonging, whether the result of imprisonment or other circumstances. Shibutani was interested in the particulars of behavior that arose as a function of emotion rather than emotion for its own sake. In fact, as this chapter will demonstrate shortly, Shibutani saw his own emotional involvement with wartime incarceration as a source of insight and a phenomenon in need of scholarly framing. Stalked by memories of wartime mistreatment and painfully aware of the gap between what he had observed in camp and what JERS had published, Shibutani found in SI a means to analyze aspects of camp life that had previously been considered unmeasurable and to present them clearly and precisely. Equally important for Shibutani, this method allowed him to account for the dynamic interplay between power and race, not least with respect to Japanese Americans in the 1940s. Nikkei men who had volunteered for the armed forces at the outset of the war were reclassified as 4-C enemy aliens, imprisoned along with their families, subjected to the Loyalty Questionnaire and draft, forced to serve in segregated units, and then celebrated by the United States for their exemplary service. And yet, they also were unwelcome in the mainstream once the war ended. As Shibutani saw it, the implications of SI and its associated texts were profound. First, SI allowed for the idea that the identity of the individual, like that of the group, was neither static nor inherent. Second, insofar as identity formation was reciprocal, with large- and small-scale cultural and interpersonal factors affecting one another, it could be conceptualized as significant at every level of social interaction.

After Shibutani earned his doctorate in 1948, the University of Chicago offered him a job to study and teach sociological pragmatism there for three years, after which he took a job at UC Berkeley. His new colleagues at Berkeley had just finished a long, tense battle over the combining of comparative history and sociology into a single department. As a result, that department proved an uncongenial environment for Shibutani, who seems to have been driven primarily by research problems, which for him were also social and political problems, rather than by a concern for career advancement. It has been pointed out, for instance, that disillusionment with academic life lay behind Shibutani's decision to resign from Berkeley in 1957.[72] Free from academic politics, he went on to write *Society and Personality*, one of his most important methodological meditations. Far from an attempt to secure a plum job (he had just resigned from one, in fact), this book was an opportunity to examine sociological methods without having to worry about administrative or departmental politics. In short, Shibutani used scholarly independence to resolve methodological issues he grappled with over the course of his career, even as far back as during his work for JERS. Still, bills come due, and even a sophisticated and important work like *Society and Personality* could not meet Shibutani's needs. By 1961, he was back in academe, having accepted a position at the University of California, Santa Barbara, where he would remain until his retirement and where he would write both *Improvised News* and *The Derelicts of Company K.*

Disciplinary Practice and the Lingering Presence of Personal Experience

Even after he had completed his training at Chicago, Shibutani did not publish on the complexities of wartime incarceration that had so struck him at the time. Rather, he continued to think and write about Symbolic Interactionism, which he regarded as a powerful analytical, and thus political, tool. In fact, nearly two decades would elapse before he used that tool to frame and present his own experience. There are a number of possible reasons, but a consideration of Shibutani's publications suggests the most important: at some point in the early 1960s, methodology and personal experience came into alignment in a way they simply had not before. Shibutani would ultimately present this alignment primarily in scholarly terms, suggesting that his grasp of SI had developed to such an extent that he could finally use it to account for phenomena that previously had defied articulation. But, as this chapter notes below, he also acknowledged that his own feelings about unjust incarceration required their own kind of reshaping, one that had not been apparent to him until much later. It is as if prior political commitment, wartime personal experience, and later methodological investigation eventually coincided in a way that transformed Shibutani. In that transformation, intuition, feeling, and professional responsibility combined to allow the reframing of that experience with an eye toward making it present to others who might otherwise think of themselves as standing at some distance from it.

Having acquired a disciplinary framework more attuned to the complexities he had experienced while working for JERS, and armed with the means for designing his own studies of race relations, Shibutani used SI both to review earlier analysis of wartime experience and to make significant contributions to the field of sociology. The first of these combined contributions, *Improvised News*, is perhaps the subtlest example of how the lingering experience of wartime incarceration shaped Shibutani's postwar work and of how he deployed that experience to change the sociological view of individuals in society. It therefore deserves close attention. Basing his work in part on the observations and field notes he had made for JERS, Shibutani was able to mate his earlier interest in social cohesion and disjunction to a fascination with rumors that he developed while imprisoned. The result is a text that tracks impromptu social reconfiguration. Tracing the behavioral patterns of groups thrown into disarray, Shibutani hoped, would ultimately reveal "some of the processes whereby new social structures come into existence."[73]

While *Improvised News* used sixty examples of situations involving rumor, its central hypothesis came primarily from four case studies Shibutani conducted regarding Japanese Americans and their wartime experience.[74] Indeed, he framed the whole book as having its roots in that experience: "Although this book is not written as a research monograph, it is the product of a fairly lengthy investigation, including some four years of field observation." This observation, he added, "began on December 7, 1941, with records of rumors among the bewildered Japanese in the San Francisco Bay Area, who suddenly found themselves suspected of being enemy agents." Racism and hysteria were the stimulus, Nikkei Americans and their family members were the sample group, and the camps were his laboratory: "Observations were then made in a succession of unsettled contexts: evacuation of the Japanese from the Pacific Coast, days of confinement in relocation centers, mass migrations from the camps to the Midwest and East, an interlude in the U.S. Army, and Japan during the first year of military operation."[75] In short, *Improvised News* was the product of extensive participant observation that began even before Shibutani joined JERS and extended through his military service, having gained force and direction during his time in prison.[76] Not that he approached the attack on Pearl Harbor and its aftermath with the same academic distance that Thomas and other senior scholars had. On the contrary, Shibutani's journals indicate precisely the same sorts of anger, confusion, fear, and resentment as do the surviving diaries, letters, and oral histories of other inmates. Rather, time brought a set of academic instruments with which he eventually found himself able to address wounds that had long refused to heal. SI made those wounds clearer and brought into focus their cultural and social impact. Most importantly, though, it also allowed Shibutani to extend his analysis of wartime racism and hysteria to similar dynamics he had later observed in other groups, enabling him to see how the experience of eviction and unjust incarceration could provide the focal point for a larger study of sociocultural disruption: "To make this study comparative, data have been drawn from many other sources; nonetheless a disproportionate share of the cases still deals with the fate of various categories of Japanese during World War II."[77]

Shibutani then concluded this passage by noting that "somewhat lengthy summaries of four of the original cases have been included; key insights were derived from them, and the materials are not available in any other published source." Two points stand out here. First, the mention of "lengthy summaries" recalls both participant observation and Thomas's way of approaching that method. In this moment, Shibutani was effectively rewriting how one should discuss the "important sociological event" that was wartime incarceration. A proper account for that event, he implied, should provide not only summaries of the cases, but also "key insights"—that is, analysis that in his text derived from SI.[78] Second, and perhaps more importantly from a historical standpoint, Shibutani made clear that his data were being published for the first time. He needed to do this because he knew that readers would likely compare his findings with Thomas's JERS-based publications, which remained the standard sociological texts on the topic. He anticipated, in other words, that readers would perceive *Improvised News* as at least to some extent a study of wartime incarceration with its roots in JERS, so he attested to the novelty both of his findings and of his data. He attested, in short, to the divergence between a non-Nikkei outsider's survey of wartime incarceration and his direct experience of that event. Still mindful of the disruptions of Executive Order 9066, but now energized by a method designed expressly to allow the analysis of such disruptions, he returned to his direct and lingering experience of mass imprisonment and focused it through the lens of SI.

Especially important for Shibutani's analysis were population density and the lack of formal channels for relaying large-scale information (for instance, dedicated news sources that could address changing circumstances accurately, consistently, and in detail). These two factors forced and then fueled reliance on informal sources (i.e., rumors) within Nikkei communities along the West Coast. Extrapolating from the behavior of these communities, Shibutani wrote, "If unsatisfied demand for news is excessive, collective excitement becomes intense, and rumor construction occurs extemporaneously through spontaneously formed channels."[79] He had observed this phenomenon firsthand, both on the coast and at Tule Lake. For example, on July 11, 1942, he wrote in his journal about a conversation with another inmate: "She passed on two rumors: (1) there is a curfew at 10 for all women in Tule Lake and (2) Tule Lake is only a temporary center."[80] Shibutani's interest in rumors, which later became the topic of his graduate writing, showed up repeatedly in his wartime journal and reports. In a July 21, 1943, report about the first six months in camp he wrote: "Rumors of all sorts were rampant, and it became difficult to determine what to believe."[81] Another, more innocuous example, which Shibutani discussed in *Improvised News*, was the vigor with which evacuees attempted to comprehend their forced removal from the West Coast.[82] Less benign instances include the energy devoted to figuring out who might be *inu* versus a trusted member of the Japanese American community.

The heart of the matter, for Shibutani, was the dual role rumor played, as both a symptom of social breakdown and a factor contributing to it. Regarding life in camp, Shibutani noted, population density and a lack of reliable sources for information combined to generate a twofold improvisatory transmission of information. First, population density made for efficient relay, particularly when the lack of privacy bred an environment in which even the slightest deviation from social norms was met with profound suspicion, even paranoia. Second, speculation, combined with political and social instability, promoted a hunger for the credible. That is why, according to Shibutani, rumors tend to persist "where institutional channels are not completely trusted. . . . This is especially true when the rumors appear more plausible than the official announcement."[83] Building on firsthand experience and observation, Shibutani produced a foundational study of that breakdown of trust. Demonstrating that rumors were far more than faulty communication, it showed that in the absence of definitive sources, people share what information they have in an attempt to organize seeming chaos. In order to explain that organizational impulse, Shibutani referred to a figure who had loomed large in his thinking from an early age: "A public, as Dewey (1927) puts it, consists of *people who regard themselves as likely to become involved in the consequences of an event and are sufficiently concerned to interest themselves in the possibility of control*."[84]

Improvised News is thus nothing less than a progressive analysis of important sociological phenomena, of which wartime incarceration was one notable example. The book demonstrates an important continuity of interests for Shibutani, of course, but it also demonstrates that wartime incarceration lent urgency to those interests. That is why Shibutani treated his subject not as a mere intellectual curiosity, but as a barometer of alienation. He observed, for instance, that the organizational potential of rumor was largely illusory, as hunger for the credible gradually became credulity. As Shibutani pointed out, uncertainty over plans to imprison the entire Japanese American community on the West Coast prompted widespread and occasionally bizarre speculation, such as over unjustified FBI raids: "Although published accounts of spy rings, huge stores of firearms and ammunition, and disguised Japanese admirals were frightening to those outside the Japanese communities, to the people within the charges were so preposterous that questions arose as to what constituted the *real* reasons for the arrests."[85] Presenting laughable news reports of high-ranking military officers secretly embedded within the Japanese American community, formal news outlets became suspect: "The reasons given in the newspapers were patently absurd; then, why were people being arrested? Answers were provided by a flood of rumors."[86] From the outset, fundamental questions concerning citizenship, legal status, racism, and economic disadvantage had plagued the Japanese American community. Yet, since no fully credible news source existed, members of the community improvised their own, more plausible scenarios. Most such rumors pertained to the time frame for incarceration, while others (especially around April 1942) had to do with how life in the camps would be: articles one could bring, provisions to be offered by the government, and so forth. Using rumor to navigate such circumstances could be exhausting. Continually generating criteria for social formation was exceedingly taxing. Hence, Shibutani wrote, "As one locale after another was evacuated, many arrived at the centers with a sigh of relief; at last the uncertainty was over."[87] Lending his analysis a subtly ironic twist, Shibutani described Executive Order 9066 as having derived, at least in part, from "improvised news" by whites after the bombing of Pearl Harbor.[88]

Still, although ineffective as a means for stabilizing the community, rumor was nonetheless a sophisticated phenomenon. The product of a group that was bound up in the consequences of wartime incarceration, rumor became a meditation on powerlessness. Shibutani wrote, for instance, that people were wryly aware of the unreliability of the information they generated and shared: "The Japanese interned in relocation centers . . . sometimes referred to their unsettled way of life as *dema-kurashi*, literally 'existence through rumors,' but pronounced 'democracy' in a heavy Japanese accent." The artifice of pronunciation demonstrated the self-consciousness of rumor-mongering, its status as a reflection on the desire, in the absence of genuine potential, for control. According to Shibutani, the rumors seemed to assuage fears as much through an illusion of order as through the explanations they offered: "For some individuals participation in rumor construction may on some occasions be more cathartic than instrumental. Rather than making a serious effort to define the situation, they are merely relieving their tensions by giving vent to inner dispositions."[89] More than mere self-soothing, ironic recognition of rumor allowed inmates to voice their disenfranchisement by appropriating, reframing, and critiquing the ideal of representative government. That is, it allowed a supposedly polite and tractable people (if one viewed as simultaneously treacherous) to articulate resistance in the midst of injustice. Having long been interested in rumor, as Sakoda recounted, Shibutani found that topic continuing to linger in his social conscience years later. And only once his methodology had become sufficiently refined and robust could he finally act on the feelings that had stayed with him throughout the years.

Shibutani recognized that the long-term effects of such instability and suffering could result in a fundamental dislocation of one group from the system to which it was supposed to belong. After the bombing of Pearl Harbor, he wrote, "rumors developed among the Japanese that the U.S. Army planned to kill everyone of Japanese ancestry in Hawaii. Many fully expected retaliation from outraged Americans and were immobilized with fear."[90] This was due in part, he suggested, to the tendency of people "to dissociate communication content from their evaluation of sources." This dissociation fueled the transmission of rumor by undermining the rigor with which people customarily tried to treat information: "Acceptance of material from channels that had once been suspected rises with time, just as belief in reports from sources that had originally been rated high in credibility often decreases."[91] The fragmentation that followed would feed itself, driving an afflicted community into ever-greater instability, so long as its circumstances remained unsettled.

To some extent, then, *Improvised News* gave Shibutani the chance to return to wartime hardships that had neither been subject to a full public reckoning nor faded from personal memory. It also enabled him to work through some of the societal and methodological implications of wartime incarceration that Thomas had not explored. In so doing, it allowed him to return to his own past and that of his fellow Nikkei as part of an attempt to strengthen the American social and political fabric. Linking his core case studies to other examples, Shibutani made wartime incarceration an object lesson in what happens when people are deprived of the opportunity either to control or to opt out of their circumstances. Rumor correlated with a lack of belonging, and unjust mass imprisonment was something that might happen to any group that fell out of public favor; only accidents of history directed that disfavor specifically at people of Japanese ancestry. Shibutani aimed to do more than document unjust treatment; in fact, several of his examples involved more banal kinds of indeterminacy (e.g., Case 44, which dealt with the 1948 Republican Party convention).[92] Instead, he was interested in addressing the underlying dynamics of social fragmentation:

> The manner in which popular perspectives are shaped becomes a question of crucial importance in periods of social upheaval. One of the characteristics of modern mass societies is that men face one ambiguous situation after another. They are constantly sensitized to news precisely because they have to get their bearings as they go along. Ours is also a generation in which manipulation of outlook through ingenious propagandistic devices is commonplace, where ruses, unsubstantiated testimony, and doctored evidence play decisive parts in local and national life.[93]

Shibutani wrote as someone whose life had been transformed by such devices, ruses, and testimony. (For instance, he had a significant interest in what he had called "social disorganization" and "the breakdown of governing values" while at Tule Lake.[94]) He wrote as a pragmatist for whom the myriad complexities of emotional and cultural experience affected the health of the society to which a person might belong. The empathetic component of his project thus lay in its aim of separating social disorganization from a specific historical, racial, or religious circumstances and making that phenomenon something that any reader might identify with.

Crises and failures might not be averted, but perhaps they could be turned to some advantage: "What makes decisions in such unsettled times so important is that crises are the crucibles out of which many innovations emerge. . . . In studying the manner in which people mobilize to act in such contexts we are trying to get at some of the processes whereby new social structures come into existence. The study of rumors is important, then, not only in itself but also in what it tells us about social change."[95] Identifying how groups responded to various pressures, Shibutani sought to identify how one might prevent those pressures in the first place. Far from a purely disciplinary exercise, the writing of sociology was for Shibutani a mechanism one might use to reinforce a civil society. In and of itself, rumor was a problematic coping strategy that inmates used in an attempt to give meaning to their experiences. Writing about rumor, by contrast, resulted from the painstaking development of more useful (i.e., demonstrably productive) tools to accomplish that same task later. Afterlife, in Shibutani's case, enabled harmful behavior eventually to provide models for its opposite.

The Derelicts of Company K (1978) performed much the same function, but in this case the afterlife of wartime incarceration became a much clearer and important presence in Shibutani's analysis. In fact, it played a solo role in the narrative of his chosen subjects, rather than serving as one key example among many. As he had in *Improvised News*, here too Shibutani laid out the injuries visited upon Issei and Nisei, with particular attention to anti-Japanese sentiment and its effects after the bombing of Pearl Harbor. He discussed the fears of the older generation concerning their poor English and visible difference from people around them, as well as the humiliation they repeatedly suffered as a result of these characteristics. He also talked about the rise of rumor, that hallmark of social disincorporation, such as the widespread idea that "the FBI refused to allow wives of prisoners to speak to their husbands in Japanese; suspects were not allowed to change their clothes or even to go to the toilet; in a raid in Concord old people were forced into their yard without bathrobes on a freezing cold morning; some FBI agents forced a girl with mumps to get out of bed in order to search beneath her." Such rumors had a direct, material impact: "Issei busied themselves destroying anything in their homes that might possibly be forbidden, and those who thought they might qualify for arrest packed their suitcases and stoically prepared for jail." Persecution also fueled intergenerational and interpersonal conflict: "Considerable resentment developed against certain individuals suspected of being informers; they were accused of taking advantage of the situation to strike back at their personal enemies."[96]

Shibutani enumerated such topics in order to demonstrate how wartime incarceration was an injury that Japanese Americans had endured both collectively and individually. That injury, he demonstrated, had shaken the faith many Nisei had in the American political system long before the soldiers he was discussing found themselves in uniform. Furthermore, the prospect of military service threatened to accelerate a loss of traditional features of Japanese American culture that was already well under way. Wartime incarceration, Shibutani observed, had helped drive the forces of social disincorporation far beyond small groups of disaffected Issei: "For some Nisei this [imprisonment] was proof that there was no future for them in the United States; it confirmed the contention of those Issei who had insisted that they would never be treated as Americans, no matter how they themselves felt."[97] This was a position Shibutani himself knew well. In a journal entry from June 29, 1942, he reflected on the rage he felt on hearing that Nikkei servicemen were barred from visiting family members: "What the hell, if they can't trust a Nisei to the extent of not letting him come into the Western Defense area, why did they draft them to begin with?" In the same journal entry, Shibutani wrote in response to the censorship of their mail: "I was griped as hell and wondered where our great democracy was."[98]

The result, which Shibutani documented meticulously in *The Derelicts of Company K*, was a collection of alienated individuals that barely functioned as a group and, over time, became increasingly chaotic, at times even anarchical. It is precisely this type of change in attitudes over time that Thomas was not able to capture in her more strictly quantitative accounts of Japanese American wartime experience, but that had long preoccupied Shibutani. No less important, that change in attitudes was the direct result of government malfeasance based on racist hysteria, and its very irrationality completely eroded any investment members of Company K might otherwise have had in the collective endeavor that military service presumed. In sum, Shibutani demonstrated how Executive Order 9066 and its aftermath further alienated a significant element of the Japanese American community long after the end of World War Two.

The Derelicts of Company K deviated significantly from triumphalist narratives of Japanese American military service that were the norm at the time,
most notably those about the celebrated Japanese American 442nd Regimental Combat Team. Consequently, Shibutani was careful to demonstrate
how demoralizing life in general had been for members of the company
throughout the 1940s. Describing racism leading up to mass incarceration,
Shibutani mentioned a sign in the window of a barbershop: "Free Shave to
Japs—Not Responsible for Razor Slips."[99] He also described how in California many people were arguing that Japanese Americans should be incarcerated for the duration of the war, after which they could then be deported.[100]
Shibutani linked the company's compromised morale to the psychological
state of Japanese Americans who were trying to reestablish themselves after
being released from the camps, noting that "the prevailing view [among Nik-
kei] was that they were still vulnerable and on trial." Individuals were afraid
to make a wrong move, for fear that doing so would "jeopardize the safety
of everyone." He continued: "Resettlers generally agreed that they should
dress neatly, leave large tips, and avoid boisterous conduct."[101] Shibutani's
goal with such observations was less to lament injustice than to frame the
conditions under which conscription was reinstituted for Japanese American men in January 1944. That is, following the model of Blumer, Shibutani
aimed to lay out how American life had placed Japanese Americans "over
and against" its institutions, giving scholarly form to the afterlife of injustice
not only for his subjects but also for himself.

To that end, Shibutani also provided details about how Japanese American men in the military were treated both during and after their service. He
described an incident that occurred on November 11, 1944, when a barber
in Parker, Arizona "refused to serve a crippled Nisei veteran and ejected him
forcibly from his shop." At the time, according to Shibutani, the man was on
crutches, wearing a uniform as well as his service ribbons; when questioned
by reporters, the barber said he would do it again even if it meant his shop
would be closed down.[102] The result of such hostility—hardly a rarity in the
United States—weighed heavily on Japanese American soldiers: "To outsiders
most Nisei soldiers looked alike. They were short, stocky, dark skinned, and
uncomfortably like the enemy in the Pacific. They wore American uniforms;
yet they seemed out of place, incongruous." And yet, despite being thrust
together under similar circumstances, these men were hardly inclined to co-
here: "since they had been treated alike on the basis of ethnic identity, they

were forced to act together as a unit" despite their frequently very diverse backgrounds. The result was a cohort in which "differential acculturation [class status, education, proficiency in English, etc.] resulted in considerable heterogeneity."[103]

Where *Improvised News* offered a range of examples demonstrating sociological fundamentals, some twelve years later *The Derelicts of Company K* addressed group dynamics very differently, though it, too, offered broadly applicable pronouncements. It dealt exclusively with Japanese Americans, for one thing. For another thing, it took a subset of Japanese Americans who more or less completely contradicted a growing popular discourse that stereotyped Nikkei as mild-mannered and industrious. Shibutani opened with the declaration that "although this book is about soldiers, it is not a saga of heroes." Instead, it concerned itself with what he called "a tawdry backwash of a gigantic war," a "'fuck-up outfit.'"[104] He then offered two reasons for this. First, he wanted to provide "a chronicle of one of the more disorderly units in United States military history, and one objective is to learn how it deteriorated to this point."[105] The importance of this project for American culture in 1978 is difficult to overstate, for that project implicitly rebuked the concept of the model minority by discussing the record of a group that presented a "stark contrast to the exemplary performance of most Nisei troops in World War Two," not least the 442nd. Writing about Japanese American soldiers with "a formidable record of discord," Shibutani produced incontrovertible evidence—as if that were needed—that Nikkei were just people prone to all the usual vices as well as virtues. Any suggestion to the contrary was the result of what he called "hero-making" at the level of mass culture. Japanese Americans, he observed, had been treated as a kind of "Cinderella" in the popular imagination, having been reviled and then celebrated.[106] *The Derelicts of Company K* was at least partly an attempt to set the historical record straight.

Shibutani was setting the record straight both historically and methodologically, though, as he pointed out elsewhere in his introductory remarks, "this study differs from most previous investigations of morale in that attention has been focused on the subjective experiences of the demoralized men themselves." He then added, as if recalling JERS and its quantitative emphasis, "many disorders have been studied from the outside—statistics of the damage done, the number of people who defected, opinions of officials and observers."[107] But morale is an elusive topic, ill-suited to such a quantitative, macrosocial approach. Consequently, the second purpose of *The Derelicts of Company K* was to provide "sociological generalizations concerning the process of demoralization" based on participant observation and its more qualitative emphasis. Still, that emphasis had larger applications. Thus, while he had produced a study of Nikkei men in their twenties, Shibutani took pains to point out that "most of the behavior patterns described have been observed before and are likely to develop again in many other historical contexts. The record is to be taken, then, as a case study that will serve as a vehicle for a broader investigation of the breakdown of collective undertakings."[108] That breakdown was less a product of supposed troublemakers than a failure of those in power to safeguard the very idea of a collective undertaking in the first place: "Many insurrections have succeeded not so much from the adeptness of revolutionaries, but from the inability of the privileged to mobilize their resources to defend their interests."[109] Wartime incarceration was one such episode. Rather than ensure that Japanese Americans actually enjoyed equal protection under the law, rather than ensure that these vulnerable people were treated fairly and honestly, those in power had instead demonstrated repeatedly and at every level that there was no such thing in American society as far as Issei and Nisei were concerned. And this demonstration, as much as the personal failings of any of Company K's constituents, led to the extraordinary dysfunction of that group. Those constituents served as a warning to people who might otherwise see themselves as having little or nothing to do with this supposedly anomalous group. Generalizing outward from his experience as a Nikkei citizen who suffered the corrosive effects of institutionalized bigotry, Shibutani employed pragmatic sociology as a way to strengthen the fabric of society. And he did so through engagement with the afterlife of wartime imprisonment, which could shed light on all manner of social and political problems if framed properly and analyzed rigorously.

Afterlife and Shibutani: Time, Method, and the Presence of the Past

One might reasonably ask why, if Shibutani was so self-aware, it took so long for the afterlife of wartime incarceration to express itself openly in his work. Shibutani himself answered this question in *The Derelicts of Company K*: "Because of deep emotional involvement in the events, the intensity of which I could not appreciate at the time, I was unable to understand many things that now appear obvious."[110] That involvement is a complicating factor for anyone who pursues participant observation, as Shibutani suggested elsewhere in his book: "It requires both enough identification with the subjects being studied to comprehend and to feel *their* definition of the situation and at the same time sufficient detachment to realize that this particular view is but one of several possible interpretations." Doing so, however, was of paramount importance, for while it might be difficult to remain "reasonably dispassionate, especially in the midst of some of the exasperating circumstances described,"[111] only that method was well suited to the work Shibutani had in mind, work that was sociological, to be sure, but also was socially and politically engaged. No less important, perhaps, that method would allow access to varieties of experience—including emotion—that linger even after the events that provoke them have passed.

That political engagement was a very real concern for Shibutani. Reviewing the state of the literature in his most famous work, *Society and Personality: An Interactionist Approach to Social Psychology* (1961), he said, "scientific research may be regarded as a type of activity that has evolved gradually in the efforts of men to find more effective ways of coping with their difficulties." To talk about how people behave in groups was, he suggested, a way of solving problems and, as such, had an ethical dimension. These remarks cast important new light on Shibutani's concern about civil liberties violations, which he expressed clearly in his Tule Lake journal among other places. For instance, he wrote on May 13, 1942, that "a threat to our civil rights is a threat to the rights of all elements of the American population because it sets a dangerous precedent for the others to follow."[112] Talking about how people behave in groups also carried an obligation; anyone wanting to address the topic in a useful way should do so as rigorously and dependably as possible, which meant acting scientifically: "The demand for scientific knowledge, however, often arises in those areas in which common sense proves inadequate, as men attempt to improve upon practices hitherto resting on popular beliefs."[113] Because he viewed knowledge production as inherently political, Shibutani had to move past readily available narratives—the sort one might obtain through formal questionnaires, for instance—since "a man could do things for reasons of which he himself was unaware, and having performed the deeds he could subsequently invent plausible explanations."[114] According to this argument, the scholar's goal should therefore be to study people at close range, observing not only their material and political circumstances but also their unselfconscious day-to-day functioning. In so doing, he or she would be able "to reduce the diverse things that men do to a limited set of *general principles*, principles that will account even for the fact that men continually explain their deeds—to themselves as well as to others."[115] Only by reducing human behavior to that set of principles could Shibutani put his lingering memories—that afterlife of wartime incarceration—and those of others to broader use. Such was the complexity and painfulness of his experience that that reduction took time and occurred in stages—first with *Improvised News*, and later with *The Derelicts of Company K*.

Afterlife and Methodological Innovation

At stake in this chapter is the way in which the afterlife of wartime incarceration began with Shibutani as a generalized sense of injustice and its costs for Nikkei on the West Coast of the United States, but eventually grew into a topic for scholarly study and, thus, political engagement. Whether in the study of rumors or analysis of social disincorporation, his own personal experience of officially sanctioned mistreatment metamorphosed from traumatic experience into a call for action, or a specific form of knowledge production. For Shibutani, the action that was likeliest to result in large social and political gains was academic, because it provided a robust theoretical foundation for rigorously analyzing phenomena, thus transforming emotional investments into durable intellectual and political engagements. SI gave him the means to understand how an individual might be impacted by a group, and vice versa. This goes for Nikkei waiting for trains in the initial stages of their eviction from the West Coast, for Japanese American men conscripted by a government that had just barely finished calling them traitors, for members of the Republican Party in the 1940s, and for whites in California following the bombing of Pearl Harbor. SI gave Shibutani the means to recognize the basic humanity of both Nikkei and non-Nikkei and, with that, the flaws and peculiarities that, unchecked, kept them from forming a more perfect union. That is to say, it provided for a scholarly kind of empathy. Dogged by the very real imperfections of an earlier union, he eventually returned to the impact of those imperfections in order to avert their recurrence, along the way making durable the afterlife of his experience.

Personal Disclosure as a Catalyst for Empathetic Agency

In the wake of the September 11, 2001, attacks, Secretary of Transportation Norman Mineta wrote a letter to all U.S. airlines directing them to increase security but forbidding them from using pre-flight racial and ethnic profiling. The latter, he said, would discriminate against Muslims or people of Middle Eastern descent. In subsequent public addresses he expanded on this directive, citing not only the idea of basic civil liberties, but also historical precedent. Referring to his own experience as a prisoner at the Heart Mountain camp during the Second World War, Mineta pointed to a historical injustice that he himself had endured, demonstrating both the damage that bigotry and hysteria can cause and the hollowness of their foundations. Mineta's decision to draw on, and at times to disclose, his personal experience with wartime incarceration was more than just part of his work on behalf of Japanese Americans, particularly in support of the Civil Liberties Act of 1988. Like many other Nikkei who became politically active in the 1970s and 1980s, he has invoked the memory of unjust imprisonment across a range of circumstances in order to advocate change in both law and culture.

Taking Mineta's public presence as a case study, this chapter will show how Nikkei North Americans have increasingly approached the afterlife of wartime incarceration as a means for producing coalitions across significant political and cultural divides. Driven by the lingering presence of injustice, a striking number of Japanese Americans have turned their experience into a perpetual reminder of how failures both of government accountability and of the public sphere, the place in which government and civil society meet, can afflict virtually any group in moments of crisis.[1] They have achieved this in large part by recounting personal experience, a practice that necessarily emphasizes the individual. To discuss his own disclosures, as this chapter will do, is not to declare Mineta exceptional. He was but one of many Nikkei who worked tirelessly to secure redress and, perhaps more importantly, to keep the memory of wartime incarceration alive even after they achieved that goal. Furthermore, he also was but one of many Nikkei who began to speak about the personal impact of Executive Order 9066 and its aftermath publicly in pursuit of shared political engagement.[2] However, Mineta provides a particularly high-profile and well-documented example of a larger political and cultural shift toward a kind of activist disclosure among Japanese Americans in the late twentieth century. Furthermore, his career also demonstrates some of the ways that Nikkei public engagement with personal experience has continued to grow and extend to include larger social and political issues far beyond the achievement of redress.

For many readers, talk of disclosure might sound peculiar. As Harry Kitano noted, Japanese Americans born in the early twentieth century tended to demonstrate emotional reserve that bordered on opacity.[3] The proliferation of personal stories about wartime incarceration, and the willingness of so many Nikkei to relate those stories publicly, marked a significant personal and cultural change. As Yasuko Takezawa has shown, this change resulted partly from new intergenerational and political dynamics that redress produced within the Nikkei American community.[4] However, it also arose from the recognition that such disclosure might be important *outside* that community. Japanese American legislators and activists came to realize that a key element of making the afterlife of an event politically engaged involves presenting that afterlife as a lived experience. As this chapter and those that follow will show, such first-person address has been meant to cultivate empathy in people for whom mass incarceration is geographically or historically remote. By giving such people opportunities to identify with aspects of the experience of Nikkei North Americans and to act on that identification, an empathetic response enables agency to become more readily transmissible. Thus, one might suggest that disclosure had become a necessity, and not just for individuals who experienced injustice. Starting in the last quarter of the twentieth century, Japanese Americans also came to approach disclosures about wartime incarceration as essential for those with whom they came into contact; they began to approach personal revelation as a way to help other individuals and groups recognize their places in an important but fragile social fabric. They were, in short, pursuing a goal similar to Tamotsu Shibutani's, which was to demonstrate that the privileged often fail to safeguard not just the rights of others, but the very idea of rights.

Like those of other Japanese Americans who increasingly worked to prevent such failures, Mineta's own disclosures repeatedly framed government not as opposed to the public sphere, but as a guarantor of it. He did so by calling on government to serve and respond to the public more actively and with a greater sense of obligation. Furthermore, like other Nikkei, he increasingly argued that what happened to 120,000 American citizens and their relatives during World War II could easily happen to others. In this respect, Executive Order 9066 and its aftermath have come to exemplify the personal as well as political and economic costs of failing to safeguard and enhance democracy and the debates that allow it to endure. As many Nikkei would point out, that cost accrues not only to the targets of injustice, but also to society at large, which denies itself the social, political, and economic contributions of those it has marginalized.

Through an examination of personal and political testimony as well as other primary sources, this chapter traces Mineta's growing willingness to consciously relate both his experience of wartime imprisonment and his lingering feelings about that experience in order first to achieve redress and later to prevent such injustice from occurring again. His testimony and legislative work can thus be described as an example of how Nikkei came to recognize the political significance of their and their family members' experiences. By recalling his own past, Mineta, like his fellow survivors of Executive Order 9066 who also have chosen to speak out publicly, helped demonstrate that the afterlife of wartime incarceration could reshape both political culture and laws.

Like Tamotsu Shibutani, Mineta and his generation approached that afterlife differently over time. His work began as an explicit engagement with helping those on the margins of American economic and political life that implicitly stemmed from his own experience of bigotry and, at times, generosity. With the pursuit of redress in the 1980s, however, the origin of his engagement became increasingly open, metamorphosing from a personal justification for legislative action into an object lesson in the combined fragility and importance of the public sphere. As Mineta strove to change how those around him engage with one another, he also changed how he himself might do so. As he encouraged others to express the long afterlife of historical events, he also gave increasing voice to his own experience. To better understand that change, this chapter will begin with a discussion of Mineta's biography and early political career.

The Origins of Afterlife and the Beginnings of Transformation

Prewar life for the Mineta family was consistent with that of most Nikkei of their generation. His parents, Kunisaku and Kane Mineta, could not become citizens because of the 1924 Exclusionary Law. As a result, the family was politically and economically marginalized from the start. Over time and with a great deal of work, though, they gained a foothold on the West Coast. When Mineta's father had first arrived by ship in 1902, he landed in Seattle and spent a year and a half moving south along the West Coast, working on farms and in lumber camps along the way.[5] By 1928, he had enough money to acquire a home in San Jose, as well as establish a thriving insurance business and a strong presence in the local Japanese American community. He was, however, an Issei, and the 1913 Alien Land Act barred him from buying his own home. As a result, he turned to a man named J. B. Peckham, who had helped several other Japanese Americans circumvent the Act. Peckham's method was simple, if one that took time for his clients: he would purchase the house in his own name and then transfer the deed to his client's eldest child on that person's twenty-first birthday.[6] As a result, by the time Norman Mineta was born in 1931, he and his four siblings belonged to a solidly middle-class San Jose family that commanded the respect of their fellow Nikkei.

That middle-class existence came to an abrupt end after the bombing of Pearl Harbor, which shattered Japanese American hopes of having stable homes, jobs, and a place in the local community, as well as access to bank accounts, education, and any real claim to due process. Mineta would later recall the day Pearl Harbor was attacked: "It was just after 12:00 noon, and the phone was ringing off the hook. My dad was a leader in the Japanese American community. People were wondering, 'What's going to be the impact of this attack on Pearl Harbor?' People were starting to come over to the house, as well." Being in a position of community leadership could be a mixed blessing, though. Mineta added that "next-door to our home was a home where the executive director of the Japanese Association of Santa Clara County lived. Now this was just a social organization, but . . . their daughter Joyce came running in about 1:30 saying, 'The police are taking Papa away! The police are taking Papa away!'"[7] Mineta's father ran out to see what was happening, but by then the FBI had already taken their neighbor. Events would soon hit closer to home when Mineta saw his older brother, a sophomore in college, with tears in his eyes and his draft card in hand. Less than a year earlier that card had read, "Ready, fit, and able to serve," but now the Selective Service Office had issued him a new card reclassifying him— like all Japanese American males of age—as "4C: Enemy Alien."[8] This was only a foretaste of what was to come in the wake of Executive Order 9066.

The lingering aftereffects of camp and of the emotional toll it took on the family were vitally important. Early memories of the violation of rights would leave an indelible mark on Mineta, although it would take time for to manifest itself fully. When they were finally released from the prison camp at Heart Mountain, like most other Nikkei the Minetas concentrated on reestablishing themselves. They moved back to San Jose and reinstalled their children in school. Later, after graduating from UC Berkeley and performing his postwar military service, Norman Mineta settled once more in San Jose, a place that would spark and nurture his interest in public service. While working in the family's insurance business, he joined local Methodist organizations and served on the city's Human Relations Commission. During his time on the commission, he helped form a Municipal Housing Authority to assist people who were displaced by the construction of an interstate highway. As a result of this work, in 1967 the mayor of San Jose asked Mineta to consider filling a vacant seat on the City Council. Mineta's father expressed his concern by observing that "the nail that stands up gets hammered down" and asking his son if he would be willing to withstand such hammering.[9] This episode demonstrates two important traits common among Nikkei who had lived through wartime incarceration: a cultural distaste for attracting attention and an awareness that their status as citizens was always contingent.[10] Both of these traits led many of that generation to believe they had better just keep their heads down and not attract attention.

Despite the warning by Mineta's father about the risks of life as a public official, Mineta felt he owed something to the San Jose community. He later explained that "when we were evacuated in '42 there was a group formed that saw us off at the station and when we returned there was another committee that worked to help make things easier" to return the coast.[11] For him, San Jose at that time had been a haven from xenophobia, exemplifying the potential of a communitarian ethic. This is why he had gone out of his way to participate in civic and political activities as a young man: he believed that his work would gain traction there. Convinced of his ability to effect change, he considered the pursuit of that change an obligation.

In addition, Mineta tried to make an impact well beyond the confines of that community. His approach to governance might have derived from his experience as a Nikkei citizen, and he might have pursued issues important to his Japanese American constituents, but his work also addressed the lives of those outside Japanese American circles. Mineta's identification with marginalized citizens turned out to be a defining trait in much of his governmental work over the years that followed.[12] Though no less shaped by wartime imprisonment than were older generations, Mineta was activated by the sense that something had yet to be done—a lingering feeling that transformed into action, spread outward from Nikkei into American society. In particular, he seems to have intuited the power of empathetic agency from early on. In 1971, he testified before the U.S. Commission on Civil Rights. As the newly elected mayor of San Jose, Mineta wanted to point out the negative impact of a recent U.S. Supreme Court decision, in *James v. Valtierra*, that governments must first hold referenda before they could build low-income housing.[13] His goal was not to promote new legislation, but to demonstrate the administrative trap in which local politicians now found themselves. He cited statistics showing that the demand for such housing exceeded supply, and that consequently San Jose and other cities like it were faced with an impossible choice: to hold a costly referendum in which wealthier citizens might simply vote down affordable housing, to ignore the requirement of the referendum altogether, which he called an "un-American" prospect, or not to provide any such housing in the first place.[14] He refused to accept this last course. Moving from the first-person singular to the plural, he declared: "As a Mayor, I believe we the city, working with our City and County Housing Authorities, have a responsibility to try and promote the development of adequate housing for all citizens within our economy, including the low income."[15] Where civil society failed to safeguard its most vulnerable constituents, government would be obliged to intervene.

Though formally dedicated to economic problems, Mineta's testimony addressed marginalization in general. Having run through his statistical evidence, he moved beyond income and available-housing numbers in an attempt to cast light on an underlying flaw in the relationship between government and civil society. For him, that flaw lay in the link between economic privilege and race: "In San Jose there is a correlation between being poor and being a member of a minority group. . . . Of the approximately 14,500 persons whom the Kaiser report identified as having an unmet low-rent housing need, our city staff estimates upwards of 85% of that number are members of minority groups."[16] Mineta was careful to frame the matter as a consequence of institutional blindness. Noting that the Valtierra decision effectively allowed "the total community [to] deny to a smaller portion of that community the low-rent housing it needs," he then suggested that the Supreme Court's decision had entrenched an ultimately untenable view: "I am not a lawyer, but to my mind this constitutes discrimination, not only against the poor, which is bad enough; but due to the correlation between being poor and being of a racial minority, it constitutes discrimination against our racial minority citizens as well."[17] As a member of a family that had been subject to exclusionary laws and had narrowly skirted the wartime confiscation of its hard-won home, Mineta recognized the fragility of access to housing. The bulk of his audience could, by contrast, take such things for granted, since they were largely white and middle-class elected officials, civil servants, and enfranchised citizens. Acting as someone whose own access to housing had been both contingent and violated, he aimed to represent people in analogous positions. His argument was that even when it was constrained by the electorate, the government nonetheless had an obligation to those who do not have an equal voice in the public sphere. Government therefore had to take the initiative and act on behalf of those people, despite the Supreme Court's decision.

Mineta seemed largely content to continue in this vein, bolstering civic communitarianism at a local level. Certainly that would have been consistent with his career up to that point. In 1971, Mineta had become the first Asian American mayor of San Jose, having served as a City Council member since 1967. Yet Jim Ono, a Japanese American attorney and friend, had plans that would put Mineta on the national stage. In January 1974, Ono attempted to convince his friend to run for a seat being vacated by Republican Charles Gubser, who served in the House of Representatives for the 10th congressional district, which included San Jose. Mineta declined, saying that he wanted to serve out his term as mayor.[18] Ono persisted, however, and enlisted twenty other people to join him at Mineta's house the next night to persuade him to run for Gubser's seat. They succeeded, and he went on to win the general election with 51 percent of the vote, becoming the first Japanese American from the mainland elected to Congress.[19] As a result, he found himself working on a much larger scale, and that work would gradually clarify how the persistent memory of wartime incarceration might allow him and other Japanese Americans to engage in the public disclosure of private experience in pursuit of redress.

Personal Disclosure as Political Action

Election to national office greatly expanded the scope Mineta had for working on behalf of marginalized groups. Though his actions, like those of many other Nikkei from his generation, have been largely centrist-communitarian, they still demonstrate a genuinely activist disposition. Mineta's work with respect to passage of the Civil Liberties Act, his post–September 11 attempts to ward off profiling, and his role in having Heart Mountain rededicated as a commemorative site all depended on the afterlife of Executive Order 9066, which became a more prominent and complex feature of that work over time.[20] He and other former inmates undertook such work partly in order to address the lingering memories of the Japanese American community. But, like other Nikkei subject to mass imprisonment, they also pursued that work in order to recuperate civil society and make government more responsive. That is to say, they turned their attention outward toward American political culture as a whole.

Mineta's decision to pursue national political service has necessarily bound his actions to limits the electorate might set. But that decision also allowed him to influence both legislation and debates about it on a larger scale, and so shape the limits of the electorate at the same time. The resulting compromise is evident in his record. In the early and middle portions of his career, his work beyond the Civil Liberties Act mostly concerned infrastructure and the like. For instance, from 1992 to 1994 he chaired the House Public Works and Transportation Committee, after having led its Aviation Subcommittee between 1981 and 1988. At the same time, though, he maintained an interest in ensuring minority representation, such as when he cofounded the Congressional Asian Pacific American Caucus (1994), for which he also served as the first chair.

Though the work of Mineta and his fellow Nikkei in Congress advanced the welfare of both Japanese Americans and citizens in and beyond his district, their labor also had a far-reaching effect on society and politics nationwide. Perhaps the most famous was the 1988 Civil Liberties Act. Though the work of multiple authors and the result of multiple iterations following the 1982 release of the report *Personal Justice Denied* by the U.S. governmental Commission on Wartime Relocation and Internment of Civilians (CWRIC), the Civil Liberties Act had a transformative effect on many Japanese Americans. That effect is most visible in the highly personal disclosures in the testimony of hundreds of people before the CWRIC as well as testimony in support of the Civil Liberties Act. As noted above, those disclosures were a remarkable departure from tradition for most of the people who spoke. And yet, these people recounted their experiences and voiced their lingering feelings because they came to realize that doing so could revivify the past, crystallizing the afterlife of wartime imprisonment and making it available to people who might otherwise never understand the full force of that injustice. Because the first-person singular voice of afterlife is such an important part of its efficacy, this chapter will now turn to Mineta's testimony and statements to the press. Although Mineta was but one of hundreds who ultimately decided to engage in public disclosure, the trajectory of his governmental work and the character of his public statements are a particularly clear example of how effective that change could be and, thus, why it occurred in the first place.

Like many other Nisei, Mineta did not undertake the public disclosure of his private experience lightly. Having been raised in a family that felt the customary pressure to leave memories of wartime incarceration buried, he knew how big a departure from common practice this was. However, he also recognized the potential disclosure had to advance the needs both of Japanese Americans and of the communities in which they lived. Mineta also knew that disclosure had to be made in a way that would demonstrate the illegality of Executive Order 9066 as well as its economic, social, political, and even emotional toll. (Though it heard wrenching personal testimony, the CWRIC had primarily addressed constitutional and judicial questions in its 1982 report.[21]) In addition, disclosure had to counter stereotypes that, having lodged themselves in the popular imagination, resurfaced in the late 1970s and early 1980s in the wake of recession, the collapse of American industrial production, and a growing trade imbalance with Japan. More than a public recasting of Japanese Americans, Mineta's public recitation of his personal history also testified to the persistence of wartime memories for a group of people who had first been dehumanized and stripped of their rights, then later held up as an ideally passive "model minority" unaffected by that dehumanization.[22] For Mineta, therefore, the importance of this task outweighed any cultural inhibitions he might have felt, insofar as personal disclosure might similarly linger in the minds of non-Nikkei observers, creating a productive discomfort that came from identifying with former inmates in surprising ways.[23]

Identification can move one to act by increasing the sense that something needs to be done. In this way, agency becomes both more visible but also more freighted. That is, it becomes more contagious. Hence, in sharing his story in public forums, Mineta aimed to do more than scold or admonish. He also aimed to ignite a sociopolitical engagement in his listeners, Nikkei or otherwise, and then to point out a way they could act on engagement. To do so, though, he believed he had to tell people what had happened at ground level, which he did in public appearances and congressional testimony that not only recounted the injustice West Coast Nikkei suffered but also shed light on how wartime incarceration continues to burden Japanese Americans. Mineta's testimony provides a sense of how the public airing of private suffering helped set the stage for redress and the important work that has followed it (which Chapters Four and Five discuss in greater detail).

In a 1987 interview with the *Los Angeles Times*, Mineta framed the mass incarceration of Japanese Americans as an example of the destabilization of any large community that became the target of racist hysteria and underhanded economic competition. By depriving citizens and their family members of basic legal rights, Executive Order 9066 had opened the door to virtually every kind of suffering, including the dispersal of Nikkei families.[24] Plus, it had done so with frightening speed and devastating force. Mineta described how the absence of reliable information within the Japanese American community about what to expect had led to panic feeding rumor and vice versa. In the Mineta family, Kunisaku had gathered his wife and children to tell them they might be broken up, and that he had heard that Japanese Americans like him and his wife who were ineligible for citizenship might even be traded for prisoners of war in Japan.[25] The story is remarkably similar to what Shibutani had recounted, but the venue was different. Where *Improvised News* presented the findings of a sociological study of group dynamics, Mineta's narrative was highly personal and played out colloquially on television and in the pages of newspapers. As he and other Nikkei who testified before the CWRIC and in support of the Civil Liberties Act recognized, those differences were critical for making their narrative the topic of public debate.

As "relocation" approached, the only thing the Mineta family was certain of was that prisoners were permitted to bring only a few possessions.[26] Mineta recalled that he and his family practiced for that fateful day by packing suitcases and determining what each member could carry.[27] They were careful, however, to avoid packing anything on the list of so-called contraband: irons, radios, cameras, and knives and scissors longer than four inches. On the day of departure, Mineta, then ten years old, put on his Cub Scout uniform.[28] Since Nikkei were scheduled to leave the train station during the lunch hour, he recalled, several of his friends ran five or six blocks from school to say goodbye. Military police with bayoneted rifles were stationed nearby. The train itself was dark, the shades pulled down to prevent the people on board from seeing where they were going. Throughout the long ride, passengers were instructed to stay put, the exception being Mineta and the dozen or so other young boys dressed in Scout uniforms.

When the train finally pulled to a stop, Mineta and his fellow prisoners were taken to the Santa Anita Assembly Center, a hastily repurposed former horseracing track. There, stables served as temporary housing for prisoners, who occupied one horse stall per family while they waited for the camps to be built. Mineta's family, he recalled, was somewhat luckier than the majority of prisoners: because there were not enough horse stalls, and because they were among the last to leave the train, they wound up occupying a barrack. When he visited his less fortunate friends who slept on straw mattresses in the stables during the height of the summer heat, he wondered how they could bear the discomfort, especially the stench of manure.

After they arrived at Heart Mountain, his family of six lived in a single fifteen-by-twenty-foot room. Though the space was small, at least it was clean. Cots were shoved in side by side, and the Minetas used their suitcases as night stands. More disturbing than the lack of privacy and space, though, was the bright searchlight that passed regularly across the room's window, shining directly in one's eyes. More than just a physical disruption, the light was also a continuous reminder that the Minetas were prisoners, a message reinforced in daylight by armed guards along the perimeter of the camp.

Although some politicians had argued that the prisons were designed to protect Nikkei during this period of racial hysteria, the fact that the guards faced inward suggested otherwise. The full extent of Mineta's status as a prisoner received confirmation when he and a friend went to watch a riot that had erupted after authorities came to search the barracks for contraband flatirons. After the guards opened fire on the prisoners, Mineta and his friend saved themselves by hitting the ground, but several others were wounded.

People nevertheless found ways to make the best of an awful situation. For example, Mineta recalled that at Santa Anita inmates took showers where horses had previously been washed. The names of many of these horses remained on the stalls, Seabiscuit and Man o' War among them, and as a source of amusement, the boys would wonder out loud, "Who are we going to take a shower with today?" Physical activities also were an important part of daily life for children. As Mineta recalled, at Heart Mountain, "we would get in large boxes and get blown by the wind and see how far we could go. Once I was swept under the barbed wire and past the fence. A guard in a jeep picked me up and took me to what you could call the brig, and then I got chewed out by my father."[29]

Still, the indignities of incarceration were many and varied, and Mineta took pains to reiterate them in many of his public speeches and in testimony before his congressional colleagues. In one recollection, he spoke of a family friend who had waited all day at the train station in Salt Lake City, Utah, to hand them a box of her father's favorite cigars, a small reminder of life on the outside. When the train stopped, she passed the box to one of the armed guards, who then handed the box to a military officer, who opened it and promptly broke each cigar in half under the guise of inspecting the box's contents.[30] By recounting such episodes, Mineta aimed to demonstrate the profound impact of Executive Order 9066 and its aftermath, and to show how that impact was as much cultural and emotional as economic and political. Doing this in formal testimony and in public interviews, he and his fellow former inmates made the previously private and largely invisible afterlife of wartime incarceration visible and understandable to others. And though such testimony would eventually engage with civil liberties in general, the widespread presentation of such narratives began mainly as a way to advance the cause of redress, although he would reiterate his personal testimony in the years to come, most notably after 9/11 as well as at the recent dedication of Heart Mountain as an educational center.

Setting the Legislative Stage

On June 20, 1984, Mineta testified before the House of Representatives Sub-committee on Administrative Law and Government Relations, which was considering H.R. 4110, a version of the Civil Liberties Act introduced by Representative Jim Wright (D-Texas) in 1982. Mineta had two goals in mind that day: to reinforce the account of wartime incarceration he had presented in other venues, and to link it with the legislative and legal concerns at issue. He began with an account of the work by the CWRIC and then provided a summary of H.R. 4110 and its senate counterpart, S. 2116. Following this, he asked a series of questions about the constitutionality of wartime incarceration and, finally, recounted details from the lives of Nikkei who were irrevocably changed by imprisonment. The structure of Mineta's testimony allowed him to move from the abstract to the concrete and from the juridical to the personal.

An examination of the last part of Mineta's comments sheds light on the importance of this approach. Toward the close of his legal and legislative account, Mineta posed a basic question. Even if a few individuals of Japanese ancestry had been genuinely suspect, he asked, how could it be legal for the U.S. government to "lock up 120,000 innocent and loyal Americans without a trial, without regard to the Constitution?" He noted that the reason Japanese Americans had been incarcerated was "because this was the group that popular opinion—and indeed the California Congressional delegation—demanded to have locked up," rather than because of any genuine threat.[31] Both government and civil society had failed Japanese Americans and their family members, but that had been preventable, as had been its long-term impact. To support his claim, he pointed out that few Nikkei were imprisoned in Hawaii, even though that was "where the military dangers were the greatest." By addressing both the unconstitutionality and the inconsistency of Nikkei wartime incarceration Mineta had laid the foundation for a discussion of the concrete effects of Executive Order 9066.

Before moving on to that discussion, though, Mineta emphasized the magnitude of the situation. He did so, however, by invoking categories of experience, rather than specific examples:

> Mr. Chairman, I could speak on this subject for quite awhile but my time is limited. I could tell you about some of the loyal and brave men I know; men who left the internment camps to fight bravely to defend this nation.

I could tell you of the old women torn from their homes of decades and forced to live in cold, spartan barracks only to oblige the prejudice of greedy neighbors.[32]

As a result, he was able to suggest that Executive Order 9066 had imposed countless individual miseries on its 120,000 innocent targets. He then proceeded to demonstrate the depth of suffering that people encountered, talking about both his own family and that of his future wife. He described how in early 1942 the man who would become his father-in-law, Saijiro Hinoki, was arrested by the FBI, which refused to give the family any information about his whereabouts for two months.[33] As Mineta then pointed out, the effect of such authoritarian treatment was both profound and durable. The years such treatment forced Hinoki and his fellow Nikkei to spend in a desolate prison camp, Mineta implied, amounted to a form of social death, replete with its physical counterpart: "Those who knew him said Mr. Hinoki never regained his lost will to live. He died a few years after leaving camp."[34]

No less powerful was Mineta's testimony regarding his family:

My father was not a traitor. He sold insurance from a small office in our home on North Fifth Street in San Jose, California. My mother was not a secret agent, she kept house and raised her children to be what she was, a loyal American. Who amongst us was the security risk? Was it my sister Etsu, or perhaps Helen or Aya? Or perhaps it was my brother Al, a sophomore pre-med student at San Jose State.

Localizing his audience's attention still further, he addressed his own status: "Or maybe I was the one, a boy of ten-and-a-half who this powerful nation felt was so dangerous I needed to be locked up without trial, kept behind barbed wire and guarded by troops in high guard towers armed with machine guns." Elaborating on the patently ludicrous suggestion that a little boy might constitute a threat to national security, Mineta asked his fellow members of Congress, "What was it I had done that made me so terrifying to the government?" In the span of a few scant paragraphs, Mineta brought home to his fellow legislators not only the scale of the injustice, but also the personal, even individual toll it had levied on one of their own.[35]

He did so because the proposed reparations could hardly compensate Nikkei for material and economic losses, a point he stressed at the beginning of his remarks. Instead, he suggested, financial payments should be made for another reason: "Although the loss of property and income from the internment is estimated at perhaps as high as $6.2 billion in comparable current dollars, these payments [authorized by H.R. 4110] are intended, in my mind, not as compensation for lost property but as liquidating damages resulting from the profound abridgement of basic constitutional rights."[36] The term "liquidating damages" is key here. It signals that reparations would serve as a penalty for the government's failure to honor its constitutional obligations to Nikkei citizens and their family members.[37] By localizing the effects of Executive Order 9066, then, Mineta was not simply cultivating emotional identification on the part of his fellow representatives, senators, and other citizens. He was also documenting losses caused by the failure of government to check the excesses of civil society, losses that, while intangible, nonetheless persisted and demanded a response. That is why his testimony moved carefully from the abstract to the concrete and from the juridical to the personal: by doing so, Mineta reframed the psychological and social fallout of wartime incarceration as phenomena with identifiable legal standing, byproducts of governmental misbehavior.

In order to bring this point home, he once again expanded his view from the personal back to the Constitution, concluding his testimony with an important comparison. After describing his own situation, he remarked that "murderers, arsonists, even assassins and spies get trials. But not young boys born and raised in San Jose who happen to have odd sounding last names. Is that what this country is about?" Referring to the inscription on the façade of the Supreme Court Building, he claimed that it encapsulated what advocates of redress were asking for: "It does not say Equal Justice Under Law Except When Things Get Sticky. It says Equal Justice. And that is what we ask for, Mr. Chairman. No more. No less. We have waited forty-two years. The time has come."[38] Mineta thus framed adherence to the Constitution as a contractual obligation. The failure of government was both shameful and harmful, and thus it warranted recompense. That was particularly important because, as Mineta pointed out, "our government had labeled us—and by us I do mean all 120,000 of us—as vaguely untrustworthy and a danger to the republic."[39]

In this way, Nikkei public disclosures made the individual's afterlife of wartime incarceration—that first-person singular experience that refused to retreat into the past—into something that could cultivate a first-person plural engagement. For Mineta, empathy has been elastic, expressing his thoughts in one moment, expanding to include the group in another. It also became a model, as in his discussion of "women torn from their homes of decades and forced to live in cold, spartan barracks only to oblige the prejudice of greedy neighbors." In fact, examples such as this last one are particularly important since they allowed Mineta to nest one form of empathy within another, to work outward from his own anger, sorrow, and pain toward the feelings of others. In so doing, he was able both to cultivate first-person plural identification and to model it, while also modeling what he perceived as the proper response: vigorous engagement with governmental obligation.

Afterlife, Disclosure, and the Timing of Engagement

Nikkei legislators did more than just argue for redress. For instance, testifying before his colleagues, Mineta also provided an example of its justification. Here, having reached his fifties and speaking as a seasoned congressman, was a former 11-year-old boy wrongly punished for treason by the government in which he now served, a government that he believed had an obligation to protect the most vulnerable members of society. The metamorphosis from child to adult, from prisoner to congressman and from the margins to the center was implicit, but it was also inseparable from the losses Mineta and his fellow Nikkei had suffered. Consequently, his testimony in support of the Civil Liberties Act created an opportunity for empathy and identification on the part of his audience. The presence of so many Nikkei speaking of their experiences before Congress allowed listeners and observers to extrapolate outward to all Japanese Americans, imagining others, similarly aged, who were also incarcerated but either had not or could not testify; others who, older when Executive Order 9066 was issued, had no opportunity to regain their lost economic and social standing; and still others who died in camp. Testimony like Mineta's drew back a curtain on the suffering and loss Japanese Americans and their family members had endured. It exposed the previously untold complexities of experience behind the convenient historical narrative that many people had entertained for so long.

Though remarkable, Mineta's testimony was not exceptional. It illustrates that Nikkei survivors of mass incarceration had come to recognize the importance of personal disclosure. Combined with his role as a member of the House of Representatives, it also illustrates the complexities of how personal experience can linger over decades and result in moments of important political work, which in turn produces further personal transformation. The most obvious part of this work lies in the demonstration, noted above, that a boy subject to farcical suspicions might become a trusted member of the House, now testifying about those suspicions and the imprisonment they caused. At the same time, Mineta's presence in hearings on the Civil Liberties Act, and in the House more generally, exerted new force on the predominantly white, middle-class bodies around him, not only challenging the forces that regulated him unjustly before, but also challenging the forces that continued to regulate him at the time, in this case by continuing to deny reparations for unjust incarceration. What had been lost became implicit and undeniable in what was present. Along with his fellow Nikkei legislators and their supporters, Mineta brought to mind the stolen homes and businesses, the money squandered and the lives laid waste by Executive Order 9066. And yet, he and his colleagues did so to win allies, not browbeat naysayers, by inviting people to "imagine otherwise" in the present.[40] They stood ready to move into the future by at long last beginning to acknowledge the past—and by continuing to do so.

The issue of time was critical in Mineta's testimony, since it addressed some of the objections against the Civil Liberties Act. Though he was successful, Mineta pointed out that that success was hard won. Inmates, he said, had spent the first twenty years after incarceration reassembling the shards of their prewar lives rather than pursuing legal remedies: "Our main goal was to rebuild our lives, rebuild our businesses, and regain our standing in the community. We were shamed and held up to public humiliation by the internment, and frankly we just did not want to think or speak about it."[41] Mineta added that by the early 1960s, many inmates had gotten back on their feet and began thinking again about what had happened to them during the 1940s. Yet the greatest change in their approach to imprisonment, he said, stemmed from intergenerational differences. Persistent memories gradually led the older generations to rethink what had happened to them, and as they did so, "our children began to ask questions about the missing years, the silent years that were never discussed at home."[42] He explained that the movement for redress had originated in the need of individual families to get the past out in the open, and in the feeling of many inmates that their status as full-fledged citizens had never been properly restored. In this way, he and other Nikkei who testified regarding the continued impact of unjust imprisonment turned that long silence into a further argument for redress. As Mineta explained, "All our energies went into rebuilding. That rebuilding process began to end in the early 1960s. That is, it took twenty years for us to get back what this government took from us in 1942." Far from expressing equanimity in the face of injustice, the silence of Japanese Americans who had been interned instead testified to the damage done to them and their families, damage that now demanded redress. Long after the initial injury, he declared, Nikkei citizens were asking the subcommittee to "to give us back our honor."

Mineta argued that, although redress was a long time coming, it would also be valuable for the nation as a whole: "Every citizen of this land will benefit from our rededication today to equal justice."[43] That rededication was the first step in a larger project. Though difficult, pursuit of the Civil Liberties Act had brought scrutiny of the government and of a historical circumstance that was unknown to many and uncomfortable for others. For Mineta, that scrutiny would give people the chance to work through their discomfort, making it productive in the sense of leading to more equitable behavior in the future.[44] His mention of "every citizen" indicates that both elected officials and members of the electorate would be involved. For him, to address an injustice committed by the government was also to address a failure of the public sphere. As a result, every citizen could benefit, not just from equal protection under the law, but also from that productive discomfort. By offering both liquidating damages and a verbal apology, the government would counteract some of the damage it had done to Japanese Americans and their family members. At the same time, it engaged in its own version of "imagining otherwise," by rejecting what Mineta called in a 1988 speech "the sad precedent [that] still stands that our government can round up and jail its own citizens, solely on the basis of race."[45] For Mineta wartime incarceration could be projected back onto civil society and onto government itself, in order to move toward a more perfect union.

Like many others who testified in support of redress, Mineta drew on examples of the combined social, political, and psychological impact of forced incarceration, and thus the need for redress, from his own family. For instance, he read out a letter from his father to friends (later published in the *San Jose Mercury Herald*) in which the elder Mineta recalled, "'We all felt so strong while we are staying at the station with you and many other friends but the train started and with the exchange of good bye then became so lonesome and when I looked Santa Clara Street from the train, I thought this might be the last look at my beloved home city.'" The poignancy of this moment for many Nikkei was brought home by the next two lines from the letter: "'My heart almost broke out and suddenly hot tears just pouring out. We whole family cried out and could not stop, until we get out of our loved county.'"[46] More than just a touching detail, Mineta Sr.'s letter demonstrates the emotional force behind lingering memories, even for members of an older, less activist generation. Beyond that, Mineta's decision to recount the contents of that letter demonstrates how the trauma his father endured could in turn sharpen the afterlife that drove Mineta himself to fight for redress. It also demonstrates how aspects of agency could become contagious within, and by implication beyond, a given family. In this way, testifying before Congress provided a chance for non-Nikkei to identify with the suffering of Japanese Americans and their family members, thus extending empathetic agency to the general public.

Empathetic Agency

Such divergences from the reticence of many former inmates about their wartime experiences ultimately served several interlinked purposes. First, by humanizing Nikkei experience, they helped people like Mineta "restore honor" to those who had endured wrongful incarceration as a result of Executive Order 9066, thereby ending decades of silence and shame. Second, they enabled Japanese Americans testifying before Congress to emphasize a communitarian strand of political culture. Third, they brought history out of books and into the lives of congressional representatives and their constituents. By anchoring his legislative work in a deeply personal experience, for instance, Mineta attempted to make the experience of his unjust incarceration weigh on the consciences of his fellow representatives and senators, some of whom were unaware of the extent of that experience even after having worked with Mineta for years. Fourth, the legislative and even social benefits of sharing personal experience and its lingering impact also helped change Nikkei cultural values (and the perception of those values) by demonstrably shrugging off many of the generations-old inhibitions that had helped maintain the illusion of equanimity for so long. Fifth, by exemplifying cooperation across racial, political, and historical divides, personal disclosure helped advance communitarianism in both government service and the public sphere that would once more be put to the test in later years. Such cooperation would also see repeated engagement with personal testimonials.

The disclosure of personal experience in a public setting would ultimately prevail, but only after considerable time and prolonged work by grassroots activists, Japanese American organizations, and members of the House and Senate. The Civil Liberties Act, passed on August 10, 1988, had required well over ten years of labor to garner support both within and outside the Japanese American community. Work began in 1978, when at its national convention in Salt Lake City, the Japanese American Citizens League (JACL) adopted a resolution "to undertake a legislative program seeking an apology and redress payment of $25,000 per individual evacuated and interned during World War II." Not long thereafter, leaders of the JACL flew to Washington, D.C., to meet with Japanese American elected officials and enlist their support for redress. In addition to meeting with Mineta, the JACL also met with Senator Daniel Inouye and Senator Spark (Masayuki) Matsunaga, both from Hawaii, and Representative Robert Matsui, from California. In Japanese, Mineta summed up the sentiment of the group as *komatta ne*—roughly, "We're in trouble here." The implication was that the pursuit of redress would face significant obstacles, and not just from outside the Japanese American community. Although these Japanese American politicians felt they faced a long and perhaps even unwinnable battle, they agreed that their first step must be to educate the public about what happened to Nikkei during the war.[47]

Their concerns were warranted. Even within the Japanese American community, there was resistance to pursuing redress. Many people continued to offer the same counterarguments raised in the JACL's deliberations. For example, when Mineta solicited feedback from his constituents in San Jose, most doubted that the commission would accomplish anything concrete, and many even wondered why he was bringing up the topic in the first place. Some still considered wartime imprisonment an embarrassment both for the U.S. government and for former inmates, who were ashamed not only of having been incarcerated but also of having had their patriotism called into question. The result was an adamant inertia among these people. According to Mineta, many constituents told him, "This happened in '42, why are you bringing this up now? Let's let it die, forget it."[48]

But the core group of legislators and activists was undeterred, having realized that reluctant JACL members were a minority that Mineta later described as "maybe not even 20%" of the organization.[49] More pressing were the lack of knowledge and the likely resistance of non-Nikkei legislators and their constituents. So, as Japanese American legislators moved forward with their plans, they made educating the public a critical part of their strategy. Senator Inouye later explained that they used as precedents two recent commissions that had studied and educated the public about critical events: the 1963–1964 Warren Commission on the Kennedy assassination and the 1970 President's Commission on Campus Unrest, or Scranton Commission. Drawing on these models, Mineta's staff helped Senator Matsunaga adapt the structure of a Hawaiian Native Claims Act he had cosponsored with Senator Inouye to include the creation of the CWRIC.[50] The resulting bill passed in both houses of Congress and was signed into law by President Jimmy Carter in 1980. The report released by this commission in 1983 affirmed Mineta's reading of events by concluding that "the reason the evacuation and incarceration occurred was because of historical racial discrimination, wartime hysteria, and weak political leadership." Mineta cited this conclusion when he presented the report to the House Subcommittee on Governmental Affairs on August 16, 1984, and listed the five recommendations the CWRIC had proposed: (1) a formal apology from the government, (2) pardons for those convicted of violating the incarceration order, (3) formal review for applications of administrative relief, (4) a $1.5 billion trust fund to finance educational, social, and humanitarian programs, and (5) payment of $20,000 from a $1.5 billion trust to each of the approximately sixty thousand surviving prison camp inmates.[51] He also summarized the commission's findings in the first-person plural during testimony he gave in 1984: "We were not traitors, we were farmers and businessmen, homemakers, and teachers. We were not secret agents. Nearly twenty-five thousand of us were fourteen years old or younger. Nearly six thousand of us were born in camp."[52]

In support of the commission's recommendations, Mineta and other public officials testified before Congress and their own Nikkei constituents, encouraging the latter not to give up and emphasizing the historical importance of their participation. To put it another way, the lingering memories of Nikkei seeking redress led to the formation of a commission, which in turn recognized the something-to-be-done that Japanese American activists and legislators had discussed, thus providing a concrete example of the impact of empathetic agency. In a speech to the National Coalition for Redress/Reparations, an organization founded in 1980 and comprising the JACL, the National Council for Japanese American Redress, and Nikkei members of Congress, Mineta declared, "To give up now would be to fail our parents, and defraud our children of their heritage. We have endured pain and indignity."[53] In a later speech in San Jose, he told his audience that fighting for redress was essential to have their wartime experiences "heard" and "understood around the nation and appreciated throughout the world."[54] As an example, he told his audience of encouragement he had received a few weeks earlier from the principal of a high school in Kitzingen, West Germany, and from the 1,400 French citizens from Bruyères who had written to President Reagan urging him to sign the Civil Liberties Act.[55] The goal Mineta and his colleagues had in mind was to extend the educational, social, and humanitarian impact of wartime incarceration, rather than draw a line under it.

Gathering Legislative Allies

Once the CWRIC report was issued, Nikkei legislators and their allies worked to translate its recommendations into legislative language. This took years, largely because various members of Congress were resistant to the idea of redress. Given that resistance, Mineta and his colleagues sought congressional cosponsors who could help create broader support for legislation and neutralize claims that the intentions of Nikkei legislators were self-serving. Cosponsorship also would help demonstrate that addressing historical injustice need not be a zero-sum game, since a range of non-Nikkei representatives and senators would be endorsing legislation. And while securing cosponsors and supporters was no less laborious than persuading Nikkei to pursue redress in the first place, over time it became increasingly evident that such labor was beginning to have an effect.

The search for cosponsors led to unexpected allies. Representative Tom Kindness (R-Ohio, and at the time a member of the Judiciary Committee), for instance, told Mineta in the early days of the redress campaign that he remembered having heard about incarceration and that somehow his former boss was involved. When to Mineta's astonishment Kindness later revealed that that boss was Karl Bendetsen, one of main architects of incarceration, Mineta recalled thinking to himself, "Oh crap. Here's the guy [Bendetsen] who engineered the evacuation and was the SOB who put us in camp."[56] Kindness became an ally nonetheless. Mineta and his Nikkei colleagues also established an important alliance with Representative Jim Wright, who had been a fighter pilot in the South Pacific during the Second World War and had heard about the American prison camps when on leave in 1944.[57] Wright told Mineta that he had been deeply moved by the bravery of Nikkei soldiers fighting in Europe, particularly Japanese American soldiers in the 442nd Regiment and the 100th Battalion, who, after two failed attempts by other units, had successfully rescued the so-called Lost Battalion, suffering hundreds of casualties in doing so.[58] As the third-ranking Democrat in the House and a decorated veteran, Wright knew he could help convince others, especially Southern members of Congress, to support the legislation.

In 1983 Wright himself introduced H.R. 4110, which directed Congress to accept and implement the CWRIC's findings, while Senator Matsunaga simultaneously introduced a companion bill in the Senate, S. 2116.[59] Knowing that he had to win the votes of as many as 218 of the 435 members of Congress, Mineta gathered more than 125 cosponsors, a move that proved important to counteracting congressional opposition. (Mineta characterized a letter against redress that was circulating through Congress as arguing "there's a bill being circulated about forming a commission, this is a waste of taxpayer money, this happened in '42."[60]) Empathetic agency is neither automatically nor universally effective, and Mineta knew there were about 150 members of Congress that he would not win over no matter what he said, and therefore he concentrated his energy on the remaining hundred-plus members.[61] He and his colleagues sought to sideline recalcitrant members in part by convincing House Parliamentarian Charlie Johnson to assign Wright's bill the number 442 in reference to the highly decorated Japanese American regiment.[62]

Empathetic Agency beyond Redress

Empathetic agency is vital for bridging differences. This comes through in Mineta's work after the Civil Liberties Act. He had long sought more than just an increased Asian American engagement in the public sphere; he also wanted the public sphere to address the needs of Asian Americans and other marginalized groups more vigorously and visibly as well, which is why he sought to extend Japanese American afterlife to non-Nikkei. If convinced that both government and civil society had failed, if made aware of what had been lost and sensitive to what remained out of place, Americans in general might stand a better chance of repairing their tattered polity and preparing it for future challenges. By bringing wartime experience into view for others, Mineta gave them the opportunity to empathize with those on the margins of society and, in so doing, to imagine otherwise.

Although evident in Mineta's cultivation of Kindness and Wright, this desire to extend the reach of the afterlife of Executive Order 9066 is even clearer in his relationship with another member of Congress, Republican Senator Alan Simpson of Wyoming. While Kindness and Wright had experienced more or less indirect resonances—their own experiences engaging the imprisonment of Nikkei at a distance—Simpson even more fully modeled the effect that Mineta hoped to achieve with H.R. 442: not simply the acknowledgment and correction of a historical injustice, but a personal investment in mutual respect. Hence, when Mineta sought to underscore the importance of that kind of understanding, he frequently told the story of his relationship with Simpson, whom he had first met while at Heart Mountain.

Simpson responded in kind, recounting his own experience of wartime incarceration from outside the camps. As Simpson recalled that first meeting, his scoutmaster had announced one day, "We're going to go out to the Jap Camp for a Scout meeting." Although many of the boys did not want to go, their leader was insistent.[63] When the boys gathered to get to know one another, Simpson and Mineta quickly bonded. They talked about boyhood activities they had in common—knot-tying, carving wood, starting a fire without matches, and earning merit badges—and pitched coins and played mumblety-peg with a penknife.[64] This shared experience allowed the two to negotiate significant political differences. For instance, Mineta's published accounts addressed not only their childhood meeting and mutual support of the Civil Liberties Act, but also their disagreement over a subsidiary component of the Act: the provision for monetary damages. Though a cosponsor of the Senate bill for a formal apology, Simpson opposed a financial remedy. Rather than stress this considerable difference, though, Mineta emphasized that their relationship was cooperative, concluding one interview by declaring, "I consider Alan a good friend, although we are philosophically worlds apart." To some extent this was a collegial gesture of respect, but Mineta also made it something more when he added that "it's a small world, when you consider that in 1943 we met as Boy Scouts in an internment camp." In this moment, Mineta engaged in subtle parallelism, comparing the fact that he and Simpson shared in limited ways a sense of wartime incarceration with the way his ideas about governmental responsibility diverged from Simpson's. In this way, he implicitly provided further evidence of how Executive Order 9066 continued to play out in the present. Consequently, in recounting moments such as that early meeting in camp, Mineta recognized his role as an example not only of injustice, but also of how individuals and groups might work through that injustice to achieve a greater degree of political and cultural equity.

When President Ronald Reagan finally signed the Civil Liberties Act in August 1988, the accompanying congressional signatures demonstrated the ability of a group that has been subject to grievous injustice to seek redress and engage in the shaping of political and social standards. (Those signatures included both Mineta's as speaker pro tem of the U.S. House and Matsunaga's as president pro tem of the U.S. Senate.) Mineta framed the success of Japanese American activists and legislators in conciliatory terms.[65] The Civil Liberties Act was part of the larger afterlife of wartime incarceration: the continued presence of a marginalized group within the society that has wronged it, the potential agency of that group, and the ability of that group and those around it to achieve a shared recuperation through empathy.

The agency of at group is greatest when the group can work with others, which is why Nikkei seeking redress kept promoting parallelism between former inmates and other citizens whose rights had not been violated. Parallelism shed light on commonalities among different people, and those commonalities allowed for partial identification and potential empathy on the part of people not directly impacted by Executive Order 9066. Empathy increased the likelihood of support for the Civil Liberties Act among non-Nikkei even when they disagreed with parts of it. In this way, non-Nikkei identification with Nikkei experience created the opportunity for future political engagement based on both similarity and difference. As a child, Alan Simpson could identify with Mineta in terms of geographical place, age, and interests. That identification allowed him also to sense a key difference, which was that Mineta had been imprisoned as a child while he himself had not, despite the two of them having virtually everything except race in common. That difference led to a second similarity, which was support for the Civil Liberties Act's call for an official apology. And this mix of similarities and difference enabled the two men to negotiate one more difference: whether or not to provide liquidating damages. Linking his personal history with Simpson's, Mineta changed the political engagement of Simpson, a man of very different ideological inclination, making his colleague's agency more closely resemble his own. In other words, Mineta's pursuit of the Civil Liberties Act turned out to be contagious beyond Asian America. His cultivation of an empathetic frame created an expanded opportunity to "imagine otherwise."

Beyond Redress

Recall Mineta's discussion of how younger Japanese Americans helped motivate their elders to voice the afterlife of wartime imprisonment. That discussion demonstrates the value of empathetic agency: it has the potential to be expansive as well as unifying. Mineta seems to have recognized and then seized on this potential after the passage of the Civil Liberties Act. Even as his legislative career drew to a close, for instance, he kept building on the awareness and strategies he and Nikkei colleagues had developed in the 1980s. In fact, as his later governmental work shows, redress seems to have made clear the power of the afterlife of wartime incarceration for Mineta, who continued extending its effects to others. In 1995, he resigned his seat mid-term to take a position as vice president of Lockheed Corporation. Nonetheless, he still maintained a presence in political life as chairman of the National Civil Aviation Review Commission, which was tasked with reducing congestion in airports and improving air safety.[66] Such was the impact of personal disclosure in support of the Civil Liberties Act that it continued to figure prominently in Mineta's public profile even years later. In 2000, President Clinton recruited Mineta to become Secretary of Commerce, making him the first Asian American to serve in a presidential cabinet. Even in this supposedly neutral post, Mineta's early history played a role in his appointment and policies. The president, declaring that "politics and public service have a way of calling the best back," made clear that he was appointing Mineta because of his ability to lead and his in-depth understanding of economic strategy, but that he also valued Mineta's commitment to the marginalized and dispossessed, his "deep concern for people—for the people in places who are not yet fully participating in this economy." As evidence of such concern, Clinton cited Mineta's commitment to social justice after his own wartime experience, talking about how, when he was released from camp, "young Norm vowed to work to make sure that kind [of] injustice could never happen to anyone else."[67]

That narrative can easily become problematic, as when, despite being a Democrat and having been in the Clinton cabinet, Mineta was also appointed to President George W. Bush's cabinet, this time as Secretary of Transportation. Once again, Mineta's early personal history figured in his governmental work almost as prominently as his administrative and political skills did. During Mineta's swearing-in ceremony, President Bush said he believed that Mineta had amply earned the unusual distinction of serving in two cabinets, citing a life of "determination, courage and service." "As a child," Bush continued, "Mineta lived in an internment camp. As a young man, he wore his country's uniform in Korea and Japan. From there, he went on to become a mayor, a Congressman, and a Cabinet Secretary."[68] What Nikkei activists and legislators produced in support of the Civil Liberties Act, others still had to interpret, and not all interpreters are equally subtle. Thus, Bush's comments tread dangerously close to reasserting the model minority stereotype. And yet, they also demonstrate a new willingness to include the afterlife of unjust imprisonment in a larger historical imaginary.

Mineta continued to express that afterlife during his time in the cabinet and in more recent speeches, not only because it was accurate, but also because it enhanced his ability to implement larger social policies. As secretary of transportation, Mineta was responsible for infrastructure and regulatory practice, but he also addressed political, historical, and racial issues. For example, at the August 18, 2001, meeting of the Organization of Black Airline Pilots, he spoke about the need to break down remaining racial barriers to full economic (and social and political) inclusion in aviation. To avoid the suspicion that he was simply giving this issue lip service, Mineta declared, "I, too, know a little something about racism, ignorance, and discrimination, as my family and I were among the 120,000 Americans of Japanese ancestry forced from our homes and into incarceration camps by the United States Government during the Second World War." Building toward his conclusion, he reminded his audience that "more than two-thirds of us were American citizens, but we were branded enemy aliens by our own government and our most basic Constitutional rights were violated, simply on the basis of our race."[69] By cultivating empathy among another historically marginalized group, Mineta sought to establish a collective endeavor that bridged differing professions and histories in order to acknowledge and then align the afterlives that linger in seemingly distinct groups.

Having seen how effective parallelism based on personal experience could be, Mineta had become even bolder about embodying the issues he addressed as well as cultivating empathy in the members of his audience and demonstrating a common ground between them. Thus, in his speech to the Organization of Black Airline Pilots Mineta extended the analogy between the Japanese American and African American experience of discrimination and injustice by comparing the 442nd Regimental Combat Team with the Tuskegee Airmen. Both groups, he claimed, were "American citizens [who] were told they were not worthy enough to fight for their country in her time of need" but who nonetheless "responded with incredible courage and bravery." Reporting that he was often asked by other Americans to explain why Japanese American inmates volunteered to fight for the country that had imprisoned them, he said that the answer was evident in the similar actions by the Tuskegee Airmen: "They fought a dual battle—the enemy of democracy abroad, and the enemy at home. They persevered because they had an abiding faith and core belief in the freedoms our great nation had promised" and "a sustaining hope that, one day, that promise would be fulfilled." Rallying his audience to continue the struggle for equality, he asked, "How much of our nation's progress toward equal justice and equal opportunity did they purchase with their sacrifice?"[70] While noting that many of the achievements of the civil rights movement were built "on a foundation constructed in no small part" by minority servicemen during World War Two,[71] he emphasized that there was much more to be done to increase professional and economic opportunities for minorities. In aligning the interests of Nikkei and African Americans, he also advanced a model of widespread cooperation, among Japanese Americans, among members of different minority groups, among senators, as the most effective method for achieving political and social transformation. In such moments, Mineta suggested that different sorts of afterlife could unite seemingly disparate people, serving as a call to further action in the present with an eye toward the future.

Achieving such collective action is especially difficult for groups that have traditionally been at the margins of both government and civil society. Recognizing that difficulty early on, in 1971 Mineta framed his concerns before the U.S. Commission on Civil Rights as a matter of governmental "responsibility" to all of its citizens, especially those who are economically and politically most vulnerable. That is also why, in that same testimony, he emphasized the relationship between race and class. This was more than an attempt to represent only the Nikkei citizens who elected him; rather, it was a commitment to serve all marginalized and underrepresented people. But the character of that work changed after the pursuit of redress. From the late 1970s onward, Mineta referred significantly more often to his and his family's experience of prewar bigotry and wartime incarceration. Thus, his testimony on low-income housing demonstrated his engagement with marginalized people that derived from his personal experience, while his speech before the Organization of Black Airline Pilots made both that engagement and its personal origins entirely explicit.

Analogy is a powerful mechanism for pointing out commonalities among diverse groups. It also underscores the importance of those commonalities. In 1988, as work on the Civil Liberties Act was coming to a head, Mineta gave a speech at San Jose State University in which he addressed that importance. After talking about exclusionary laws, wartime incarceration, and the postwar troubles his family had encountered, he moved on to a topic that might have struck some as divisive: "All of you have probably heard Americans of Asian ancestry described as 'model' minorities—hard-working, law-abiding, and an example for other minorities to follow." Rather than celebrate this image, though, he criticized it: "This stereotype—and that's what it is: a stereotype—has caused understandable resentment and conflict with other minority groups, and has thrown up yet another barrier in our efforts for full acceptance in this nation." The model minority, he suggested, is nothing but a rhetorical stick with which to beat other marginalized groups. He declared unambiguously that "Asian Americans are not 'model' minorities." Instead, he said, "I often think that a better description of us would be the 'invisible' minorities."[72] Defining Asian Americans as tame, the model minority stereotype both effaced the complexities of the category

"Asian American" and denied the existence of significant political action by people of Asian ancestry. As such, it also was a convenient mechanism for denying the demands, even diverse ones, Asian Americans might make of the government: "The Reagan Administration wanted to change the forms for the 1990 Census, and rather than acknowledge the different Asian American communities, the preferred option of the Census Bureau was to lump them all together. But without a group-by-group analysis, the data would be of little use to social service agencies and others which allocate our scarce resources."[73] Noting the differences among Chinese and Hmong immigrants, for instance, he went on to recount a successful collaborative campaign to reject the bureau's proposed changes.

In the San Jose State University speech, Mineta also argued for coopera-tion by various marginalized groups, not just Asian Americans. Noting the hard work that had yet to be done (even from a centrist vantage point), he declared that "to reach this dream, Asian groups must work with black, Hispanic, Native American and other minority and women's groups who share our concerns for civil rights and search for a political voice." This was, he said, a problem for more than one specific community. It was a question of access to the public sphere and, thereby, government for all marginalized groups: "If we act separately, the term 'minority' will remain an accurate one. But, working together, we are a formidable force." He then cautioned against excess compartmentalization, adding that "an even greater threat to our effectiveness than not working together is working at cross purposes. If we allow ourselves to be pitted group against group—blacks against Asians, Vietnamese versus Koreans, new immigrants against second- or third-gener-ation citizens—we all lose."[74] Even among those with the most to gain from collective action, a failure to identify with one another and to collaborate would only lead to further disenfranchisement.

In light of this declaration, Mineta's discussion of the bigotry directed at Nikkei Americans is particularly noteworthy. Having talked about that mani-festation of racism, he proceeded to address the needs of other marginalized groups in the United States. This allowed him to suggest something of vital importance for how we understand the afterlife of wartime incarceration: that it was a concentrated example of something that many people experienced and, Mineta acknowledged, continue to experience. Speaking directly of Asian Americans, but indirectly about others as well, "no matter how hard we have struggled, it never seems to be enough. And the struggle is never over."[75]

This is the voice of someone who remains a centrist and a communitarian, but it is also the voice of someone whose approach to political action grew increasingly vigorous, personal, and disclosive over the course of his career.

Pursuing the Civil Liberties Act seems to have awakened something within Issei and Nisei. Mineta once remarked that it was not these older members of the community who drove redress and its cultural work, but rather the Sansei (third generation). He declared that they had "finally forced their parents to come out of the closet" to talk about the experience of mass wartime incarceration.[76] And yet, first- and second-generation Japanese Americans were central to this shift. Having pursued redress at least partly in response to the questions from the younger generation, they found the redress movement raised new questions and sharpening old ones. Questions by Sansei also lent a new sense of urgency to ideals Mineta had long held. He initiated empathetic agency in his colleagues, in fellow Nikkei, and non-Nikkei, but he did so at least partly because he had experienced it himself in conversations with younger Japanese Americans who felt the burden of injustice outweighed the prohibition against disclosure. Having worked to change how those around him might change their thinking, he had changed his own well—and had been changed by those around him—thus becoming both a vector for empathetic agency and one of its beneficiaries.

Mineta sought not simply to create new opportunities for minorities but also to safeguard their rights, specifically in terms of his own experiences. In the wake of September 11, 2001, he realized that an alarming number of Americans were once again responding to a national crisis out of fear and prejudice, a response he later characterized as "Take all these Arab Americans and Muslims and put them in camp."[77] His use of the singular "camp" is instructive. A standard term among Nikkei, "camp" is a synecdoche for unjust imprisonment and the hardships it caused. Mineta's decision to prevent such prejudice and injustice from becoming institutionalized, like his earlier and continuing decision to speak about Executive Order 9066 and its aftermath, echoed far beyond the Nikkei community.

To forestall anti-Muslim and anti-Arab bigotry, on September 21, 2001, Mineta issued his condemnation of racial profiling without first clearing it with the president's staff. That he did not seek the approval of the White House is telling. More than the actions of someone free from House rules, Mineta's initiative illustrates the extent to which his own lingering experience of injustice had come to exert ever-greater force on him over time.

He had long stated his opposition to indiscriminate racial categorization. For example, in a 1983 editorial, he wrote: "The incarceration's dependence on an 'imprison-by-background' policy is itself absolutely condemning."[78] Soon after Mineta issued his ban on profiling, the president invited him to a White House meeting with a group of Arab Americans and Muslims, representatives of communities that were feeling increasingly vulnerable as a result of the public's ignorance and distrust.[79] Given a rash of attacks on people of Middle Eastern and South Asian descent there was reason to be fearful. Mineta addressed these attacks and the sentiment underlying them directly, decrying those who would mistreat someone merely "because he looked like the enemy." Looking "like the enemy" was an accusation that Nikkei heard frequently during World War II and that, as Mineta well knew, had helped generate support for Executive Order 9066.[80] Alarmed by perceptions of some Americans after 9/11 that Muslims and people of South Asian and Middle Eastern descent "looked like the enemy," he was determined to do what he could to stave off these growing sentiments. This was a project that he would repeatedly stress, as in a speech the following October to the Detroit-based Arab Community Center for Economic and Social Services (ACCESS), in which he assured the audience that, regardless of the security measures that would eventually be developed, "our national policies will not be driven by, or tolerate, racial and religious scapegoating."[81] Of course, day-to-day reality shows how intractable racism and religious bigotry can be.

In essence, Mineta fought as much against complacency as prejudice by trying to extend empathetic agency once again. In his speech to ACCESS, for instance, he observed that journalists and historians had "taken to describing September 11 as the new Pearl Harbor," an analogy he acknowledged was applicable in that in both instances the United States had been attacked without warning. But he remarked that as a Japanese American the analogy to Pearl Harbor was important to him for another reason: "It highlights one of the greatest dangers that we face as a country during this crisis—and that is, the danger that in looking for the enemy we may strike out against our own friends and neighbors."[82] Once again, Mineta drew on personal experience of hysteria and bigotry in order to invite his audience to empathize with him, to extrapolate from his experience to that of others who now found themselves the targets of racism and religious bigotry, and then to reflect on their own political and social impulses.

Mineta's public disclosures thus engaged not only the past and present but also the future, as if he were trying to inoculate American society against racism and religious bigotry. In his speech to ACCES he spoke once again of his experience during World War II to highlight the human impact of racial profiling. He recalled that when his family had left the Japanese Methodist Episcopal Church in San Jose on December 7, 1942, and heard the news that Japan had bombed Pearl Harbor, they, like most other Americans, were "outraged by the attack and fearful." But, he added, "we had an additional cause for fear—because we knew that many of our fellow Americans would not distinguish between us and the pilots flying those planes that bombed Pearl Harbor that day." As predicted, "that same afternoon, agents of the Federal Bureau of Investigation began rounding up leaders in our community and shipped those people to INS detention centers. And in the weeks and months that followed, we saw our status as Americans slowly but surely called into question."[83] Standing before that audience, Mineta once more demonstrated concretely how fragile basic rights can be.

For Mineta, later retellings of his own narrative were further instances of personal disclosure designed to inoculate both civil society and government against repetition of their mistakes by calling on his listeners to rededicate themselves to a fully open and equitable public sphere. The wartime incarceration of Nikkei, he said, represented "a warning to all of us how dangerous misguided fear can be." For that reason, he noted, "as the events of September 11 unfolded just over a month ago, I know that I was far from alone among Japanese Americans in wondering how this Nation would respond. And our greatest fear was that the backlash we had experienced would be visited on our Arab American, South Asian American and Muslim neighbors." Formerly imprisoned Japanese Americans, he suggested, had fought for the Civil Liberties Act not only to win recognition that what was done to them was wrong, but "to build a national commitment that nothing like the internment would ever happen in this country—to anyone— ever again." "As an American of Japanese ancestry," he said, "I know that commitment can be broken. I have seen it happen." And the abandonment of that commitment was precisely what the small group of violent individuals hoped to achieve: "They believe they can use the forces of terror and fear to make us fail our most basic principles, and to break our most sacred promises to each other."[84]

Heart Mountain and Beyond

In August 2011, largely as a result of Mineta's support, the camp at Heart Mountain reopened as a museum. Redesigned to educate visitors about its use during the war, the site houses wartime artifacts, oral histories, and photographs. Although the museum functions to preserve Second World War history, at a dedication ceremony in 2011 Mineta emphasized that it was established with an eye toward the future rather than the past, explaining that converting Heart Mountain into a museum was intended to educate visitors and therefore help prevent repeating past mistakes. "I know from my own work that it can happen. It came very close on September 11, 2001. I was Secretary of Transportation. I grounded all the airplanes." Grounding the airplanes, he said, was the easy part; regaining the trust of passengers without demonizing an easy target would be more difficult. As he told the crowd gathered for the Heart Mountain ceremony, "there were a lot of people who were saying don't let Middle Easterners or Muslims back on the airplanes. And they were even talking about even internment and rounding them up. Phrases and thoughts that were similar to something that many of us had experienced."[85]

And yet, in this same dedication speech, Mineta was also quick to point out that others had been confounded and disturbed by this wartime act, gesturing to the man standing behind him as a notable example. This man was Alan Simpson, his longtime friend and sometime legislative ally. Retelling the story of how the two Scout troops had come together, Mineta recollected that his troop leader had originally invited several troops from the outside to visit for one of their jamborees, only to be met with the response, "We're not coming in there. Barbed wires. Military guard towers. Machine gun mountings. Searchlights. They're prisoners of war. We're not going in there." But Mineta's troop "leaders wrote back and said, 'Hold it: These are Boy Scouts of America. They wear the same uniform you do. They go after the same merit badges you do.'"[86] As a result, those confused but curious Boy Scouts from Cody, Wyoming, had ventured behind the fences and barbed wire of Heart Mountain to try to understand how other Scouts could be both so similar and yet so dissimilar that they were imprisoned.

Mineta's presentation, like his other public collaborations with Alan Simpson, addressed the experiences of individuals in camp, rather than abstractions. In so doing, it was designed to cultivate empathetic agency across differences including race, age, class, and political affiliation. In this way, the refusal of personal experience to exist solely in the past, the nagging complexities of a historical event, led many Nikkei to give voice to that experience, to make the afterlife of injustice visible, and to do so in order to work against its repetition in the future.

THREE

Canadian Redress as Ambivalent Transnationality

In May 1987 the National Association of Japanese Canadians held a conference to link the pursuit of Japanese Canadian redress to wider political and civil rights initiatives. Among the speakers was Charles Paris, head of the Canadian Council of Christians and Jews, who gave a talk entitled "Never, Never Forget." Not long after, the president of the Japanese Canadian Citizens' Association of Greater Vancouver, Dan Tokawa, addressed the group: "This past year a member of the Vancouver Parks Board put forward a motion to rename Victory Square after Halford Wilson. Now that was shocking, I'm sure, to all of us. . . . There was only a day or two that we had to respond before a decision would have been made. . . . The motion could have easily been passed."[1] The failed initiative Tokawa mentioned would have commemorated an infamous bigot. In addition being a member of the Vancouver City Council in the early 1940s, Wilson was a vocal advocate of incarcerating all Nikkei in British Columbia. Before the bombing of Pearl Harbor he had even suggested forcing them into ghettos, pointing in 1941 to the work of the Nazis as a happy precedent.[2]

The timing of the proposed honor was particularly bad, given the fraught state of debates between Japanese Canadians and their federal government over redress.[3] The ignorance it demonstrated, however, helped galvanize a community that had begun taking greater control of historical discourses that long portrayed them as passive. The community was able to exert such control in part because of debates earlier in the 1980s, as the movement for redress began to grow. Consequently, although the Vancouver initiative arose abruptly and with little opportunity for debate, Nikkei in Vancouver as well as elsewhere in Canada were able to mobilize sufficient support to defeat the planned renaming. (Victory Square remains Victory Square.) The ability to pursue such quick and effective political engagement was a long time in the making, and it belies the complexities of the community. As Tokawa's statement suggests, emotion not only ran high, but it also was a key to the success of the opponents.[4]

Empathetic agency depends on a nagging sense of what might have been, but that differs from person to person, even when people empathize with one another or have had similar experiences. Conflict arises as they debate what action they might want to take, if any. They debate strategy, but also the aims of the group itself as well as the aims of its individual constituents. And, being about aims, debates of that sort also are about how the group sees itself and wishes to be seen. As a result, those debates demonstrate how the cultural work necessary for people to assert a shared identity is especially complicated in places that constitute what Kornel Chang has called "borderlands," or realms in which ideas of nationality, geographical origin, and class come into question.[5] In such places, even the most basic terms of debate may be contested, leaving groups fragmented, as was the case with the struggle for redress in Canada during the early 1980s. As this chapter will show, that struggle necessitated public discussion of what happened to Nikkei in Canada after the bombing of Pearl Harbor, but it also necessitated discussion about what, if anything, the term "Japanese Canadian" might mean. Memories of wartime and postwar mistreatment lingered in the minds of people forcibly dispersed from British Columbia, but that afterlife, like the experiences that produced it, followed a different course from what occurred in the United States and thus helped shape an ambivalent and complex Nikkei transnationality.

Scholars such as William Hohri, Mitchell Maki, and Alice Yang Murray have documented the redress campaign of U.S.-based Nikkei at both the level of the individual and the community.[6] By describing work of the Japanese American Citizens League and others from 1978 onward seeking a formal apology and redress payment, as well as other, subsequent collective political work, they have shed important light on a community in pursuit of reparations.[7] In addition, they have described the role of the individual by stressing the importance of personal testimonials in both educating the public and eventually persuading Congress to pass the 1988 Civil Liberties

Act.[8] Although Canadian reparations may be less familiar to some readers, Roy Miki, Cassandra Kobayashi, and Maryka Omatsu have written important histories of the struggle for justice in Canada.[9] This chapter addresses the complexities of citizenship and belonging as expressed in the latter narrative. Sometimes described as if a kind of coda to events in the United States, that narrative in fact reveals a community engaged in profoundly complex and sophisticated self-reflection.

Redress and the Beginnings of Debate

On Tuesday, March 22, 1983, the *New Canadian*, a Nikkei newspaper, published an article, "Japanese Canadians Still Keep Low Profile after Evacuation Trauma," that documented how wartime removal from the West Coast of Canada, coupled with postwar dispersal, had nearly obliterated a cohesive Nikkei community.[10] To be sure, some sense of group identity persisted, as the continued existence of the *New Canadian* at that time indicates. Furthermore, a number of Japanese Canadians had eventually returned to British Columbia. But in general the community was dispersed, and its engagement with Japanese language and cultural traditions was attenuated, which the article attributed to prolonged, endemic racism, especially its institutionalization after the bombing of Pearl Harbor.

The article was remarkable because it appeared in the *New Canadian*, a self-proclaimed "independent organ for Canadians of Japanese origin" that had long been a kind of community newsletter. As activist, poet, and scholar Roy Miki recently remarked, the paper "had been slumbering for years" before the article ran.[11] With the exception of several incarceration-related features in the late 1960s and 1970s, the *New Canadian* tended to run birth and death notices, articles about Nikkei high school athletic feats, international human-interest features, and classified ads for cooks, private drivers, and babysitters, as well as commercial ads for Japanese Canadian businesses.[12] Consequently, its readers were unaccustomed to seeing such emotionally and politically charged fare in its pages.

For Canadians of Japanese origin, like Nikkei in the United States, the immediate challenge following incarceration was basic survival. What property they had owned had largely been sold off, despite government assurances that this would not happen. In addition, the government resisted virtually every attempt to secure compensation for the associated losses. Inmates had been forced to pay the costs of their own incarceration, which were deducted from the meager earnings they received during their exile, thus reducing what little savings they might have been able to generate.[13] The government also attempted to deport them, including those born and raised in Canada, to Japan. And, perhaps most important, Nikkei were then subject to a form of ethnic cleansing after the war, as the government tried to prevent them from ever again "concentrating" themselves in one province.[14] As they struggled to restore their economic and political stability, the *New Canadian* had modeled a largely middle-class, politically risk-averse way of life that would pose little threat to its readers' place in Canadian politics and society.

And yet, the 1983 article on the virtual invisibility of Japanese Canadians signaled an important change that had begun in the *New Canadian* and, by implication, its audience. The article addressed a historical event that had long held painful memories for Canadian Nikkei, though many of them still refused to speak openly about it. Breaking with recent tradition, the paper was becoming an important forum for Nikkei news and debate, so much so that by the winter of 1984 it was a primary source for updates on the internal politics of Canadian redress. This shift toward an increasingly public engagement with the afterlife of wartime mistreatment demonstrates that the tenor of life among Japanese Canadians had begun to change as the fight for redress gained momentum.[15]

Besides being a type of journalism that the *New Canadian* had not displayed in recent memory, the 1983 article also was a reprint from the *Los Angeles Times*, which had run it a month earlier.[16] Newspapers shared articles regularly, even before the rise of aggregation, and a significant portion of the content in the *New Canadian* (including many of the articles discussed in this chapter) had been either syndicated or drawn from wire services. But in this case, that sharing tells us something important about the interplay of personal experience and racialization in the early 1980s.[17] The *New Canadian* considered the piece sufficiently timely and important to merit a national audience that had, until recently, turned to the paper more for its human-interest stories than for news. In addition, the *Los Angeles Times* also considered the subject important enough to run. The apparent common interest is noteworthy, because the two papers did not operate on the same scale; they did not share the same journalistic aspirations, either. Plus, one served a specific, if fragmented ethnic and racial subgroup distributed across Canada, while the other addressed an extremely diverse audience mainly in the Los Angeles Basin. And yet, one factor drove the presumption of a shared audience and shared interests for these two newspapers: the presence of a large and increasingly politically engaged Nikkei readership. Furthermore, both papers recognized that their respective audiences had an important connection. Consider, for instance, the comparative nature of the article, which was written by Stanley Meisler: "Unlike Los Angeles, Vancouver no longer has a Little Tokyo."[18] Both the tone of the article and the different venues in which it appeared reveal the transnational dynamic between communities involved in the fight for redress.

The Limitations of the Transnational Frame

To write about the discourse of Japanese Canadian redress in a strictly comparative transnational frame is risky. On a theoretical level, doing so risks eliding the histories of inequity in the nation-states a transnation occupies. At the same time, writing of the transnational can sometimes produce a subject that is undifferentiated, as gender, age, education, sexuality, and other variables drop out of or are simply omitted from the account. Accordingly, discussion of transnationality risks producing a kind of transcendental subject—the hypothetical transnational individual—who comes to resemble the late-capitalist norm of the wealthy, white, hetero consumer of global wares.[19]

Although such risks are daunting, the diasporic transnational frame also has significant benefits. First and foremost, it has the potential to destabilize convenient nationalist and nativist narratives—narratives that might under other circumstances obscure the histories of colonialism and oppression that continue to weigh on marginalized groups.[20] This potential was summed up by Miki. Writing about the difficulty of defining "Asian Canadian," he observed that the term,

> when dislodged from its foreclosures [i.e., applications that reproduce white nationalist claims], becomes a revolving sign which re-articulates and thus exposes discourses of both globalization (i.e. towards Asian markets and economies, for instance) and a reactionary nationalism (i.e. as a "yellow peril" that is asianizing white Canada). "Asian Canadian" then becomes both a localized subject—of research, cultural production, interrogation—

and a double-edged site: where relations of dominance threaten to be remobilized (more of the same), *or* where critiques of the nation can posit future methodologies of resistance and collective formations.[21]

As Miki points out, writing about identity in this manner can reinforce prejudices, but it also harbors the potential to destabilize those same prejudices by interrogating their contested status.[22] Consequently, he goes on to suggest, "these marks [hyphenated references], in turn, would call for an acknowledgement of linkages, not through some prior cultural homogeneity, but in the warp and weave of the nation's formation—a condition that attests to the burden of representation in such a term as 'Asian Canadian.'"[23]

The same can be said for the term "Japanese Canadian" and, for that matter, "Nikkei transnationality." "Japanese Americans," like "Asian Americans" in general, have long been a dominant academic paradigm. Despite the potential limitations, however, approaching the discourse of Japanese Canadian redress using a transnational frame—and, with that, writing of "Nikkei North American" engagement with wartime injustice—will at the very least provide a focal point for addressing some of the confusion, not to mention the disagreement, involved in identity formation. For the most part, discussions of redress have dealt with strains *among* Nikkei over whether and how to pursue official governmental action. This chapter attends to a less familiar aspect of redress: the ways it called into question what, if anything, might have constituted Japanese Canadian identity in the early 1980s.

This chapter does not actually answer that question. For one thing, doing so risks reifying the comparative dynamic I trace through the years 1983–1984. That comparative dynamic was a means, not an end, and Japanese American cultures were not a model so much as a point of departure. For another thing, the transnational identity I propose for Nikkei north of the 49th parallel was and in many respects still is a question rather than an answer. That the idea of Japanese Canadian identity remains contested has, in fact, been part of what renders its forms of political engagement supple and sophisticated. In this regard, Nikkei Canadian identities, by virtue of their porousness and mutability, support Kandice Chuh's observation that "*undecidability rather than identity* provides the grounds for unity, and identifying and contesting the forces that control intelligibility, that affiliate meanings, emerge as crucial tasks for Asian American studies."[24]

To write of a transnational or broadly North American identity therefore does not imply a unitary cultural and political outcome. On the contrary, pursuing redress taxed Canadians of Japanese ancestry and those around them. To quote Miki once more, "In creating and sustaining their call for justice, they [Nikkei in Canada] stretched to the limits their ability to transform their insecurities and anxieties into a national movement that captured the attention of Canadians."[25] But it also tapped into an acute awareness of how one might be simultaneously like and unlike others. As Henry Yu has noted, "Asian Canadian consciousness is an uncommon form of identity, not because those who might find themselves in a category parallel to 'Asian Americans' are unconscious, but because they may be more conscious of other modes of political and community engagement that are more powerful. . . . My home, as much as I cherish it, was stolen from someone else, and to be 'Canadian' is a term loaded with the history of colonialism and expropriation."[26]

Instead, I approach the transnational frame as a way to examine one specific moment in group self-examination that eventually led not just to a clearer sense of that group (Canadians of Japanese ancestry) but also to a clearer sense of how it and its constituents relate to others. That group self-examination was fueled in part by the 1983 publication of *Personal Justice Denied* and by the debates, legislative work, and lobbying that followed south of the 49th parallel. This was so not because the United States occupied an ideal position. The American political landscape served as a model for many Nikkei in Canada as much to show what did not apply north of the 49th parallel as to show what might. Rather, debate and political action in the United States had achieved a critical mass, one that spurred Nikkei in Canada to ask what exactly they constituted, politically, culturally, historically, and otherwise.

Such questions took on particular importance before an official decision—i.e., one that would be representative at a large scale—even to pursue redress. (The National Association of Japanese Canadians formally voted to pursue redress in 1984, following prolonged and often acrimonious debate.) As the redress movement gained momentum in Canada, it both benefited from and contributed to profound changes in the national political landscape. In order to do so, however, that movement had to undergo significant and often painful, but ultimately beneficial, changes. As Miki once said of that time, "a broader neo-colonialist perspective brought into view the inequality of representations of different subject positions in the body politic. The Japanese Canadian redress movement, a strategy to redress the injustice of internment in the 1940s, developed within that context, perhaps even thrived on the changes going on." No less important, he adds that "other communities of color, including Chinese Canadians, Afro-Canadians, and Natives, became more vocal in asserting their histories, which had thus far been neutralized, denied, or otherwise erased."[27] Consequently, to discuss Nikkei North Americans as this chapter does is not to establish a constellation of minor groups revolving around an American sun; nor is it to posit a unified, static group. It is, instead, to map in the simplest possible terms a set of seismic changes that occurred for Nikkei in Canada, beginning with a clear and forceful prompt and extending through continuous further action.

The Meanings of "Japanese Canadian"

Kandice Chuh has suggested that "*transnation* designates cross-border collectivities and identity formations, and *transnationality* refers to the conception and condition of membership in those organizational forms."[28] Accordingly, Nikkei in Canada might be said to have been a transnation that engaged with the place of their ancestors (Japan) as well as the one that might issue them a passport (Canada).[29] In the late 1970s and early 1980s it also engaged with another key place: the West Coast of the United States, where the bulk of Nikkei who had also been subject to officially sanctioned racism during World War II once more resided. As a result, the transnation to which Japanese Canadians belonged had unclear boundaries and varied constituents. Nikkei north of the 49th parallel recognized aspects of a shared experience, from prewar racism to post–Pearl Harbor imprisonment, which linked them with their southern neighbors. But in the 1980s they also increasingly recognized historical differences that set them apart. These included government structure (a parliamentary system that perpetuated an imperial imaginary), as well as differences in both wartime mistreatment and continued official harassment after the war.

People of Japanese ancestry who lived north of the 49th parallel did not think of themselves in terms of a larger, purely Nikkei collective at that time. On the contrary, they occupied what Russell Leong has called a "parallel Pacific": "contested spatial, political, and cultural conceptions of peoples and places. Parallel Pacifics can also include those of Asian and Pacific descent, as well as native nations within the Pacific diaspora."[30] But insofar as wartime incarceration and the pursuit of redress raised the question of

Japanese origins and character, that question came to the fore in critical moments. As a result, a Nikkei North American imaginary began to take shape, one that was subsidiary to a larger parallel Pacific. That imaginary arose not from local historical and cultural circumstances, but those circumstances repeatedly activated a sense of connection with U.S. and Japanese interlocutors. For this reason, the transnationality of Japanese Canadians was complex and ambivalent.[31]

The complex cross-border Nikkei engagement is ironic. For one thing, it manifested itself in a community that was falsely defined as inherently transnational at the time of the bombing of Pearl Harbor.[32] The primary justification for mass incarceration was that Japanese identity transcended geographical and political differences, and that it therefore would remain immutable, even in people who had been born and raised in North America. Of course, the contrast between reality and racist essentialism could hardly have been starker. On December 21, 1941, for instance, Vancouverite and columnist for the *New Canadian* Muriel Kitagawa wrote to her brother that "we're Canadians and can expect decent treatment from decent people."[33] And yet, the legacy of injustice on both sides of the border eventually produced a sense of common cause between Nikkei Americans and Canadians.

A second and related irony of this cross-border dynamic is that injustice further complicated the relationship to Canadian citizenship of people of Japanese ancestry. Defenders of wartime incarceration, including those in Canada, have often spoken of how it sped the process by which people of Japanese ancestry knit themselves into North American societies. Even people who recognize the inherent racism of Canadian and American wartime policies have accepted this argument at times. For example, the Canadian-born linguist and former U.S. senator S. I. Hayakawa once suggested that "whatever injustices there were in the relocation, it accelerated the absorption of Japanese Americans into the mainstream of American life by one full generation," a comment published in the *New Canadian*, among other places.[34] Such statements recapitulate aspects of the racist transnation that had originally served to justify incarceration, insofar as they suggest that a large group of supposedly alien souls moved inexorably toward a degree-zero national identity. In truth, the situation in both Canada and the United States was more complex, as this chapter and Chapter Five will make clear.[35] For instance, in pursuing redress, Canadian activists sought less to affirm their citizenship credentials than to find alternatives to the narrative of an ever-more-assimilated immigrant group. Crucially, Nikkei Canadian activists did so by comparing themselves to Nikkei elsewhere—in the United States, but also in Latin America.

In the course of trying to identify potential types of redress, and then of trying to select which type to pursue, Nikkei North Americans looked to one another. The result was circuitous movement among local, regional, national, international, and transnational identities. Initially constituted by immigration, then fragmented by imprisonment and postwar dispersal, Japanese Canadians eventually re-formed as a group in ways that called into question the very idea of such an identity. Thus, a country that forcibly tried to render one segment of its population invisible ultimately produced a group that would be much more vigorous, visible, and politically engaged than it had been at the outset of the Second World War. Even as it was repeatedly subjected to totalizing narratives, that group drew on the afterlife of its constituents' experiences to subvert those narratives and, thereby move toward a narrative and a political engagement that was its own.

And yet, immigration, fragmentation, and re-formation inextricably linked Japanese Canadians with their American counterparts. This is not to imply American exceptionalism, but simply to note that a community north of the border, which was profoundly diminished as a result of government mandate, did at times adopt strategies and draw on lessons from the United States. Nonetheless, Japanese Canadians ultimately remained self-consciously distinct. Their historical experience was, as they repeatedly pointed out, only similar to that of Japanese Americans. Consequently, they had to address internal problems, cultural and economic challenges, that differed in various respects. As many of the leading figures in the fight for redress in Canada recognized, they also had to work within a very different political system. That provision, they also noted, remained in place, a continuing threat to any group deemed sufficiently dangerous.[36] As a result, the transnationality of Nikkei North Americans was necessarily provisional and its contours were and still are in flux. In some ways it has been more of a question than a thing about which one could ask a question. Nonetheless, a common engagement with Nikkei wartime experience and its aftermath, as well as with Japan as a country of origin, did exist north and south of the border. And that engagement proved critical to the formulation and reformulation of Japanese Canadian political action.

The dynamics of Nikkei transnationality and of redress are complex, but one particular moment is especially important: the year following the 1982 publication of *Personal Justice Denied*, which presented the findings of the Commission on Wartime Relocation and Internment of Civilians (CWRIC). As noted in Chapter Two, the commission's report was tremendously important in the United States, but it also was influential in debates in Canada because it validated long-standing Japanese American claims of injustice publicly and in detail. Putting to rest any doubt about the trustworthiness of Nikkei citizens and their family members, the report established an unambiguous point of reference for wider cultural and political work. It also established a solid legal foundation for redress. The product of a commission rather than a single individual, built on testimony from hundreds of eyewitnesses and drawing on evidence that had long been suppressed by government agencies, *Personal Justice Denied* documented government misfeasance and the need for an official response. Furthermore, the commission had been tasked with making recommendations for how the U.S. government should address the legacy of Executive Order 9066. As a result, its findings established a standard by which any official action could be judged.

In the months following publication of the commission's findings there were important changes in the Japanese Canadian community. Those changes have generally been thought of as local or national, but they also had a transnational component. Debates about redress in the *New Canadian* from late 1982, when the commission's report was made public, through early 1984, when the most divisive internal debates among Japanese Canadians had begun to subside and the National Association of Japanese Canadians (NAJC) moved officially to seek redress, shed light on this transnational component. Before examining the discourse of Nikkei North American identity at a time when it was undergoing rapid and profound change north of the 49th parallel, though, a basic history of the redress movement in Canada is in order.

Afterlife, Postwar Nikkei Life, and the Redress Movement

Japanese Canadians had long discussed how best to claim their place in Canadian society, but the idea of an organized redress movement did not take hold until the late 1970s. After the war, most Nikkei struggled just to feed their families. As was the case in the United States, many initially felt that seeking redress would just cause further trouble, so they wondered: What's the point? What good would come of this?[37] But, as was also the case in the United States, younger generations wanted to know more about their families' pasts, including the afterlife of wartime incarceration. With that in mind, in the mid 1970s a group of Sansei formed the Japanese Canadian Centennial Project (JCCP) with the main goal of unearthing and publicizing the history of Nikkei in Canada.[38] It is worth noting that a Shin-Issei (new first-generation) named Michiko Sakata initiated the JCCP, having met a Nikkei man utterly shattered by his wartime experience.[39] Drawing together Nikkei from across Canada, the project eventually resulted in a 1977 exhibition entitled *A Dream of Riches*. Such was the impact of the show that Masumi Izumi has even suggested that "Japanese Canadian communities did not reorganize themselves nationally until 1977."[40]

When Japanese Canadians gathered to talk about their hundred-year history, younger generations felt the anger and pain in the speeches, particularly those about wartime incarceration. As Maryka Omatsu stated, "For the first time curious sansei demanded an explanation. The sansei, holding the issei's soft hands or looking deep into the nisei's avoiding eyes, could sense that lying just below the surface was a bitter truth."[41] Younger Japanese Canadians soon became a driving force in the pursuit of redress. As Miki has recounted, in 1981 several of the more activist members of the JCCP began to discuss the formation of the CWRIC, the cultural and political place of Nikkei in Canada, and possible courses for pursuing redress.[42] Though initially an informal group, and one that never claimed any particular authority, these people (including Miki) eventually formed the JCCP Redress Committee, which published a pamphlet, *Redress for Japanese Canadians*, to ensure that Nikkei would be as informed as possible. They also organized community forums and letter-writing campaigns as debates over redress began to heat up in 1983.

As a result, Nikkei in Canada were becoming ever more aware of themselves as an identifiable group with political potential that derived from a shared history and cultural patterns that extended across generations. In September 1983, for instance, the *New Canadian* described a community meeting about redress as being "attended by several Isseis as well as many Niseis and Sanseis. About half of those present seemed to be of the age to have directly experienced the wartime mistreatment."[43] In many ways, then, the 1977 commemoration of a century of Japanese Canadian life reopened earlier conversations about the future of the Japanese Canadian community: "The Centennial was a year to confirm our pride in our heritage, to celebrate our 100 year history and contribution to Canada, and to re-establish our bond as a community. It was a year of reunification."[44] That reunification, however, took less the form of a concrete, stable identity than of a generalized sense of both commonalities and differences within and without the community.

The timing was auspicious. Soon after, the redress movement in the United States achieved its first major victory, the establishment of the CWRIC, which initiated hearings in 1980.[45] As Miki later wrote, "we were fascinated by the unfolding of the issue in the U.S., specifically the dramatic hearings organized by the U.S. Commission on Wartime Relocation and Internment of Civilians." Those hearings galvanized a group of people involved with the Centennial Project to form the JCCP Redress Committee, which eventually reconfigured itself as "an activist collective driven by the belief that the question of redress should be faced by Japanese Canadians."[46] The JCCP Redress Committee's work culminated in a 1984 brief to the NAJC advocating individual compensation for the victims of wartime bigotry. Other groups related to redress, such as the Sodan-kai ("Study Group," a non-partisan organization), also formed around the time *Personal Justice Denied* appeared in print.[47]

The next four years saw significant debate among Japanese Canadians. The starting point for that debate was the form redress should take. Some argued in favor of an official governmental apology coupled with blanket compensation. That might help fund a community foundation.[48] Others advanced two main arguments for individual compensation: first, the Canadian government-appointed custodian tasked with safeguarding Japanese Canadian property during the war had sold off virtually all of the valuable parts of that property at fire-sale prices; and second, an earlier response to these losses was an abject failure. The Royal Commission on Property Claims, also known as the Bird Commission, a governmental body formed in 1947 to address the misfeasance of the custodian, offered paltry sums upon application in a process that ended just nine months after it began. In addition to providing minimal financial compensation, the Bird Commission required applicants to produce receipts that would demonstrate the financial value of what had been lost. Having just been released from prison camps after being abruptly uprooted and relocated eastward, most Nikkei were not in a position to produce such documentation and, consequently, received even less than the commission was empowered to provide.[49]

Two main problems hindered later Japanese Canadian attempts at securing redress. The first was internal divisions that plagued the Nikkei community. In some cases, the divisions were primarily philosophical, pertaining to whether and in precisely what way people should seek redress. Others, however, were of a more specifically political sort, pertaining to who would lead the fight and on what occasions.[50] These divisions complicated matters, particularly given a second problem that activists faced. Specifically, the 1980s also saw significant government opposition. For instance, various current or former members of the government questioned the need for redress. Perhaps the most infamous of these was Wilson, who in the spring of 1983 came out strongly against redress, citing his long-standing belief that there was no appreciable difference between Japanese and Canadians of Japanese origin.[51] Others, such as Pierre Trudeau, prime minister from 1980 to 1984, adopted less overtly racist language while still rejecting outright the need for redress. In 1984, for instance, Trudeau remarked that "we could mount pressure groups across this country in many areas where there have been historic wrongs. I don't think it's the purpose of government to right the past. . . . It cannot rewrite history. It is our purpose to be just in our time."[52]

The election of Brian Mulroney in the autumn of 1984 brought renewed hope to the NAJC and its allies, since Mulroney had indicated his support for redress the year before. However, the redress movement continued to encounter difficulties under the new government. In particular, the office of the Minister of State for Multiculturalism, which was tasked with resolving the issue, attempted to preempt a large and expensive individual-compensation settlement of the sort that was beginning to look likely in the United States, particularly after June 1983, when the CWRIC recommended that the American government provide such a settlement.[53] In the winter of 1984–1985, the Multiculturalism Directorate of Canada presented a plan that included an official apology and the establishment of a governmental foundation to address Canadian racism in general. In an attempt to bypass the NAJC, representatives of the government informed the organization that if the community did not accept the offer it would simply implement this plan and consider the matter finished. No individual-compensation package, they said, would be forthcoming; neither would any sort of community foundation.[54]

The next eighteen months would see an exhausting bout of negotiations complicated by two main problems. The first was continued strenuous opposition to any sort of individual-compensation settlement by the Multiculturalism Directorate; the second was the directorate's attempt to negotiate with a splinter group of Nikkei that had formed in the wake of the 1983 conflicts. While the federal government continued to antagonize Japanese Canadians seeking a fuller account of history, the NAJC set about establishing hard data on the economic losses of the Nikkei community in Canada, surveyed its constituents and, as a result of that survey, formulating a position in favor of individual compensation. Negotiations continued through the summer of 1987, at which point the NAJC, exhausted by a shift in the government's position away from open hostility toward foot-dragging, broke off discussion. After the passage of a H.R. 442 in September 1987, public pressure beyond the Nikkei community in favor of redress continued to grow, and in December the government initiated talks once again. As discussions continued throughout the spring and into the summer, the NAJC and its allies held rallies and continued to apply public pressure on the government. When Ronald Reagan signed the Civil Liberties Act into law on August 10, 1988, Mulroney's ministers rushed to resolve the matter, finally agreeing to a formal settlement on August 27. After years of denying the possibility of any such arrangement, they agreed to provide an official apology, individual compensation (C$21,000), citizenship for Nikkei wrongfully deported after the war, pardons for those convicted under the War Measures Act, and the establishment of a Canadian Race Relations Foundation.[55]

A Divergent National Discourse

To write of Nikkei transnationality may seem odd, for Japanese Americans and Japanese Canadians spoke so frequently about their respective national identities. For instance, Tamotsu Shibutani complained during his imprisonment that "if we are citizens and as long as we are willing to chip in and do our share why in the hell do we have to live in a dump like this and get paid starvation wages."[56] This complaint acknowledges a legal fact, citizenship status, but it also relies on the ability (or lack of ability) to identify with a larger population. That is, it builds on the (false) presumption of community, which is why Shibutani went on to speak of citizenship not as an official designation, but as something experienced in the first-person plural: "A threat to our civil rights is a threat to the rights of all elements of the American population because it sets a dangerous precedent for others to follow."[57] Primary sources in Canada demonstrate a similar sense of betrayal that followed the presumption of belonging, however complicated that was before the bombing of Pearl Harbor. Think, for instance, of Muriel Kitagawa's declaration that, as a Canadian (though still a British subject), she and her family had the right to expect what she called "decent treatment." Not only did she declare a specific geographical affiliation, but she also went on to express the expectation of certain rights and privileges associated with representative government. She spoke, in short, as someone who did more than claim Canadian identity; she also lived one of the most basic presumptions associated with it. Her decision to do so is all the more complicated since Nikkei in Canada were declared noncitizens during the war and even for several years afterward. (Only in 1948 did they regain citizenship and finally get the right to vote.[58])

Like Mineta in his congressional testimony in support of Japanese American redress, Shibutani and Kitagawa each articulated more than just political ideals. They also expressed aspects of a specific national identity, such as Kitagawa's mention of being Canadian. She returned to this subject repeatedly in the 1940s, both in print and in correspondence.[59] To some extent, Nikkei North Americans had to carry themselves this way. Many had been born in the United States or Canada, and they were well schooled in each country's rhetoric of equality before the law, despite the uglier truths they lived. That is why, before stating her expectation of "decent treatment," Kitagawa drew a contrast with Germany, which forced its people "to work for nothing in the fields and factories far from home and children," and denounced Hitler's "system of captive labour; shooting hundreds in reprisal for one." Referring to the rhetoric of equality before the law, she closed this passage by expressing the hope that "the little peoples [will] have a chance at life again."[60]

The issue of Canadian identity became even more pressing after the bombing of Pearl Harbor, since it sharpened the question of how physical difference might relate to citizenship. Virulent Canadian racists such as Halford Wilson and Ian Mackenzie seized on that question to justify the mass expulsion of Nikkei from British Columbia. It should therefore come as no surprise that Gordon Kadota, the president of the NAJC in the early 1980s, would paraphrase the postwar Japanese Canadian attitude as having been "never again do we want to be Japanese. We are Canadians."[61] Presented with a binary opposition by their largely white compatriots, Japanese Canadians sought to minimize their deviation from the imposed norm and instead call attention to their participation in the fraught imperial politics of Canadian belonging.

Though Kadota's statement came in 1983, not 1941, it demonstrates that being Japanese Canadian was at key moments thought of as something specific that one could cultivate. While Kadota summarized a strongly defensive postwar mentality, a sense of specificity nonetheless persisted among Japanese Canadians of later generations. Communities may be imagined, but they still exert enormous pressure on their constituents.[62] For that reason, recognition of specificity persisted long after Nikkei had left the camps and the ghost towns, relocated, and tried to reestablish their lives. Already under pressure to become enculturated before the war, many of them went on to participate even more fully in supposedly Canadian cultural patterns afterward.

As a result, the question of what the term "Japanese Canadian" might mean, if anything, was on the minds of many readers of the *New Canadian*. This is evident in articles like "Questions and Answers on J. C. Redress by National Association," which appeared in the July 19, 1983, issue. Largely a reprint of a fact sheet sent out by the NAJC, this article provided background information concerning redress efforts in Canada and discussed aspects of how Japanese Americans were pursuing the matter. The NAJC had begun canvassing the Nikkei community about what form redress might take, and the purpose of the fact sheet was primarily to answer questions people might have, rather than advocate a specific policy. To that end, the organization asked and then answered basic questions on redress, such as, "When is the campaign being carried out? Now." It listed the options available, discussed the implications of each, and compared those options with developments in the United States. It also spoke of the need "to give JCs a sense of place and a sense of confidence," which were "traumatically disrupted in 1942."[63] The NAJC also spoke of the need to clarify the Canadian-ness of Nikkei citizens. It addressed the peculiarities of Canada's governmental structure as well, pointing out that "the class action option is not yet a viable alternative in Canada, not like in the U.S."[64] Even though the article was about the constitutional and legal obstacles to Canadian redress, it also discussed "a sense of place" that had been "traumatically disrupted" and drew comparisons with U.S. precedent. Such engagements came with the investigation of a specifically Japanese Canadian sense of self, even as that sense was inseparable from aspects of the larger Nikkei diaspora.

The imagination of a specifically Japanese Canadian community was also present in the first-person plural language of the NAJC's statements, which noted regarding the individual-compensation option that "the question here is how much should we demand, if we take the individual route." As for why Japanese Canadians should take action so long after the war, the NAJC statement argued that "our history would not be complete without a full resolution of that detention injustice."[65] The most important goal of this article was to promote a "national Japanese Canadian consensus" about redress, which also meant activating a Japanese Canadian collective identity that would include not only the NAJC's membership, but also "most community groups in Canada, including local chapters of the Japanese Canadian Citizens' Association, cultural centers, community groups, churches."[66] The idea of a collective identity was no small matter in 1983, when the question of redress gave rise to some of the most vigorous dissent among Japanese Canadians, even as it aggravated the perverse and long-standing suspicion among other groups that all people of Japanese origin were somehow essentially identical in terms of culture and politics. And yet, despite that dissent and the frequently rancorous environment that it contributed to, redress and its revivification of history helped to promote the imagination of a specifically Canadian Nikkei community by raising questions of cultural, political, and social unity.[67] In essence, then, afterlife provided a means to unify, provisionally, people driven by personal experience, which in this case is both shared and idiosyncratic.

One part of the Japanese Canadian imagination of community is particularly important: the recognition that Canada treated its Nikkei citizens and their family members in a particularly vicious manner. As Meisler pointed out in his *Los Angeles Times/New Canadian* article, "American civil libertarians will hardly take any solace in the fact, but no matter how harsh American treatment of Japanese-Americans may have been during World War II, Canadian treatment of Japanese-Canadians was worse."[68] Nor was this observation limited to outsiders, as Meisler pointed out:

> Sitting with a few friends at a dinner in Kamo's restaurant on Powell Street, Tamio Wakayama, a 41-year-old photographer, put it starkly.
>
> "The community in the States," he said, "was not so thoroughly trashed as the community in Canada."[69]

The damage Wakayama referred to resulted from Canada's more punitive postwar measures, which included forced "repatriation" for many, as well as a drive to keep the remainder of Nikkei from returning to the West Coast.

This attention to differences of circumstance was widespread, as is evident in a profile of two camp survivors, Shiro Uchida and Roy Uyeda, that ran adjacent to an article on the CWRIC's recommendation of individual compensation in the *New Canadian* on June 28, 1983.[70] Entitled "When It Was a Crime to Be of Japanese Descent," the article made a blunt comparison with the United States, declaring that "Japanese Canadians fared worse than those in the U.S.," and described the postwar dispersal policies under Prime Minister Mackenzie King. The author of the article then pointed out the historical factors that made Canadian redress more difficult to achieve, especially the constitutional differences between the two countries: "Unlike the U.S., where Japanese Americans are claiming in their lawsuit [brought in 1983 by the National Council for Japanese American Redress (NCJAR), which had split from the JACL] that their civil rights were violated, the War Measures Act made it perfectly legal for Ottawa to force Canadians out of their homes and ship them around the country."[71] According to this last statement, Nikkei in British Columbia were unquestionably Canadians who were wrongly stripped of their citizenship and then subject to unjust imprisonment and postwar deprivation. As Vic Ogura wrote in an editorial in the *New Canadian* during the following autumn, "History has recorded that they [Japanese Canadians] were innocents victimized by their own country of birth and allegiance."[72] Building on this idea of dereliction, the June 28 article also suggests that the xenophobia of Canada's government produced an experience different from that encountered by Japanese Americans. Not all discussions were so explicitly comparative. In an article entitled "Redress Options," Maryka Omatsu wrote laconically of the various injuries visited upon the Japanese Canadian community, including "the restriction on returning to the coast for seven years."[73] But the discourse of redress in Canada still acknowledged that wartime incarceration in North American took two different forms, as explained above, and that the histories of the Nikkei communities on either side of the U.S.-Canada border thus diverged in important ways.

The divergence was critical for what Omatsu called "the re-emergence of Japanese Canadian consciousness." That reemergence came partly, she said, from the JCCP. But it also came from a reevaluation of the history of Nikkei in Canada, the racism they had endured, and the government-sanctioned injustices they had suffered. As Omatsu wrote, "In the process of evaluating our history in this country, the destructiveness and pain of the war years and their aftermath is being acknowledged and discussed openly." Addressing injustices was vital: "Talk of redress for the wrongs perpetrated on the Japanese Canadian community is daily gaining acceptance."[74] Acceptance varied from person to person and region to region, though, and conflicts over redress within the Japanese community—particularly regarding who should represent the community—became acrimonious during the fall of 1983.[75] Nonetheless, as a topic redress helped advance awareness of the specifics of wartime incarceration and postwar bigotry in Canada, and that encouraged people to differentiate Japanese Canadian experience from that of Nikkei in the United States. Rather than produce a uniform definition, the result was to pursue a prolonged consideration that individuals would participate in as they wanted or could. As Frank Moritsugu suggested in an October 18, 1983, editorial in the *New Canadian*, "if this process has to take some extra time, better that we feel we've been part of the process—'we' being each Japanese Canadian who wants to be."[76]

The importance of differentiation extended beyond the Japanese Canadian community, too. As Kadota pointed out in a March 25, 1983, profile in the *New Canadian*, a bigoted transnationalism continued to plague public debates about wartime incarceration and its targets. The idea Kadota had in mind, one common among non-Nikkei Canadians, placed a vaguely white imaginary against a largely cohesive Nikkei one: "What bothers me about dealing with the media about these issues is that although they're supposed to be well informed, they actually have narrow preconceptions about Japan and Japanese Canadians. Basically, it doesn't differentiate between the two." Kadota linked this inability to distinguish between culture, nationality, and race to fears of economic and political diminishment that were prominent in North America at the time: "To most Canadians, Japanese Canadians are still Japanese. . . . They don't see them as Canadians. . . . It's part of a black-and-white mentality, a kind of intolerance that comes from fear of other people. From suspicion. And it gets worse in bad economic times when people feel threatened."[77]

Kadota's job as head of the NAJC therefore involved educating the non-Nikkei public: "I'm always being interviewed. In the last six months there's been a lot of interest in the Redress Committee which is trying to get financial compensation from the federal government for the 23,000 Japanese Canadians who lost their property during the Second World War." To advance the cause of his constituents, Kadota had to emphasize the specifics of their history, from the number of people affected to the particulars of how they suffered.[78] Part of this involved advancing a Nikkei history and experience that were discrete, identifiable, and above all beholden neither to Japan nor to the United States but that still addressed both. Like activist groups including the JCCP and the Sodan-kai, he sought to help establish the idea of a specifically Japanese Canadian community, with its own history, culture, and values, not in order to set the contours of that community in stone, but rather to destabilize racist preconceptions.[79]

Ambiguous and Ambivalent Transnationality

The Japanese Canadian community never saw itself as entirely separate from its counterpart in either the United States or Japan, but neither did it see itself as of a piece with Nikkei elsewhere. Instead, Japanese Canadians associated themselves with analogous cultures at the same time as they distinguished themselves from those cultures. A September 30, 1983, editorial in the *New Canadian* spoke of "the Japanese on both sides of the Forty-Ninth parallel . . . looking seriously at the question of redress."[80] Commonality both enabled and necessitated differentiation. This is a corollary of the shared audience that led the *Los Angeles Times* and the *New Canadian* to run Meisler's 1983 article on Vancouver: Nikkei in Vancouver or Toronto recognized that they were both like and unlike those in Los Angeles or Seattle, and vice versa. After the publication of *Personal Justice Denied* that knife-edge similarity and difference helped produce a diasporic transnationality that worked through and beyond any given nation-state.[81]

The tendency to speak comparatively was due in no small part to the fact that *Personal Justice Denied* laid out the conditions of Japanese American incarceration so authoritatively and in such detail that it raised questions about the circumstances Japanese Canadians had found themselves in during and after the war. Given the sense of inevitability that so many Japanese Canadians had felt about the wartime Orders-in-Council, how could advocates of redress overcome resistance within the community?[82] Differences over redress had sometimes been acrimonious even in the larger and more politically active community of Japanese Americans. Furthermore, since the Canadian government's policy was to fragment and disperse, there was some question as to just how cohesive and active the surviving community might be.[83] And then there was the issue of how non-Nikkei citizens might view wartime incarceration. The publication of Ken Adachi's *The Enemy That Never Was* in 1976 and Ann Gomer Sunahara's *The Politics of Racism* in 1981 did much to demonstrate the racist motivation underlying the forced removal of Nikkei from British Columbia. But some questions still remained about how people might frame the topic as one of injustice, as *Personal Justice Denied* had done. There also was the question of how Nikkei Canadians ought to address the racist postwar policies that further damaged their communities.

Others shared these concerns. On February 11, 1983, for instance, the *New Canadian* ran an article on Ian Waddell, the member of parliament representing Vancouver-Kingsway, who was pressing for an official government inquiry into wartime incarceration. He declared that those who had been incarcerated or displaced "were not really a threat; they were Canadians, and their only crime was that they were of Japanese ancestry."[84] Arguing that inaction would allow the injustice to fester, he made two recommendations: first, that Prime Minister Pierre Trudeau formally apologize in the House of Commons;[85] and second, "we should have a commission to listen to the evidence and hear the historical record so that history will not be changed [i.e., distorted in order to minimize or ignore the injustices visited upon Nikkei in Canada]." Waddell went on to lay out the scope such an inquiry should take, modeling it on the example of the United States while at the same time referring to that example directly: "The commission should recommend whether there should be compensation individually or symbolically, and I point out there is an American precedent for this."[86]

Canadian discussions of Japanese American circumstances did more than follow U.S. precedent or note historical divergences. They also addressed contemporary differences, for instance with respect to legal precedent and governmental structure. On April 22, 1983, the *New Canadian* ran an article on the obstacles facing redress through legal action. It began by noting that "all Japanese Canadians' eyes were on the actions of their Nikkei cousins down south and their battle for redress against the U.S. government for 'maliciously and unlawfully' depriving them of their constitutional rights during the Second World War."[87] Citing Roy Miki, who was then emerging as a leader in the redress movement, the article pointed out a crucial similarity between the two Nikkei communities: as was the case in California, Oregon, and Washington, in Canada too Nikkei present economic competition for their white neighbors, who used the bombing of Pearl Harbor as a pretext to eliminate that competition.[88] This was no simple equation, though. Having laid out the basics of the NCJAR class-action lawsuit, the article then made a contrast: "In Canada, where Japanese Canadians suffered longer than in the U.S., a similar group of second and third generation Canadians seeks redress but does not appear to have a legal position."[89]

That last sentence made two important points. First, as noted above, Japanese Canadian wartime experience differed from its Japanese American counterpart. Second, constitutional and governmental factors in Canada required that activists develop new strategies. Thus, the article quoted Miki's observation that "'the Canadian government, acting through the War Measures Act, was acting legally in that they did not exceed the authority granted them.'"[90] Referring to Miki once again, it acknowledged the necessity of pursuing "moral and ethical routes" to redress, rather than taking legal action. In explaining the case against judicial action, this article also framed a distinctly Japanese Canadian circumstance and, thus, route to political engagement. And yet, it did so by referring to American precedent, even as all involved would have recognized the significant differences between each type of Nikkei North American experience.

Ancestry, Place, and Identity

The question of Nikkei North American identity had been a topic of study for decades. In an article in the July 29, 1983, issue of the *New Canadian* entitled "All Those Books about Us JCs,"[91] Frank Moritsugu provided an annotated list of sources, stretching from a 1939 sociological study entitled *The Japanese Canadians* to Adachi's and Sunahara's books. He concluded the article by acknowledging that the character of Nikkei in Canada had long been a topic of study: "You know, we must be an interesting group of Canadians to have so much written about us."[92] And yet, as Bill Hosokawa had pointed out several years before, that character could vary tremendously even across a small area.[93] As a result, in 1983 it remained a pressing concern, with the *New Canadian* publishing a range of articles on changing tastes in food, music, and fashion among Nikkei North Americans, as well as on the cultural, political, and economic implications of Japanese ancestry. For instance, among other things the paper ran an editorial by Bill Marutani on the relationship between generational differences and the tendency to intermarry.[94] It also ran two articles about the supposed erosion of Nikkei identity among Japanese Americans: a lament on June 3, 1983, followed by a vigorous rebuttal on July 15.[95]

This last pair of articles illustrate how hard it was to define Nikkei identity, even in California, where the topic had long been important. In the first article, the late Ronald Tanaka declared that Nikkei Americans were "a society on the path to cultural as well as genetic extinction," predicting that by 2050 "Japanese Americans along with their art will have been relegated to museums and history books." There would remain people of Japanese ancestry, he said, but they would "never represent a distinct American subculture."[96] According to him, this had come about because of assimilation that was diluting the ethical and aesthetic traditions that made Japanese culture distinctive. As for the source of that culture, he said, "the Japanese in Japan Westernized together as Japanese, thus retaining their Japanese identity."[97] A rebuttal, by Patty Wada, suggested that Tanaka had "not done his homework as a responsible academician should." (Born in Poston, Tanaka was at the time a professor of English and ethnic studies at the California State University, Sacramento. Having at one time held a visiting appointment at the University of British Columbia, he also was a familiar figure among Japanese Canadians.[98]) The result, Wada said, was precisely the sort of blinkered view of Nikkei identity the article purported to critique: "In pointing the finger at us, he pinpoints his own weakness—'So what I see in Japanese Americans is the general reluctance or inability to recognize a world of our own.'"[99] She then proceeded to list Japanese American artists and initiatives to support her claim; most of these examples came from the Bay Area, which, she pointed out, "lies a mere hour and a half away from Sacramento." Even in California, with its longer history of activism by people of Asian ancestry, Nikkei identity was contested, fragmentary, and at times contradictory, rather than discrete and easy to identify.

It is perhaps ironic for a Japanese Canadian paper to run an article by a self-professed Japanese American "cultural 'hardliner'" for whom there was a properly "authentic [Nikkei] existence," and to follow it with a self-consciously Californian response.[100] Nonetheless, the argument over supposedly "heritageless Sansei" in the United States belonged to a larger debate in the early 1980s about what exactly constituted Nikkei North American identity.[101] That debate revolved around the conviction among some Japanese Americans and Japanese Canadians that difference was a liability rather than an asset, particularly in the wake of wartime mistreatment. In pointing that out, Tanaka's polemic differed from the opinions of others mainly in degree rather than kind.[102] As Wada's response suggests, though, other aspects of his argument were not widely accepted. Regardless, their debate demonstrates the difficulty of navigating the cultural and political landscape of borderlands.

Despite the widespread currency of such exchanges, the *New Canadian* was not in a position to definitively frame the discourse of Japanese Canadian identity; it lacked the resources, among other things. It could, however, provide a forum for that discourse. Consequently, as discussions of Nikkei identity and of redress gained momentum, the paper necessarily drew on American sources as well as on material from larger Canadian dailies, even as it attempted to differentiate its audience from Nikkei south of the 49th parallel. This was not because of a lack of imagination, or an inability to discern the differences between Japanese Americans and Japanese Canadians. Rather, it sprang from the recognition that engagement with the redress movement and cultural production in the United States could bolster awareness of the singular circumstances of Nikkei in Canada. Thus, in drawing on articles of this sort, the *New Canadian* helped galvanize readers, providing them with both developing ideas and the tools for acting on those ideas. And, as Japanese Canadians became increasingly engaged in debates over redress, the paper ran still more original articles and editorials. It also published repeated calls for citizens to participate in public meetings. This was particularly noticeable in the autumn of 1983, when divisions within the community were deepest.

In the wake of *Personal Justice Denied* and, later, the commission's recommendations, the *New Canadian* ran articles to cultivate and amplify a kind of Nikkei voice, such as the plea by journalist Teresa Watanabe for Asian Americans to express themselves publicly.[103] Drawing on letters to the *Los Angeles Herald Examiner*, where she was a reporter, Watanabe pointed out that virtually no one of Asian ancestry had weighed in concerning the CWRIC and its outcome. Far from exemplifying prudent silence, she suggested, that lack of a voice was crippling Asian Americans by allowing bigoted and reactionary whites to set the terms of debate. (Her argument echoed one that Warren Furutani made early in his career as an activist, as Chapter Four will demonstrate.) She then rebutted the more common objections to stating a public opinion: the inability to write, a feeling of political impotence, and even the force of cultural habit: "*But . . . there's this matter of, uh, enryo* [i.e., an ideal of self-restraint]. Well, O.K. If you're really uncomfortable about expressing your opinions . . . then at least consider writing informative letters"), disproving the usual explanations for wartime incarceration.[104] She laid out not what readers should say, but rather why they should say something in the first place. For Watanabe, just as for Miki, Omatsu, and other Japanese Canadians, political engagement could lead to a concrete outcome, but it also could help find, shape, and strengthen a distinctively Nikkei voice in political and cultural discourses.

Though originally written for a Southern California readership, Watanabe's article also provided a spur for Japanese Canadians, many of whom had previously tended to be stereotypically silent. In fact, the timing of this article was apt, coming a scant couple of weeks before the CWRIC was to issue its recommendations, and as the NAJC and other organizations had begun to canvas the Japanese Canadian community about the possibility of redress north of the U.S. border. Like the article about Roy Miki's argument in favor of "moral and ethical" grounds for redress, Watanabe's editorial also emphasized the need for people of Japanese ancestry to be vocal and politically engaged—to do more than rethink wartime incarceration, but also to act. In order to help them achieve this dual evolution, the *New Canadian* and its contributors referred to a tradition that was similar to their own, even as its differences were abundantly clear to the paper and its readership. They participated self-consciously in an important, if complex and shifting, transnational community.

Beyond Comparison

The discourse of Nikkei identity in the *New Canadian* during the early 1980s was transnational, but it was ambivalently so. The transnationality of Nikkei in Canada at that time was evident in the recognition that key characteristics, such as Japanese ancestry and nineteenth- and early twentieth-century immigration and wartime incarceration, established a common denominator with Japanese Americans. Other traits, such as religious traditions and, to varying degrees, language, also established ties with contemporary Japanese culture as well. And yet, that recognition was far from monolithic. Readers of the *New Canadian* defined themselves in relationship to Canada, Japan, and the United States simultaneously—as witnessed by the strong sense of novelty that attended the selection and tone of articles about sushi-making robots, love hotels, and the Japanese imperial family, as well as the adventures and misadventures of Nikkei abroad. Conversely, a similar sense of shared experience and culture is evident in, among other things, the decision of the *Los Angeles Times* to run Stanley Meisler's article on contemporary Japanese Canadian culture and politics.

More than just international engagement, such shared and competing interests illustrate the complexity of borderlands.[105] For instance, at times Nikkei identity expanded to all the Americas, such as in the 1981 announcement of a pan-American "Nikkei confab" in Mexico City, a meeting that eventually gave rise to the Pan American Nikkei Association/Asociación Panamericana Nikkei.[106] According to the article, the meeting would provide an excellent opportunity to gain "an insight into the different historical background of the Japanese immigration to the different countries and the present status of the Nikkei," and to consider what the future might hold for people of Japanese ancestry in the Americas. As articles like this suggest, Nikkei North American identity was in flux, more like a continuing question than a definitive statement. To be Japanese Canadian could, in some circumstances, also involve being Nikkei American, not just Nikkei North American. To quote Roy Kiyooka,

> Sounding all the old homilies (again), I want to insist that everybody is a bona fide member and an activist (each in their own way) in the ongoing histrionics of a given culture. Everybody's "bearing" is in that sense equal, and we N.A. Asians ought to act forthrightly on our own behalf. We shall have to remain vigilant if we are to insert ourselves in to the W.A.S.P. scheme of things—albeit their histories.[107]

The transnationality of Nikkei identity in the early 1980s extended well beyond the Americas. Gordon Hirabayashi, in a July 1983 editorial, remarked that the injustices visited on Japanese Canadians, to whom he referred specifically, remained important for people who did not share Japanese ancestry. For some, he said, the distance of history might justify in-action, a position he summed up as, "Why raise the issue now? We have recovered well. We live in a more enlightened era. Such a thing can't happen again. So let's forget it."[108] He then recounted a recent episode in which a teacher in Eckville, a hamlet outside Edmonton, Alberta, had recently been revealed as a Holocaust denier. Noting the surprise this news provoked, he pointed out how easily complacency can yield to renewed bigotry. Thinking across a spectrum of injustices, Hirabayashi pleaded for broad cultural and transnational political engagement:

> It is not just in Canada. See the Los Angeles Times reprint of John Tateishi's cogent plea for remembering. And in Japan Susumu Hani, director of "Prophesy," which pieces together the on-the-scene footage of the Hiro-shima and Nagasaki bomb destruction of property and human beings, made available by the U.S. Strategic A-Bomb Survey, states: . . . even in Japan people think of Hiroshima and Nagasaki as tragedies of the past. But Hiroshima and Nagasaki have a message for today and tomorrow."
>
> How much more is a tragedy likely to be repeated if it is forgotten? Who remembers the holocaust better than the Jews who suffered and survived? Who remembers the uprooting and the indignity of being labeled enemies in your own country [better] than the Japanese Canadians? Who remem-bers what the nuclear bomb really means but the Hiroshima-Nagasaki vic-tims? If these people do not speak out, how can others know?[109]

In a way, Hirabayashi was arguing for more than just political engagement across racial, religious, and linguistic lines. Writing in the *New Canadian*, he was arguing for a particular kind of Japanese Canadian identity, one that extended beyond food trends or noteworthy hotels. He was arguing for a Japanese Canadian identity that was expansive, that defined itself as transnational not simply in terms of physiognomy and culture, but also in terms of its ability to empathize and to engage with others whose seeming differences belied fundamental commonalities.[110] He was arguing for a new kind of Canadian, which was also a new kind of American—one that is more fully human.

FOUR

Hakomite and the Cultivation
of Empathy as Activism

Recall for a moment Norman Mineta's statement crediting postwar generations of Nikkei for political action around the topic of Executive Order 9066 and its aftermath. Mineta suggested that it was the Sansei "who finally forced their parents to come out of the closet and tell us these stories."[1] This statement demonstrates how people who did not experience incarceration directly could nonetheless be profoundly affected by it. Mineta's statement also suggests that such engagement can produce mutually reinforcing agency. The silence of former inmates provoked curiosity and anger, which produced questions, which encouraged speech and other sorts of action (e.g., the pursuit of redress), which reinforced the desire by members of a younger generation to know and say more.[2] Even the indirect agency of many Issei and Nisei could be contagious and give rise to more active, or at least familiar, types.

Though indirect, the engagement with Executive Order 9066 by Nikkei born after the Second World War has taken on a forensic character. For instance, California Assemblyman Warren Furutani (b. 1947) once spoke of the first large-scale trip to the prison site at Manzanar, in 1969, as exhuming the Japanese American experience of World War II: "We started walking around, and it was like discovering a shallow grave, where the elements had blown the top layer off, and then the grave was exposed, and you could see a whole history."[3] Rather than an exercise in longing, the hallmark of nostalgia, work by younger Nikkei has more closely resembled the grimly determined efforts of someone surveying a crime scene. They seek to reconstruct a tragic narrative rather than recall a bygone golden age. That reconstruction is partly an exercise in historical study, and partly an exercise in imaginative engagement with gaps in the historical record. For that reason, the engagement of younger Nikkei with wartime incarceration has also retained a deeply emotional, almost sacral, character that comes through especially clearly in annual trips to Manzanar, visits that both former inmates and later generations call pilgrimages. And, as with other kinds of spiritual engagement, what remains hidden is as important as what is unearthed. This chapter discusses the simultaneous rigor and almost religious zeal with which members of younger generations have sought to discover, interrogate, and relay the experience of their forebears, as well as how that zeal has in turn helped transform older Japanese Americans.

It is impossible to say how empathy works for each person who experiences the afterlife of Nikkei wartime incarceration, but the experiences of Sansei and Yonsei activists can provide some idea, since they experienced that afterlife most closely and for the longest time. The integration of a fragmentary past into the present is directly related to embodiment, which has been an integral aspect of Nikkei North American political engagement. Mary Douglas once wrote of the "two bodies," one physical and the other social, suggesting that embodiment was produced by their alignment.[4] Standing before his colleagues or speaking to reporters, for instance, Mineta provided a physical example of someone who survived profound and far-reaching injustice. Others who experienced either the circumstances surrounding that incarceration (e.g., Jim Wright) or limited aspects of it (Alan Simpson) provide a similar manifestation. Points of contact among their very different circumstances allowed these people to embody aspects of a critical historical moment and its persistence in the present. One of the most important results of embodiment is a spatial and temporal operation that transforms an abstraction (something "there and then") into a concrete reality ("here and now"). The goal of that transformation, as demonstrated in the growing Japanese American willingness to discuss the lingering past of injustice, is to activate an awareness of history that is emotional and dynamic, something to be both lived in the present and carried into the future.

Mineta's comment about younger generations, like the involvement of members of those generations in the passage of the Civil Liberties Act, indicates the impact that embodiment can have on younger members of a historically marginalized community. That initial stage of embodiment is not always activist or even intentional, as the mention of older Nikkei being brought out of the closet by their children and grandchildren suggests. Yet embodiment provokes a crucial parallel engagement on the part of younger generations. This engagement involves reaching back to something members of a younger generation know is there but cannot perceive directly or wholly. They sense that lingering presence of the past, but substantial gaps of understanding remain as the ghostly matter of history reveals itself only reluctantly.[5] In cases such as the metaphorical exhumation that Furutani described, viewing the past through a glass darkly produces a sense of obligation to amplify or relay that past to other people who have not experienced it themselves, even indirectly, or who may not even know it is there in the first place. That obligation and how it has driven postwar Nikkei to a kind of imaginative engagement with the past form the subject of this chapter.

Black Activism and the Search for a Japanese American Voice

Unlike Mineta, neither Furutani (a Yonsei) nor Victor Shibata, the Sansei cofounder of the formal Manzanar pilgrimages, had been imprisoned under Executive Order 9066, yet both of them were alive to the history and politics of wartime incarceration as well as its emotional and familial toll. Their actions, and the actions of other Nikkei born after the war, thus testify to the powerful afterlife of Japanese American imprisonment, even in its earliest and vaguest forms. Furutani is a case in point. One of many Japanese American activists in the late 1960s and 1970s, Furutani demonstrates especially clearly the personal and political dynamics at issue. In many respects, Furutani's upbringing was not exceptional for his generation of Japanese Americans, not least in how his parents' history conformed to what he called the "standard" story of older generations, with life neatly divided into "camp" and "post-camp," a shorthand that illustrates how deeply ingrained the afterlife of injustice is for this community.[6] His maternal grandparents worked on farms near Elk Grove, California, picking hops and fruit. His paternal grandparents worked and lived in Hawaii. Like a number of Issei and Nisei had also done, Furutani's parents met in a prison camp (Rohwer, in Desha County, Arkansas). Their budding relationship was put on hold when Furutani's father left camp to join the 442nd Regimental Combat Team.[7] Upon his return, the two got married in New York and made their way back West by way of Chicago and Minnesota, eventually settling in Gardena, California.[8]

At the same time, Furutani's upbringing exposed him to a diverse racial and ethnic cohort that allowed him to interrogate what Japanese American identity could become. Though the family resettled in a largely Nikkei neighborhood, Furutani has said they "did not orbit around the Japanese American community."[9] Furutani Sr. had several non-Nikkei friends, mainly Polish and Italians and mostly from the New York area. According to Furutani Jr., he had a "cool Dad" in part because, as a Sansei, Furutani Sr. was interested in jazz, motorcycles, and racing cars. His Nisei mother, however, brought some of the older traditions to bear on the family, thus keeping his father's "flights of fancy in check."[10] Somewhat atypically, the Furutanis' social networks were tied to their specific neighborhood rather than the Buddhist churches of Gardena, where Nikkei in the area tended to go for community support. And during the 1960s, Furutani attended a diverse high school: equal parts Japanese American, black, white, and Latino.[11]

During the mid-1960s, Furutani became more self-consciously political. He started reflecting on his own family's history. And although his parents were less reticent than many other Japanese Americans of their generation, even their tendency to downplay or avoid talking about wartime imprisonment only underscored the importance of the topic. As with so many Japanese American families, "it [incarceration] was always a reference point," the place to start a conversation when meeting another Nikkei for the first time.[12] He noticed that his parents and others of their generation, for example, regularly began conversations with the question, "What camp were you in?"[13] This question spoke volumes for Furutani and others whose parents had lived under Executive Order 9066, its bland understatement contrasting with the regularity with which people asked it of one another.

Julie Jefferson, a childhood best friend, also heavily influenced his political beliefs. In junior high school, they found out that they had the same birth date, marking the beginning of shared celebrations with both families as well as conversations that would shape one another's political commitments. The two parted ways after high school, with Furutani hopping from one community college to another while Jefferson followed the tradition in her family and headed to Knoxville College, a historically black college in Tennessee. In 1965, after just one year, Jefferson returned, angry after experiencing the racism endemic to that region. Soon after, she became involved in the Black Power movement and took her childhood friend to hear Stokely Carmichael speak in the Los Angeles neighborhood of Watts, where, Furutani has said, he was the only non-black in the audience.[14]

Carmichael's speech opened up an entirely new view of race relations for Furutani. Critically important was Carmichael's call, reiterated at Berkeley and other places, that "we have to wage a psychological battle on the right for black people to define their own terms, define themselves as they see fit, and organize themselves as they see [f]it."[15] Furutani realized that Asian Americans needed to do the same thing, not simply to break down stereotypes, but also to provide their own models for identity and, thus, to take command of the discourse of what it meant to be Asian American.[16] (He recalled, for example, that his high school counselor, conjuring a stereotype about Asian Americans being good at math and science, told the young Furutani to take physics, even though Furutani had said he wanted to be an artist.[17])

In 1971, not long after the first formal Manzanar pilgrimage, Furutani described the need among Asian Americans for "ammunition and I don't mean the kind you put in a gun. I mean the kind that comes out of your mouth because when it really comes to convincing people we've got to be able to sit down with them, explain [the historical specifics of iniquity], explain other things which don't even deal with Asian Americans but deal with being a person in America."[18] Like Mineta, Furutani wanted to change perceptions of Asian Americans. But he also wanted to transform how Asian Americans perceived themselves in the first place, to move them away from a self-conception that to some extent was shaped during wartime incarceration toward one that was independent of white paradigms. (As noted in Chapter Three, people like Teresa Watanabe and Roy Kiyooka would still be arguing for this in the early 1980s.[19]) Using the example of children being bullied, Furutani defined the problem as one of ingrained passivity: "They're being beaten up because they don't fight back. And I'm sure that when they get home and tell their parents that they got beat up, the parents get mad at the kids. . . . You know, it's not even a case of why did you let them beat you up. It's 'why did you get in trouble?'"[20] Though the "why did you get in trouble" line is perhaps a Japanese American approach linked to incarceration, for Furutani in 1971 the fight against passivity required that Asian Americans throw off the white narrative they had internalized and replace it with one of their own. And for him, as for many other Japanese American activists at the time, the Black Power movement provided inspiration to do so.[21]

For Sansei and Yonsei in the late 1960s and 1970s searching for a route to political engagement, acting on that inspiration required that they draw on a history and on attitudes native to their own community. Pilgrimage to Manzanar provided excellent ammunition, an almost ideal opportunity to spur Nikkei to study their own history and its aftereffects.[22] It allowed participants to learn about their family histories and the original conditions as well as the lingering effects of wartime incarceration, and act on that knowledge. It also created an opportunity for their collective action to attract public awareness of Asian Americans as political agents. Time would have to pass before that opportunity would present itself, though. Furutani and his fellow organizers, like the Issei and Nisei before them, at first approached political activism with vague ideas of what was needed and only developed a clearer sense of direction over time.

Seeking a model for how to help mobilize Asian Americans, Furutani combed through autobiographical accounts by black writers whose approach to the intellectual, social, and political challenges of marginalization he found promising. The list included Claude Brown's *Man Child in the Promised Land* (1965), Eldridge Cleaver's *Soul on Ice* (1968), and Ralph Ellison's *The Invisible Man* (1952). Working through this list, Furutani began to wonder about the absence of similar work by Nikkei authors. In fact, during the late 1960s the only current book Furutani had found about Japanese American experience was *America's Concentration Camps* by the white author Alan Bosworth (1967).[23] For Furutani, such a lack of reflection on race from within his own community had to be addressed. Japanese Americans needed to find their own voice, rather than rely on white accounts of the injustice they had suffered.[24] Only by doing this for themselves and on their own terms could Nikkei determine a political course that addressed their specific needs and thus expressed what Roy Kiyooka called "the ardour of all such [racialized linguistic, cultural and political] displacement."[25] But first, that experience had to be made clear. The initial goal he and his fellow activists shared was thus to enable Japanese Americans to gain a clearer sense of their history, after which they could begin formulating a coherent sense of identity and then begin pursuing vigorous public action.[26]

Around this same time, Furutani and Shibata (then a student at UCLA) were en route to Oceanside to participate in an anti-war protest at the local Marine base, Camp Pendleton. They stopped somewhere to have breakfast and, reflecting on the protest movement, decided that Asian Americans needed a call to action akin to the 1966 United Farm Workers march to Sacramento or the 1968 Poor People's March in Washington. Their goal was to provide both an opportunity to talk about Asian American identity and a platform for future activism.[27] As a result, they decided a march of some sort would be in order, specifically, one that had a wartime prison site as its destination.

Manzanar and the Place of Afterlife

As a geographical site, Manzanar is ordinary. Located just west of Death Valley, it lacks visual drama. The views are pretty; Ansel Adams spoke of them during a wartime visit. Still, they pale in comparison to those in the adjacent national and state parks, so it might seem an unpromising anchor for significant political or cultural change. But this unassuming spot was also the site where ten thousand Nikkei were imprisoned from 1942 to 1945. From the end of the war until about 1970 it provided few indications that anything historically significant had happened there. A group of Paiute workers who had built the Manzanar camp were later paid to dismantle it, and the buildings and fixtures were sold and carted off for use elsewhere, leaving behind little more than a handful of concrete structures.[28] Few of the locals were inclined to commemorate their own wartime legacy, particularly since they had vigorously resisted the influx of Nikkei from Los Angeles in the first place, even going so far as to restrict the number of inmates who could visit local shops. And so, for over two decades after Manzanar closed in 1945, the site was mostly forgotten—largely obliviated physically and only selectively preserved in photographs and archival documents.[29] By the late 1960s it had all the charmlessness of any other degraded farming site along US-395, itself just another undistinguished inland California highway.

Nonetheless, Furutani and Shibata eventually chose it as the site for what became one of the most important rallying points for Japanese American political action. For all the political ardor that drove them to plan this first action, though, Furutani later admitted that the selection of Manzanar was basically by default:

> Victor and I said that we had to march somewhere, and that's when the idea came up of marching to Manzanar. . . . Logic said, 'well, it's the closest; we

can march to that.' And then in those days, you didn't have Google Maps. . . . So we took out the map, and 'half an inch equals a hundred miles,' and we sort of measured it—'aw, 400 miles. That doesn't sound too far.' . . . So we went.[30]

The pair might have chosen a more impressive place, had there been one closer by, but as luck and geography would have it, they and their fellow pilgrims wound up on a bland stretch of US-359 on a bitter December day in 1969. As Shibata recalled, "We weren't thinking about that, but it was actually good that we did it in the bad weather. You really [felt] what they went through."[31]

In fact, the 1969 trip revealed surprising avenues for inquiry.[32] Some of these were historical, such as the fact that, while Furutani and Shibata thought they were going to perform the first pilgrimage in 1969, two former prisoners at the site had been visiting for nearly a quarter century, cleaning off graves and holding services for the dead. Some avenues for inquiry were political and social, which became evident as pilgrims sought to share their experiences as widely as possible. One participant in the 1969 trip, the former inmate and fellow activist Edison Uno, wrote about the experience for the *Pacific Citizen*. Published in the national paper of the JACL, his account addressed both an organization and a constituency that many of the younger Nikkei had begun to write off, thus publicizing this action beyond the former inmates and the mainly Sansei and Yonsei students and activists who joined in the 1969 pilgrimage. In addition, mainstream papers and news channels picked up the story, publishing both photographs and clips of pilgrims tending to the site. According to Sue Kunitomi Embrey, a number of African Americans also went along in an attempt to link Manzanar to their own political and cultural struggles.[33]

The resulting trip was revelatory. Standing in that ordinary place, Furutani recounted, the pilgrims gained a new awareness of their parents' and grandparents' mass incarceration, not only because of what they saw, but also because of what they did not see. Like investigators "discovering a shallow grave," Furutani and his fellow pilgrims had to extrapolate from what they found, bridging gaps in their understanding but also coming to understand those gaps themselves more fully. The pilgrimage cast light on history, but also on just how much work lay ahead of those who unearthed that history: "We didn't understand it, because we didn't have the information yet."[34] Stumbling on a foundation here or the bed of a reservoir there, the pilgrims found in the landscape a material counterpart to their parents' mix of stoic reticence and fervent, if terse, inquiry. These younger Nikkei stood before the fragments of a terrible history they barely comprehended in 1969. And yet, the appearance of the site, especially in contrast with the mountains beyond, provided a sense of scale: "It was stark, it was weather-beaten, but it was still white, and it was interesting, because the backdrop was, literally, [Mount Williamson], and the Sierra Nevada mountains. There was an elegance to it, a starkness. It was very dramatic during a cloudy day, which provided all the environmental drama that helped fill in all the spaces relative to the limited knowledge we had."[35] Furutani's observations about the landscape illustrate the power of emotion, a critical part of the afterlife of a painful historical event. Arriving at the site of their parents' and grandparents' history armed with only a rudimentary grasp of its basic narrative and few tools for comprehending that narrative, he and his fellow marchers nonetheless strove to identify more closely with the experience of earlier generations. They began to align themselves with a seemingly lost past precisely because, standing between the impassive starkness of their surroundings and the lingering ruins of the camp, they could finally begin to comprehend the scope, if not the details, of that loss.

Pilgrimage and Hakomite

The 1969 pilgrimage was meant to be transformative, not just informative. The trip changed a remote highway just east of Inyo National Forest into a place of tragic beauty. It also changed many of the pilgrims. Both Furutani and Shibata anticipated this, since otherwise there would have been no point in going. That is why they referred to their action in religious terms. Shibata has been credited with choosing the term "pilgrimage" to describe the project, a choice that signaled the goal of drawing participants bodily toward a more immediate engagement with history.

Furutani's and Shibata's project was as much emotional as it was historically rigorous and politically pragmatic: the first large-scale Manzanar pilgrimage was a way for Sansei and Yonsei to integrate the (indirect, largely fragmentary) experience of wartime incarceration more fully into their own lives, in addition to acknowledging the sacrifices of their forebears. The pilgrimage did this in a number of ways. First, by bringing younger Nikkei to a site of incarceration it allowed them to visualize the spaces their parents and grandparents had occupied. In this way, the pilgrimage enabled Sansei and Yonsei to sharpen their earlier sense of the lingering presence of Executive Order 9066 in their own lives.[36] As participants in the pilgrimage sought and encountered fragments of a materially lost past, they also sought and encountered profound gaps in the historical record. Echoing the laconic account provided by their parents and grandparents, those gaps and the losses became at least as important as anything that might remain, since they begged for further investigation.

Second, the pilgrimage also required that participants experience in a modest way the hardships originally inflicted by Executive Order 9066. In this respect, too, the first trip was an act of faith: Furutani and Shibata described the inaugural march with the Japanese term *hakomite*, which translates "to go back"; the pilgrims did so in bitter cold between Christmas and the New Year without knowing what they would find or how it would impact them.[37] Third, and most important, arriving at Manzanar also provided a tangible instance of the challenge that younger Nikkei have faced in their parents and grandparents: seemingly still, placid surfaces that veiled an almost unspeakable injustice. But like such a veil, this stillness and silence revealed the presence of tragedy lying below the surface. The fading of history's physical imprint not only demanded inspection but also provided a warning against complacency and a call to further action that worked in exactly the way Furutani and Shibata had hoped they would, eventually spurring the foundation of a long-term program involving annual visits to Manzanar and, over time, an expanding number of related Nikkei political endeavors.

Visible Fragments of a Ghostly Past

For all the emotional weight of the first Manzanar pilgrimages, early visits still also had a significant historical component—those visible fragments of the past—which is part of the reason that Furutani, Shibata, and their fellow organizers went out of their way to include former inmates in the project from early on.[38] For instance, Furutani brought in Embrey, a fellow protester against the Vietnam War who had been an editor of the *Manzanar Free Press*, a camp paper published between April 1942 and

October 1945.[39] Likewise, two clergymen, Reverend Shoichi Wakahiro and Reverend Sentoku Maeda (Christian and Buddhist, respectively), accompanied the pilgrims on their second trip. From the closure of the camp onward, Wakahiro and Maeda had been returning annually to Manzanar. Their goal was to pay their respects to the dead who had not been given a proper burial, despite government claims to the contrary.[40] Because of these trips, the two had been able to observe changes over time and thus possessed a wealth of information about the camp, its structures, and its inmates.[41] Including former inmates did much more than give these people an opportunity to address their own memories. It also allowed them to expand on and enhance the afterlife of mass imprisonment for younger Nikkei participants by continually adding new information and reinforcing a sense of just how much remained lost. The pilgrimages quickly took on some of the character of archaeological digs. For instance, the first pilgrims found a wartime dump of sorts where plates and other domestic artifacts had been buried.[42] Manzanar in 1969 was both metaphorically and literally "a shallow grave, where the elements had blown the top layer off, and then the grave was exposed."

To a considerable extent, though, the recovery that pilgrims sought was as much emotional as it was historical. In fact, Furutani would later suggest that "we were exhuming—not the bodies, but the *experience*."[43] With each pilgrimage, Nikkei unearthed additional physical elements of the wartime narrative, which hinted at long-buried physical and emotional states. Here, the presence of Issei and Nisei pilgrims proved especially important. Besides revisiting the site of their imprisonment as free citizens, older Japanese Americans breathed life into the material fragments they and their younger compatriots found alongside the highway. When they spoke of life in camp, for instance, they voiced what still-silent Nikkei could or would not; pointing to the residue of that life, they reactivated a long-dormant site.[44] More than simply indicating noteworthy spots, they were able to explain the significance of those spots in specific, personal terms. They made Manzanar a powerful site for intersecting emotional experiences: recollection of primary experience (inmates) and empathy for that experience in those who were not present at the time (the children and grandchildren of inmates). Combining aspects of history with imaginative engagement, the pilgrimages allowed their participants to flesh out a story that had remained skeletal well into the 1960s and also to claim it, at least in some respects, as their own. The intergenerational effects of empathetic agency at Manzanar, especially in the earliest pilgrimages, thus exemplifies a dynamic recently described by Yasuko Takezawa, who has suggested that "affective bonds that bind the group together are based on the sense of past suffering."[45] All members of the group share that suffering, though to differing extents. As a result, embodiment spurs a range of experiences that converge on a few critical nodes. These nodes can either be active and explicit (e.g., recollections by Embrey, Maeda, or Wakahiro), or they can be indirect and implicit (e.g., the long silences of a Nikkei elder between meetings with other former prisoners).[46]

These diverse experiences of suffering also can be relayed over time, with the agency of one generation gaining force in the next, which could then lend that force back to its elders. The voices of former inmates necessarily would always recall the lingering silence of Nikkei who were either unable or unwilling to speak of their imprisonment; their presence necessarily sharpened the absence of others. The sense of that absence fueled a desire for clearer and fuller accounting, a desire among Sansei (and Yonsei) pilgrims to bring their older family members out of the closet. That desire spurred dialogue with Nikkei elders present on site. As a result, intergenerational empathetic agency provided a rare opportunity to change the Japanese American community by providing its individual members with a shared opportunity to change themselves. Echoing a centuries-old religious metaphor, Furutani has likened the Manzanar pilgrimages to toiling in a rich field: "Just as the camp experience bears fruit for those individuals who want to pick and harvest the lessons and knowledge to be learned, these trees blossom every spring."[47] Questions on site would lead initially to a clearer sense of the historical narrative and later to questions at home, in the company of reticent family members. Driven by a growing, increasingly complex form of empathetic agency, those latter questions would in turn help create the sense of a shared past, even as the specifics of that sharing might vary from family to family and generation to generation.

Strengthening and reshaping how the afterlife of wartime incarceration extends across generations, empathetic agency did more than reinforce a sense of Nikkei identity, as Takezawa has observed; it also catalyzed Japanese American political engagement on a larger scale, as Furutani had hoped. That stronger engagement derived in part from the empathetic and sacral elements of Furutani's and Shibata's project. Though in many ways impro-vised, the first Manzanar pilgrimage was also ritualistic, enabling younger Nikkei to self-consciously seek out aspects of their parents' and grand-parents' experiences, the places where these people had lived (and, in several cases, died), some of the conditions they encountered there, and some of the personal hardships they had endured. In this way, the voluntary repetition of the suffering wrought by forced incarceration lent Sansei and Yonsei a sense of scale. It also gave the older Nikkei who had joined the pilgrimage a way to meditate on their own experiences in the company of people who now shared critical elements of those experiences, even though they did so at a distance from the past. This meditation led to new insights for mem-bers of younger generations, who in turn asked new questions. As empathy and the historical record intersected, repetition (retracing routes, walking old paths, seeing old sights) concretized memory. Pilgrimage, in short, did not simply teach articles of faith; it made those articles part of the experi-ences of members of younger generations, part of their own histories. In addition, it provoked a renewed determination not only to unearth and publicize the history of wartime incarceration, but also to seize on the living history of Executive Order 9066 as a touchstone for other kinds of activ-ism. The resulting determination led to the 1970 founding of the Manzanar Committee, an organization dedicated to publicizing the history of wartime incarceration in the United States. It also eventually led to the founding of a subsidiary Historical Landmarks Advisory Committee, which pursued state and federal landmark status for Manzanar.[48]

Formalization and Expansion after 1969

Worried about its aging membership and about growing tension within the Nikkei community over how to address the history of wartime imprison-ment, during the 1970s the JACL set about hiring young Japanese Ameri-can activists to help it appeal to, and better serve, Sansei and Yonsei. The new recruits included Furutani and Shibata, Ron Hirano and Ron Waka-bayashi, among others. As National Community Involvement Coordinator, Furutani set up various programs aimed at younger Japanese Americans and also wrote a column for the *Pacific Citizen*, the JACL's newspaper. But he and the other young staff also drew criticism from more conservative JACL members over their support for environmental, racial, and economic activist groups, such as Cesar Chavez's United Farm Workers' union. The resulting tensions came to a head in 1972, with the appointment of a new JACL national director, Henry T. Tanaka, whom many of the Sansei and Yonsei saw as insufficiently politically engaged.[49] In response, these younger officers resigned from the organization en masse.

Despite this conflict, perhaps even because of it, during his time with the JACL, Furutani emerged as what Michi Weglyn called the "spiritual head of a growing number of Sansei and Yonsei . . . activists intensely resentful of society's inequities, past and present."[50] He was especially well placed to help develop and coordinate political work in the wake of the split between the JACL and its erstwhile younger constituents. During the 1970s, he, Embrey, and some of the other organizers of the early pilgrimages decided to take on an expanded and significantly more ambitious set of projects. One in particular stands out: seeking State Historical Landmark status for the Manzanar site. To that end, in 1971 Embrey, Furutani, and several other pilgrims formed the Manzanar Committee, which was loosely affiliated with the JACL. Though the group encountered resistance from older members of the Nikkei community, it persisted, driven by aims that were both retrospective and prospective. Looking toward the future, the committee hoped to provide a physical point of comparison for civil liberties violations in the present and beyond. For Furutani and his fellow organizers, this was less a new project than a continuation of earlier steps to shed light on the larger cultural and political implications of Executive Order 9066. According to Embrey, the first pilgrimage to Manzanar was part of an attempt to repeal the emergency detention provision of the Subversive Activities Control Act, or McCarran Act, of 1950.[51] It was, at least to some degree, part of several attempts to link the act with wartime incarceration.[52] Formulated as a part of postwar American paranoia about communism, the provision in question empowered a so-called Subversive Activities Control Board to perform a range of duties, from preventing suspect individuals from entering the United States to revoking citizenship outright. By drawing public attention to the site of mass incarceration, the pilgrims hoped to shed light on a continuing threat to civil liberties, which was no small matter for Asian Americans, given that people of both Korean and Japanese ancestry had recently been persecuted under the McCarran Act.[53] With such goals in mind, the committee's application to the California Department of Parks and Recreation offered the following language to be inscribed on a bronze plaque:

> From war hysteria, racism, and economic greed
> one hundred ten thousand persons of Japanese ancestry
> were directed by Presidential Order on February 19, 1942
> to leave their homes and relocate to
> America's concentration camps.
>
> Manzanar was the first of such camps built
> during World War II
> bounded by barbed wire and guard towers in a
> mile square, confining 10,000 men, women, and children
> of whom the majority was American citizens . . .
>
> This plaque is laid in the hope that the conditions
> which created this camp will never emerge again—
> for anybody, at any time.
>
> Then may this plaque always be a reminder
> of what Fear, Hate and Greed will cause
> men to do to other men.
>
> Tondemonai! [meaning "unexpected," but also "outrageous" or "terrible"][54]

Government-sponsored cultural and political monuments generally tend to be triumphalist, like the Washington Monument and Lincoln Memorial.[55] Publicly funded and overseen by elected or appointed officials, they are designed to reinforce an interpretive community by establishing a favorable primary narrative people can congregate around. The Manzanar Committee, by contrast, was working to commemorate a shameful episode in American history and increase awareness and political engagement outside the Japanese American community. It even went so far as to conclude the proposed inscription in the words not of an apologetic—and thus implicitly benign—government, but of its victims.[56] Consequently, the committee's suggested language met with resistance from government officials and bureaucrats.

Description and official recognition of the site came quickly (January 1972), but landmark status remained in limbo while members of the state Parks and Recreation Board deliberated and, eventually, sought to change the Manzanar Committee's text. Repeated attempts to secure approval culminated in a set-to between Furutani and the director of Parks and Recreation,

William Penn-Mott. According to Embrey, who provides one of several ac-counts, Furutani suggested that simple racism blocked final approval.[57] Ac-cording to Alice Yang Murray, members of the JACL, along with historian Arthur A. Hansen, joined the battle to win over Parks and Recreation of-ficials.[58] Eventually, the various parties arrived at a compromise in which the state and the Manzanar Committee worked together to generate the final language. Consequently, a plaque installed on site declares that:

> In the early part of World War II, 110,000 persons of Japanese ancestry were interned in relocation centers by Executive Order No. 9066 issued February 19, 1942. Manzanar, the first of ten such concentration camps, was bounded by barbed wire and guard towers. It confined ten thousand persons, the majority of them American citizens. May the injustices and humiliation suffered here as a result of hysteria, racism, and economic ex-ploitation never emerge again.[59]

The organizers of the dedication then selected the date of their ceremony to coincide with that of the 1973 pilgrimage, April 14. They also arranged for Ryozo Kado, one of the Nikkei inmates who had been tasked with building the original guardhouses, to install the plaque on site.

The timing of the dedication and the decision to have Kado install the plaque are important for several reasons, but one in particular stands out: to demonstrate the desire for the afterlife of mass imprisonment to affect as large an audience as possible. Combining government recognition, private pilgrimage, and the pursuit of public attention (in the form of news cover-age of the dedication), the April 1973 ceremony thus extended repetition, meditation, and inquiry associated with the original pilgrimage to a much larger and more diverse audience of potential political allies.[60] The work of the Manzanar Committee and its allies served to do much more than simply provide an educational site. It also treated historical awareness as a communicable source of moral and political obligation, just as Nikkei supporters of the Civil Liberties Act had approached their congressional testimony and other public discussions of wartime incarceration.

Mindful of the status of Manzanar as a physical expression of bigotry and authoritarianism, but also aware of their ability to reclaim the site in a corrective way, the organizers of the dedication ceremony wanted to convey the same basic experience they themselves had with each pilgrimage to the greatest number of people. Bringing attention to this stretch of US-395, they invited the public to follow the same historical, intellectual, and ethical path as their own Sansei and Yonsei members had taken: from (at best) minimal awareness through curiosity toward some degree of identification with, rather than just sympathy for, the targets of Executive Order 9066. In other words, members of the Manzanar Committee strove to make one particular place in the history of mass incarceration into a kind of shrine. Such people, they hoped, would see not only the future risks, but also the continued impact of McCarran-style laws and the impulses that give those laws life. As a result of directly experiencing the site and witnessing reports on the evening news, they would do so in personal, empathetic ways. In this respect, the Manzanar Committee's landmark-status project might be described as an attempt to convey the afterlife of wartime incarceration more strongly within the Japanese American community and more widely within American culture as a whole.

Legislating Fred Korematsu Day

The work of the Manzanar Committee demonstrates the recognition that empathetic agency, though deeply personal and often tied to specific moments, can also be thought of as potentially durable—whether through physical monuments or regular visits to a historical site. The pursuit of empathetic agency has also produced important legislation, such as the official day of celebration for Fred Korematsu, one of a handful of Japanese Americans who contested Executive Order 9066 at the time it was issued. Commemorating Fred Korematsu turned out to be simpler than gaining passage of the Civil Liberties Act or even winning landmark status for Manzanar. Fortunately, both of these endeavors provided precedent to which supporters of legislation could point. In February 2010, Furutani, a member of the State Assembly, introduced California Assembly bill 1775, which passed quickly. California Governor Arnold Schwarzenegger signed the bill into law the following September. The goal, however, along with the cultural mechanisms on which it depends, was more complicated.

Though celebrating a specific individual, the bill nonetheless also served a larger purpose: to "emphasize the constitutional rights afforded to all Americans regardless of race or ancestry, particularly the rights to due process and life, liberty, and property" and to "uphold the civil liberties of all citizens that are granted by the United States and California Constitutions, especially in times of real or perceived crisis."[61] What matters most about this declaration is the political and social change it implicitly presumes. Linking abstract, if important concepts, to the suffering of a specific individual, the legislative and educational work behind Fred Korematsu Day endowed its namesake with empathetic agency that could persist long after his death. Thus, establishing Fred Korematsu Day was about commemoration and about promoting sustained political engagement through a formalized afterlife.

The second youngest of four brothers, Korematsu was born in Oakland, California, on January 30, 1919, and lived exclusively in the East Bay before the Second World War. From an early age, Korematsu felt a drive to support his native land, even going so far as to pursue military service during high school.[62] He bounced from job to job until May 1942, when he attempted to elude imprisonment. He began by defying curfew restrictions and later refused to report for transportation to the Tanforan Assembly Center. He was arrested on May 30 and charged with defying military orders, a felony. Ernest Besig, executive director of the Northern California branch of the American Civil Liberties Union (ACLU), offered to represent him.[63] The case went all the way to the Supreme Court, which upheld Korematsu's conviction in 1944, stating that military necessity justified mass incarceration. This verdict stood for nearly forty years, falling only in the wake of research by Peter Irons and Aiko Herzig-Yoshinaga revealing evidence that government intelligence agencies had hidden from the Supreme Court in 1944.[64] As a result of this evidence, which proved that Japanese Americans had committed no acts of treason to justify their mass imprisonment, a pro-bono team filed a coram nobis petition in January 1983.[65] The following November, a federal court in San Francisco overturned Korematsu's conviction. The presiding judge, Marylin Hall Patel, wrote in her verdict that,

> *Korematsu* remains on the pages of our legal and political history. . . . As historical precedent it stands as a constant caution that in times of war or declared military necessity our institutions must be vigilant in protecting constitutional guarantees. It stands as a caution that in times of distress the shield of military necessity and national security must not be used to protect governmental actions from close scrutiny and accountability. It stands that in times of international hostility and antagonisms our institutions, legislative, executive, and judicial, must be prepared to protect all citizens from the petty fears and prejudices that are so easily aroused.[66]

Judge Patel's opinion framed Korematsu's case as having future utility: *Korematsu* matters, according to Patel, because future generations might turn to that case not only as a legal precedent but also as a cautionary tale about the fragility of civil liberties. That is, *Korematsu v. the United States* could provide a rallying point for continuing political engagement.

Judge Patel's decision set the record straight, bringing Korematsu out of legal purgatory,[67] but it did not end the story. In fact, Korematsu would eventually become one of the most important names associated with post-incarceration educational, legal, and political work, though it would take two decades for events to play out. The lengthy interval between his initial conviction and ultimate vindication indicates that wartime incarceration continues to linger in American society in ways one might not expect and that Korematsu continued to struggle with his wartime mistreatment, long after the war. In fact, it remained a central issue in his life.

Furthermore, the forty-year interval also brings up the greatest hazards associated with wartime incarceration: complacency and forgetfulness. The former takes a number of forms, most of which depend on the idea that wartime incarceration *was* an issue, in the sense of having mattered only as long as Executive Order 9066 was in effect or as long as scholars had not provided a full narrative of its immediate effects. As for the latter, it is most obvious in the virtual absence of Japanese Americans from popular discourses from the end of the war until the early 1960s.[68]

For Nikkei activists of the late 1960s onward, the resulting situation was anything but benign. It was precisely the kind of implicit marginalization Furutani and others sought to fight, the lingering sense that nothing serious had actually been done to this set of supposedly model citizens. Hence Furutani's desire to seize control of the narrative of Japanese American identity: when a community relinquishes or fails to take control of its narrative, that narrative becomes static, little more than a tool for tidy categorization by someone else. To unearth the history of wartime incarceration, to retrace its effects, and to point out its contemporary analogs was thus to employ precisely the sort of "ammunition" Furutani had in mind in that early interview. Employing that ammunition is not a matter of simply adding a few bricks to a scholarly edifice. It involves changing minds and changing people; cultivating a strongly empathetic identification with the history and experience of others. It is, in short, a struggle against oblivion by making history something to be lived, imaginatively, ritually, or otherwise. Empathy carries agency from one individual to another, each of whom then responds to that new (or renewed) empathy by acting on still others.

That changing of minds, the cultivation of empathy through the expression of afterlife, begins in a way that often defies articulation. As was shown in the first two chapters, it is probably most recognizable in individuals, such as Tamotsu Shibutani and Norman Mineta. But this early form of afterlife can affect whole groups. It also can yield to more purposeful and programmatic behavior. This was shown both in Japanese Canadian debates about redress and in people like Furutani. The transformation can be quick, as in the case of the Historical Landmarks Advisory Committee, or it can be protracted, as in the case of Korematsu. Over time, though, what was an internal and mainly solitary experience can metamorphose into a means of pursuing political and cultural change. For Korematsu to have engaged in legal and political work on behalf of others, especially in the name of those who suffered under Executive Order 9066, did of course involve honoring a legacy or trying to right earlier wrongs, but it also gave others the chance to use lingering memories to promote political activism in the present.

Interpersonal Identification

To extend the afterlife of injustice interpersonally rather than by means of visiting a place necessarily involves a different sort of connection. Traveling to hallowed ground allows one to stand where others have stood; to feel elements of the same environment allows one to project oneself onto the past and, in this way, approximate a generalized other's experience (for non-Nikkei visitors and onlookers). To emphasize with an individual, by contrast, calls for more direct comparison even as it defies direct physical experience. We might stand where inmates once stood, but that is the closest our experience will ever come to theirs. To link the afterlife of an event to a particular individual therefore requires that biographical details take the place of physical parallelism, the better for one to imagine what that person experienced. Accordingly, those details take on outsized importance.[69]

Korematsu became such touchstone for action because his case offered a complicated and even dynamic reaction that enabled another kind of empathetic response to mass incarceration. This is not to rank degrees of suffering or to suggest that the wartime narratives of other Nikkei are unimportant.

Instead, it is to recognize that Korematsu's wartime experience is particularly important for contemporary political discourse. His narrative deviates significantly from those of all but a handful of his contemporary Japanese Americans and also exemplifies behavior infrequently associated with Nikkei: initial public resistance, decades of silence, and then another attempt to set the record straight. That resistance was discomforting, not only for whites during the war, but also for Japanese Americans later on. Korematsu remarked, for instance, that his renewed battle against Executive Order 9066 in 1983 had alarmed many of his fellow inmates from Tanforan and elsewhere. At heart, though, the resistance Korematsu describes in his fellow Japanese Americans was more than just politically pragmatic. It also was emotional—a continuing fear of retribution.

And yet, Judge Patel's decision seemed to transform Korematsu from a troublemaker into someone admirable: "Before I won my case, the Japanese American community didn't recognize me or avoided me, and now that I won, they give me all kinds of recognition and the opportunity to speak to various Japanese [American] groups. And now I feel like I'm one of 'em, and it's quite rewarding for me."[70] Korematsu's vindication is heartening; it also shows how important even a single detail in an unusual narrative can be. Korematsu's decision to fight imprisonment struck many of his fellow Japanese Americans as an unnecessary risk. For them, living in the United States had been an almost continuous demonstration of the saying "the nail that stands up gets hammered down." And until 1983, what happened to Korematsu showed the truth in this aphorism. Losing his Supreme Court case in 1944 was only the beginning; officially labeled a scofflaw, he suffered economic and social harm for decades afterward. But once he prevailed, Korematsu quickly became a hero. Having broken the pattern of institutionalized injustice and silence, he became an inspirational figure whose losses and suffering amplified the lingering effects of Executive Order 9066 felt by so many others.

Korematsu's transformation contributed to a more fundamental shift. As Korematsu changed history, his cultural and political status changed as well. For fellow Nikkei, both former camp inmates and younger generations, his narrative spurred changes. By demonstrating the tenacity of institutionalized racism and the power of cooperation, that narrative helped people begin to transform themselves. More than an emblem, then, Korematsu also became a catalyst twice over, initially by winning his protracted legal battle and then by talking about what was required for victory in the first place: voice, action, and above all else collaboration. Hence his suggestion in an interview with Eric Fournier that "there are Arab Americans today who are going through what Japanese Americans experienced years ago, and we can't let that happen again. I met someone years ago who had never heard of the roundup of Japanese Americans. It's been sixty years since this [arrest] happened, and it's happening again, and that's why I continue to talk about what happened to me."[71] Note the relationship between empathy—Korematsu's identification with Americans of Middle Eastern ancestry—and Furutani's fight against oblivion. Rather than suggest that what had happened to himself and other Nikkei was exceptional, Korematsu was suggesting that it would be remarkably easy for the same thing to happen all over again, perhaps precisely because so many people think of wartime incarceration as a singular occurrence. Speaking in support of a new target for bigotry, Korematsu empathized with that target. A target of bigotry who ultimately overcame it, he sought to combat complacency. In short, he aimed to join with others not only against a specific instance of racial profiling, but also against the root causes of such profiling.

While the Manzanar pilgrimage was designed to provoke empathy for former inmates, Korematsu's story became a reminder of both the hazards and the power of resistance. In fact, in subsequent accounts, the risks Korematsu took and the penalties he suffered as a result became inseparable from his eventual legal victory. Those risks, like the behavior that gave rise to them, are instructive. Being ostracized in the wake of the Supreme Court decision was undoubtedly part of what made Korematsu's life history singular. Imprisoned, Korematsu suffered a double displacement as soon as it became clear that he intended to contest his incarceration:

> When I was at Tanforan, my brother said, "why don't you get some opinion about whether you should fight your case or not?" . . . So one night . . . there was a big area where everyone was meeting. So I went there and I could see them talking in groups of about five or six, and all of a sudden, they disappeared. And then I caught my brother and said, "What happened?" "Oh, they think that you're going to make it worse for them. They don't know what's going to happen to them yet, and all you're going to do is make it worse for them. They don't want you to do it." And so that's the way it went. And so nobody talked to me or wanted to be associated with me.[72]

Yet Korematsu's story also speaks to the need for fortitude. Despite what his campmates thought, he felt compelled to challenge Executive Order 9066. His resistance to social pressure became an integral part of Korematsu's narrative, not about himself but also about American identity. After recalling his treatment in Tanforan, he went on to remark, "Anyway, that [ostracism] didn't bug me because I'm an American and I wanted to fight it if I can. . . . I didn't like what was going on."[73] Casting himself in the popular image of the American as boldly unconventional, practical, and stalwart, Korematsu framed his resistance as the sort of thing any commonsensical listener might also do.[74] This reference to an important triumphalist imaginary allowed Korematsu, like Mineta and his fellow Nikkei legislators before their congressional colleagues, to assert a different configuration for the ideal political body. By indicating that that body need not necessarily be white, he was using a nationalist and traditionally racist construct against itself in order to redefine not so much what Americans might be as how America might look. He was reorganizing, not dispensing with, the dominant paradigm in order to make the afterlife of wartime incarceration available to his listeners. He also framed it as something that drove him even after his 1944 court defeat. This comes through, for instance, in his laconic account of the interval between his first and second Supreme Court battles:

> So that's the way it went. And for forty years, I was wondering, I'd like to fight it because I said, am I an American or not? Can they do this again, send them away? So it bothered me. I got married to Kathryn, and we had two children. We were active and joined the Boy Scouts and Girl Scouts, and I've been in the Lion's Club for a long time. And also there is the church group we were active in. [But] I still had in my mind, "Are we Americans or not? Are they kidding us?"[75]

Korematsu lost his battle repeatedly, and he endured the effects of that loss for decades, which he here refers to simply as a forty-year interval. In the context of his post-1983 activism, those decades of social, economic, and political harm served as an almost religious test. Like a hermit in the wilderness, Korematsu endured four decades of condemnation and all that it entailed. Yet, his reticence about those years, his unwillingness to bemoan them, makes that period a controlled absence that sharpens the listener's experience. Like the gaps that early pilgrims sensed at Manzanar, Korematsu's omissions enhance the challenge of, and thus the reward for, identification.

The moments in which Korematsu did go into detail about his difficulties matter even more, since they provide a point of entry into his narrative. For instance, although it points to a general Nikkei distaste for attracting attention, Korematsu's final judgment about ostracism in Tanforan also creates an opportunity for identification. It suggests that he may be unique, but only because he chose to act on a value system to which the United States has long laid claim and to which its popular discourse consistently aspires. It also suggests that the average listener has within herself the potential to do exactly the same thing: to spot injustice and to fight it. Korematsu aimed to do more than inspire a few individuals here and there. Addressing various audiences, both Nikkei and otherwise, in the wake of the 1983 verdict, he aimed to create coalitions. He therefore also spoke repeatedly about the help he received:

> When I was in jail, Mr. Ernest Besig from the Northern California ACLU volunteered to help me; that really was a lifesaver because no one wanted to stick their neck out to help me. I was classified as an enemy alien. Even when Mr. Besig decided to help me, the National ACLU wanted him to drop the case because the Executive Director was friendly with President Roosevelt.[76]

Korematsu was careful to note that resistance by a single individual is not enough; a critical mass of skills and voices is necessary. Moreover, that critical mass consists of individuals who face all manner of obstacles, including political and social pressure, despite coming from disparate backgrounds. According to the resulting narrative, what unites individuals and makes resistance successful is the courage of conviction. In these moments, Korematsu expanded his narrative, moving from an individual to a collective struggle. He presented himself paradoxically as a singular individual who offered a narrative not only of resistance but also of the collaboration required to realize the political potential of that resistance.

Moving Forward by Going Back

Empathetic agency has the potential to extend deep into society, binding disparate groups into powerful alliances. This is clear in, for example, in the way people with no Japanese ancestry came to identify with the targets of Executive Order 9066. The mechanisms that nurture empathetic agency can be subtle and implicit: a news report covering the Manzanar pilgrimages, for instance, or an interview on public television. They can also be obvious and explicit, such as the creation of the Fred Korematsu Institute for Civil Rights and Education.[77] Established in memory of Korematsu, the institute pursues a number of legislative and educational ends. Foremost among these is the provision of a model curriculum for use in elementary schools.[78] In and of itself, this curriculum may seem unremarkable, but viewed through the lens of afterlife—that complex set of thoughts, ideas, and actions that linger long after the events that provoked them—its significance becomes clear. Afterlife is an individual experience, even though it depends on shared experience. Whether activated at Manzanar or cultivated by the narrative of Fred Korematsu, it builds on empathy and identification. But the opportunities to provoke those states are limited. Hence the development of a curriculum: providing materials to primary school teachers, the Korematsu Institute aims to extend and amplify the afterlife of wartime incarceration across temporal, racial, and ethnic boundaries.

Afterlife and its relationship to empathetic agency have many important implications. One of the most important is the role of that relationship in social and political transformation. Rather than operating primarily on a large scale, through legislation or court cases, for instance, important though those may be, empathetic agency causes change to reverberate over time and to flow beyond the immediate confines of a given community. Such things as a visit to Manzanar (even a mediated view of the site) or a clip of Fred Korematsu speaking of his legal battles, work subtly, drawing one toward the object of contemplation. More than simply educating the listener or observer, they reshape that person, creating within her a sense of congruence, the better to make injustice as much her concern as it is the concern of those who have suffered it directly. Seizing control of a discourse, Furutani, Shibata, Embrey, Korematsu, and others have done more than define their own identity. They also have striven to give later generations the tools to change both society and themselves. They have worked to initiate a more expansive kind of afterlife that will continue long into the future in the hope that the past will not repeat itself.

FIVE

Retroactive Diplomas
and the Value of Education

A regular reader of the daily paper, Mary Kitagawa is not easily agitated by the news. But one morning in 2008 she read an article that would motivate her like no other before. The article was about how universities along the West Coast of the United States were awarding retroactive degrees to students who had been forced from those institutions after the bombing of Pearl Harbor. This news lit a fire in Kitagawa, who decided to organize a similar ceremony for Japanese Canadians who, in 1942, had been forced out of the University of British Columbia (UBC), a ceremony that eventually took place in May 2012. Kitagawa worked tirelessly for those students, even though neither she nor any of her immediate family members had been expelled from UBC during the war. On the contrary, she was a child when Secret Order-in-Council P.C. 1486 forced her family to leave Salt Spring Island, near Vancouver, in February 1942. Nonetheless, more than sixty years later she felt compelled to fight for retroactive diplomas for people who had long ago gone on to other things. As this chapter will show, the decision to wage that fight was pragmatic since, for Kitagawa, the awarding of those diplomas would achieve specific ends. However, the decision was not motivated by economic concerns since the benefit of an academic degree would be entirely political and cultural.[1]

Kitagawa's actions, like those of her American counterparts, raise an important question about the value of a college degree. Recipients of retroactive diplomas would reap none of the material benefits that the college graduate has customarily enjoyed. Well into their 80s and 90s, they could expect no increase in income; neither could they use their college contacts as a network of potential references, let alone employers. In fact, retroactive diplomas are as noteworthy for their seeming uselessness as they are for the tenacity with which Nikkei have pursued them. In this way, retroactive diplomas demonstrate the continuing presence of the past for people who have long been viewed, both by the public and by some scholars, as somehow "done" with their wartime experience.

The claim that wartime incarceration is fully a thing of the past is understandable, given the success of the redress movement in Canada and the United States. In light of this, retroactive diplomas might strike some as little more than symbolic. However, symbolism in this case is anything but empty. That symbolism tells us something important about Asian American and Asian Canadian identities: for most people of Japanese ancestry in North America the afterlife of wartime injustice continues to shape their experience, from self-identification to political engagement. And it tells us that that afterlife is something these people feel compelled to share with others, especially those who have no direct connection with the experience of wartime incarceration.

The story of the Japanese Canadian and Japanese American diploma projects is important in that it reveals how political and cultural circumstances differed for two geographically close groups. In Canada, governmental structure and policy, along with the history of the Japanese diaspora there, meant that winning the battle for retroactive diplomas required an extensive educational and public relations campaign. This is because the Japanese Canadian campaign enjoyed no official support, even from a Nikkei member of the provincial government in British Columbia. Instead, it built almost exclusively on grassroots support from local citizens and UBC students. This campaign contrasts with the more legislative approach in the United States, where Nikkei citizens occupied faculty, administrative, and governmental positions, and thus were well placed to implement retroactive diploma ceremonies.

Comparing the U.S. and Canadian campaigns also allows us to see how the recipients of retroactive diplomas in both Canada and the United States articulated similar goals: to reclaim the ground from which they were expelled, to secure acknowledgment of their intellectual and social value as individuals, and to demonstrate to younger generations, many of whom have little or no understanding of wartime incarceration, the importance of the past as a living thing. Herein lies the value of a retroactive diploma for North American Nikkei: it opens access to a space that had been denied them and also to share that reclamation with future generations so that the latter might carry the past with them.

Although much has been written about the pursuit of official apologies and financial compensation in the redress movement of the 1980s, there has been little study of the campaign for less tangible reparations. Even though they received an official apology and at least some compensation, Japanese Americans and Japanese Canadians felt this was insufficient. After the 1988 success of the redress movement, why did many former inmates and their families still feel the need to return to the topic of incarceration through public graduation ceremonies? Through an examination of new evidence, this chapter shows that retroactive diplomas were designed to recast the postwar narrative of incarceration not as one of further reparations but as a reappraisal of what education itself might signify in civil society. In particular, that retroactive diplomas provided another medium for the afterlife of Nikkei North American history to express itself. From initial pursuit through acquisition, Japanese Americans and Japanese Canadians sought to exploit the elasticity of historical time, bringing the past into the present by allowing those who suffered an injustice to reclaim ground taken from them, to receive academic recognition they had long been denied, and to celebrate that recognition alongside a new generation of students for whom a college education might previously have seemed almost a natural progression rather than an experience contingent on the stability of civil and political society.

Retroactive diplomas contrast with educational initiatives that derived from the redress movement. Of course, on some level both broadened awareness of wartime incarceration and its lingering aftereffects. Yet an important difference also is at work. Where educational initiatives have brought this historical moment into the classroom largely as a third-party topic of discussion (for example, in K-12 lesson plans), retroactive diploma ceremonies once again operated in the first person. Allowing recipients to embody the past and rebuke its injustices, they caused witnesses to participate in history, rather than simply have it illustrated for or recounted to them. For many former inmates, advanced age meant that retroactive diploma ceremonies were a last chance to take history out of books and articles and make it part of the lives of people around them, most notably far younger students and their families. Receiving a long-deferred diploma provided an opportunity to have those people see them as living history, feel the presence of that history, and carry that presence with them into the future. One might think of retroactive diploma ceremonies as similar to literary and artistic engagements with the legacy of wartime incarceration: all provided opportunities to cultivate personal, at times even physical, engagements with and revivifications of history.[2]

In order to show both how and why people of Japanese ancestry reshaped the postwar narrative through the creation of new legislation (in California) and educational policies and programs (in both the United States and Canada), this chapter employs new interviews with Nikkei North Americans. Subjects include diploma recipients; Assemblyman Warren Furutani, one of the main proponents of retroactive diplomas in California; and Mary Kitagawa, the force behind the UBC graduation ceremony. This chapter also draws on historical sources, including wartime newspapers, as well as contemporary writing about diploma ceremonies and related educational projects. Through an examination of such evidence, it demonstrates that, in addition to promoting new legislative and educational policies, retroactive diplomas and graduation ceremonies also allowed diploma recipients to embody what such policies could mean for society as a whole in the past, present, and future.

Retroactive Diplomas in the United States

In order to understand what inspired Kitagawa, or rather one aspect of it, and the challenges she faced, it is important first to understand the history of retroactive diplomas in the United States.[3] By the time Japan bombed Pearl Harbor, approximately twenty-five hundred Japanese Americans (nearly all of them Nisei) were enrolled in universities along the West Coast.[4] The University of Washington (UW), for example, had over four hundred Japanese American students, a population second in size only to that of the University of California, Berkeley.[5] When Roosevelt authorized Executive Order 9066, most students went into the temporary "assembly centers" with their families. At the same time, they were barred from studying in areas that had been designated military zones (California, Oregon, and Washington). Consequently, they were doubly displaced. There were, however, important exceptions. For instance, approximately seventy-five students from UW moved to colleges and universities outside of the restricted military zone, thanks largely to the intercession of the university's president, Lee Paul Sieg.[6]

As Allan Austin has described in detail, in 1942 a group of governmental and higher education representatives formed the National Japanese American Student Relocation Council (NJASRC) in order to assess how to best deal with Japanese American university students, a task the Department of Education (and others) suggested would "demonstrate the good will, the sense of justice, the respect for personality, and the recognition of character and achievement that are inherent in all our best traditions of American Democracy."[7] The council distributed questionnaires to analyze "not only scholastic records, but also personality factors, professional goals, successful Caucasian contacts, and special talents or interests."[8] Even so, this had a limited impact. The questionnaire, for instance, was primarily designed to determine which students were "trustworthy," the better to eliminate the possibility of releasing any student of questionable loyalty. Pupils who had studied in Japan, for instance, were ineligible.[9] Furthermore, many of the universities that were cleared to accept relocated students declined to do so.[10] And former home institutions could even hinder a transfer. The University of Southern California (USC), for instance, denied Nikkei students access to their academic records, which were necessary for transferring to another school.[11] As a result, the majority of Japanese American university students were left with no choice but to enter the prison camps rather than continue their studies.

Postwar demands compounded the problem of disrupted education. By the time Japanese American students were finally released, the thought of returning to school was unrealistic for many of them. First and foremost on the minds of Nikkei, both young and old, was housing and financial stability. Families that had owned property before the war, including farms, had been forced to sell quickly. Consequently, they received far less than market value. In addition, those who worked while incarcerated were paid significantly lower wages than non-Nikkei in comparable jobs. Others, having come from nothing, now found themselves returned to nothing, though now with the added stigma of having been incarcerated and implicitly branded as criminals. As a result, former students had to abandon thoughts of immediately resuming their studies even after resettlement.[12] It would take almost seven decades before these students would be invited back to the campuses where they had started their university lives.

The fight to address what happened to Nikkei students during the war gained momentum mainly in the 1970s and 1980s, when children of wartime prisoners started urging their parents to discuss those difficult years.[13] Not only were the children of wartime prisoners curious about their parents' 1940s experiences, but they also wanted to help right earlier wrongs, even after work on the Civil Liberties Act was concluded.[14] For some in the United States, the passage of the act marked an end to the history of wartime incarceration. Others felt additional work was still needed, though. Much of that work has been preventative, designed to help avoid a repetition of this shameful episode. For instance, the Civil Liberties Act also included educational initiatives, such as the Civil Liberties Public Education Project, which has long worked to integrate the history of wartime imprisonment into curricula.[15] Additional steps have been undertaken by individual states. California, for example, passed the California Civil Liberties Public Education Act (AB1915) in 1998, providing an annual budget of $1 million for three years. The bill was renewed in 2000 (AB1914); in 2003 its termination date was removed (AB1754).

A significant component of the educational work in the wake of the Civil Liberties Act has been done outside the classroom and has involved more first-person instruction. Retroactive diploma ceremonies are a case in point: they raise important questions about the aims and the value of learning, but they do so in a way far more personal for participants as well as witnesses. Warren Furutani explained his work on behalf of retroactive diplomas by noting, "education was the so-called key to the American Dream." Japanese Americans recognized education as a means to improve their economic and cultural lot, a fact that made the unjust denial of that means all the more tragic. Even though the additional diploma would not provide new economic or professional opportunities, he said, it would allow former inmates to "tie up loose ends."[16] That is to say, it would enable diploma recipients to rebut one of the few remaining charges against them, the implicit one that they had not deserved their place in the educational system.

Pushing against the past, diploma recipients corrected the historical record. Acting in the present, they sought to redefine the place of education itself in civil society. By reclaiming spaces and degrees that they were denied, former students were able to occupy their proper place in American society, if belatedly. The belatedness was vital. For the majority of students at graduation ceremonies, education was almost something to be taken for granted, a middle- or upper-class rite of passage, rather than a hard-won economic or cultural necessity. To participate in a ceremony with any of the recipients discussed in this chapter, by contrast, provided younger graduates with an opportunity to reflect on their own good fortune and, with that, the injustices suffered by their much older Nikkei classmates, whose hopes, dreams, and expectations had been irrevocably deferred if not outright dashed. Exposing the politics of higher education, retroactive diplomas provided an opportunity for the afterlife of wartime injustice to transform the present by making visible what might have been. It revealed to younger, largely non-Nikkei generations a group of people who had been forced to live radically different lives than they had hoped for, different lives than equity should have allowed. Diploma recipients in that sense gave onlookers the chance to imagine a different, more equitable future.

In short, retroactive diploma ceremonies not only allowed recipients to exercise their rights to their full extent and to continue their hard-won political and social recuperation, but also caused institutions as well as contemporary onlookers to participate in that exercise. Thus, retroactive diploma ceremonies allowed their participants to pursue reflexive teaching, as Nikkei former students, current administrators, and current students all enacted the value and purpose of education.[17] Extending rather than closing off the history of wartime incarceration, these ceremonies used lingering feelings about the past to propel what Jane Naomi Iwamura has described as a form of civil religion forged in the crucible of imprisonment and now governed by the belief that "the dead—which here includes a sense of what used to be (Japanese American life before incarceration) and what they had hoped to become (fully accepted American subjects)—are ever present, but only remain so through continual acts of attention and care."[18] Thus, while securing such ceremonies was laborious and time-consuming, it also was critically important for Japanese Americans and Japanese Canadians, even for those whose high school and college careers came long after incarceration. For in pursuing those ceremonies, Nikkei North Americans were tending both to their own culture and to that of their fellow citizens.

The history of retroactive diplomas began not with institutions of higher education, but with Los Angeles High School, where in 1992 Furutani helped organize the first such ceremony.[19] Furutani began this work during his 1987–1995 tenure on the Board of Education for the Los Angeles Unified School District. The response to this ceremony was enthusiastic, and support for a broader initiative grew over time. In 2003, Sally Lieber (D-San Jose) proposed AB781, which was signed into law in July of that year:

> Notwithstanding any other provision of law to the contrary, a high school district, unified school district, or county office of education, may retroactively grant a high school diploma to a person who has not received a high school diploma if he or she was interned by the order of the federal government during World War II and was enrolled in a high school operated by the school district or under the jurisdiction of the county office of education immediately preceding his or her internment and did not receive a high school diploma because the pupil's education was interrupted due to his or her internment during World War II.[20]

Unremarkable as the wording may be, it proved critical. Officially removing any obstacles to the provision of retroactive diplomas, AB781 deprived opponents of their final recourse and opened the door for California educational institutions to systematically pursue retroactive diplomas.[21]

Despite the growing support for this project in California, UW provided the first retroactive degrees initiated by an institution of higher education. The ceremony originated with a group of university faculty, Tetsuden (Tetsu) Kashima, Gail Nomura, and Stephen Sumida, all of whom are professors in the American Ethnic Studies Department, Asian American Studies area. The trio had a tradition of meeting annually to organize activities for the Day of Remembrance (February 19), the day set aside to recall Executive Order 9066 and its aftermath. Almost yearly since 1997, they arranged a panel, exhibit, or a speaker in order to promote discussion of this historical moment. In early 2007 Nomura, Sumida, and Kashima talked about the possibility of seeking recognition for 449 UW Nikkei students whose academic careers were interrupted by World War II. Nomura discussed the specifics of one such student with the committee, who expressed interest in bringing others with similar experiences back to campus for the Day of Remembrance. As a result, the planning committee started working with administrators in the President's Office, members of the Board of Regents, Office of the Registrar, UW Libraries, UW Office of Minority Affairs and Diversity, UW Alumni Association, many campus units and colleges, and the UW Nikkei Alumni Association. The Nikkei Alumni Association with other Japanese American community groups and the UW Libraries compiled a contact list of the honorees, which took more than two years but perhaps insured the high turnout of honorees and family representatives. The event, *Long Journey Home*, took place on May 18, 2008, when the UW awarded honorary baccalaureate degrees to all affected Nikkei undergraduates and inducted them into the UW graduating class of 2008.[22]

The University of Washington's decision to award retroactive diplomas demonstrated the continuing power of the afterlife of wartime injustice even in the wake of redress. Seeking to shed light on what had been lost, advocates aimed to force closer scrutiny of a shameful event that, for most, had slipped entirely from the historical record. Working against this amnesia, diploma recipients repeatedly expressed happiness that the ceremony enabled others to learn about their experiences. For example, it was reported that four Japanese American faculty members at the university had suffered under Executive Order 9066, including the sociologist S. Frank Miyamoto, a fact not widely known before the ceremony.[23] This was more than simply seeking acknowledgment of a historic injustice. It also renewed the importance of that injustice in the present, treating it both as a teachable moment and as a shared revivification. Though a happy occasion for the vast majority of its participants, UW's diploma ceremony also constituted a crucial instance of empathetic agency, as the seemingly over-and-done-with history of wartime injustice made its continuing presence felt once more.

Sharing the emotional legacy of injustice was crucial, for extending empathetic engagement with wartime incarceration to people whose families had no direct experience of it provided them with an opportunity to experience the emotional implications of mass incarceration, rather than simply possess a collection of historical, legal, and financial facts. In this respect, the UW ceremony was an attempt to reweave the local social fabric into something more egalitarian and inclusive. Not that this was necessarily bound to succeed; ignorance, racism, and apathy can be powerful. But, as in other schools in later years, UW's decision to award retroactive diplomas aimed at staving off the worst of such excesses by treating wartime incarceration and expulsion as concrete phenomena with continuing effects. That is why the citation bestowed on the former Japanese American students read, "In the dim fog of war, the threads of fear and intolerance wove a clouded shroud. We gather to dissolve that shroud and enlighten. . . . A trust was violated. We come together to restore. We acknowledge the injustice of the past, and we walk with you now into the future."[24] The presence of former students, coupled with histories of those who had died or otherwise could not attend, helped make such statements more than empty rhetoric. Cultivating an empathetic response among contemporary administrators and students, it enlisted them in carrying a personal engagement with history into the future, rather than allowing it to congeal on a printed page or in a well-rehearsed lecture. The first retroactive diploma ceremony was essentially an attempt to reverse an earlier case of social death.[25] It and subsequent efforts thus support Iwamura's suggestion that the traditional phrase *shikata ga nai* (it can't be helped) has become less a blanket pronouncement about injustice and more a call to shift attention away from lamenting the past and using it to improve the future.[26]

This same impulse governed the pursuit of retroactive diplomas by California institutions of higher education. After departing the Board of Education, Furutani remained engaged with the impact of Executive Order 9066 on Nikkei education during his time in the California State Assembly, which he joined in 2008 after a special election. A scant few months into his first term, Furutani proposed AB37, which

> would require the Trustees of the California State University and the Board of Governors of the California Community Colleges, and would request the Regents of the University of California, to work with their respective colleges and universities to confer an honorary degree upon each person, living or deceased, who was forced to leave his or her postsecondary studies as a result of federal Executive Order 9066 which caused the incarceration of individuals of Japanese ancestry during World War II.[27]

Unlike Lieber's bill, which removed administrative obstacles to retroactive diplomas, Furutani's bill made diplomas a goal to be pursued actively. It would result in what has become known as the Nisei Diploma Project, a program overseen by the Japanese Cultural and Community Center of Northern California. AB37 also encouraged institutions to award current and retroactive diplomas simultaneously: "This section shall be implemented in a cost-effective manner by incorporating, to the extent practicable, any ceremony for the purpose of conferring honorary degrees with a previously scheduled commencement or graduation activity."[28] Although he framed this stipulation primarily as a budgetary measure in the bill itself, Furutani has said that he included it in order to encourage an exchange between elderly recipients and current students graduating alongside them.[29] He sought to ensure that retroactive diplomas would not only provide their recipients with emotional closure but also revivify the past for contemporary students, thereby promoting empathetic agency. Following the passage of AB37, administrators at the University of California campuses in Los Angeles, Berkeley, and San Francisco quickly located former inmates and organized ceremonies. The California State University system soon followed.

"Lady, You've Got a Fight on Your Hands"

The difficulty facing Nikkei Canadian college students during the Second World War was compounded by the fact that Canada had no equivalent of the NJASRC. Furthermore, the climate at UBC, where seventy-six students of Japanese ancestry had been enrolled, was hostile. In spring of 1942, for instance, administrators dismissed its male students and declined to assist its female ones. Nevertheless, a handful of faculty members attempted to help Nikkei students complete the term and, in some cases, transfer to schools out east.[30] And most Nikkei suppressed not only the details of the event but also their own feelings about it until the fight for redress helped create a venue in which such things could be articulated more fully.[31] Given this history, one might be surprised not that it took so long for UBC to hold a retroactive diploma ceremony but that such a ceremony should have happened at all.[32] Some Japanese Canadians pointed to American retroactive high school and university diplomas, but as Kitagawa discovered, it would take four years of fact-finding, meetings, letter writing, and community outreach even before she could begin her search for the former wartime students. In this and other important respects, her campaign would differ significantly from those in the United States.

Still, given the success of American campaign for retroactive diplomas, Kitagawa's first course of action was to enlist the help of leading figures south of the border. She began by contacting the organizers of the UW graduation ceremony, who advised her on the type of ceremony they had held, in addition to suggesting strategies for how to engage with the mass media.[33] She then contacted Satsuki Ina, whom Kitagawa had met when Ina gave the keynote address at a 2009 conference at the National Nikkei

Museum and Heritage Center in Burnaby (just east of Vancouver).[34] A longtime activist and professor at the California State University, Sacramento, Ina was active with the Nisei Diploma Project, and in addition, she initiated and produced the documentary *Children of the Camps* (Ina, 1999), a collection of interviews she conducted about the lingering psychological impact of wartime incarceration. Kitagawa's American contacts suggested she study other ceremonies in order to learn how the various institutions had gone about locating and honoring former students.[35] They also encouraged her to find out exactly what happened to students at UBC during the war in order to confirm that they had in fact been treated unjustly.[36]

Despite these suggestions, Kitagawa had a difficult time finding out what happened in British Columbia. After conducting a preliminary search on UBC's website and finding nothing, in May 22, 2008, she wrote to Stephen Toope, the president and vice chancellor of the university.[37] Toope's office forwarded the letter to Dr. Sally Thorne, chair of the Senate Tributes Committee, a body that evaluated proposals for honorary degrees.[38] The response from Thorne and the committee was discouraging. In essence, their letter stated that UBC had not in fact expelled Japanese Canadians in 1942, but that Nikkei students, faculty, and staff left voluntarily for a variety of reasons. Furthermore, the Tributes Committee said that university policy did not allow for the type of ceremony that Kitagawa wanted.[39] Faced with this apparent dead end, Kitagawa said, she redoubled her resolve. Reading the letter from Professor Thorne once more, she thought to herself, "Lady, you've got a fight on your hands."[40]

At this point, Kitagawa realized that only external pressure would compel the Tributes Committee, and thus the university, to change its position. In order to generate that pressure, Kitagawa would have to publicize the continuing effects of Canada's wartime Orders-in-Council on Nikkei citizens and their family members, and she would have to demonstrate that UBC students were not exempt from expulsion, while also showing that UBC had neither faculty nor staff of Japanese ancestry at the time.[41] In this respect, her project dovetailed with a larger interest in recovering the story of wartime incarceration and integrating it into the narrative of Canadian history. While redress had helped draw attention to Japanese immigrants in the history of Canada, shifting the cultural and political discourse has been a complex process. As discussed in Chapter Three, the Canadian government agreed to a settlement in part to avoid being caught out by the success of the

Civil Liberties Act, and its educational outreach had thus been lackluster and of questionable motivation.[42] As recently as 2010, for instance, the National Association of Japanese Canadians produced a report critical of official curricula, which still tended to embody what Matt James has called the "amnesiac culture of memory" in British Columbia.[43] Both the NAJC and James issued their critiques several years after the provincial government revised the eleventh-grade curriculum, which included a new module on the history of Japanese Canadians.[44] Empathetic agency, though powerful, nonetheless has its limits. Reports such as the NAJC's not only speak to those limits but also change them. Not everyone feels the lingering presence of a particular historical moment, but those who do can then encourage action in others.

Thus, Kitagawa was able to align her work on behalf of former UBC students with that of Japanese Canadian organizations, which have continued to pursue an accurate account of history in the face of governmental inertia and, at times, outright resistance. She published articles in the *Nikkei Voice* and the *Bulletin* of the Japanese Canadian Citizens' Association; she gave public talks and spoke on the radio; and she sat for an interview with the *Vancouver Sun*, all of which helped increase public pressure on the Tributes Committee and its chair. In addition, she started a national letter-writing campaign, explaining her cause and its history and urging recipients to write to UBC's Senate Tributes Committee as well as President Toope. Hoping to provide added incentives for Toope and the committee, she also gathered signatures from across Canada in support of the Nikkei graduation ceremony. However, she also had to tailor that educational project to the task at hand. For instance, there were so few educational resources that many Japanese Canadians did not know the history of the expelled UBC students.[45] Furthermore, she had to explain that there could not have been any Japanese Canadian faculty or staff at UBC during the 1940s, despite a suggestion to the contrary by the Tributes Committee. Exclusionary laws in place at the time would have precluded such a situation, in any case. In the early 1940s, Canadians still had to be registered to vote in order to secure professional work, including sitting on a university faculty or being a staff member. However, an 1895 amendment to the British Columbia Elections Act barred Asians from the voters list.[46] Japanese Canadians did not gain the franchise until 1948.[47] Consequently, Nikkei faculty and staff could not have left UBC of their own accord during the war years for the simple reason that they did not exist in the first place. As for students, they were following the prime minister's orders, not various youthful whims. Finally, on October 5, 2011, after a steady stream of public pressure, UBC's president contacted Kitagawa to ask how to best honor wartime students.[48] Kitagawa then began searching for students, many of whom had not set foot on the university campus for almost seventy years.

Afterlife: Walking into the Future with the Injustices of the Past

Though the means by which Nikkei in Canada and the United States secured retroactive diplomas differed, the basic aims were the same: not only to right a past wrong, but also to promote awareness in the present and better behavior in the future. The latter task is urgent not only because of inertia as well as the reactionary forces working against it, but also because of the advanced ages of former inmates. Of the original seventy-six students forced from the UBC campus at the outset of the war, for instance, only eleven (all in their late 80s and 90s) confirmed that they would attend the special ceremony on May 30, 2012. A former university student died less than two weeks before the ceremony; others were too infirm to attend.[49] Likewise, USC's ceremony, also in 2012 (long after other California schools emulated the example of UW and the state's high schools) came too late for some, such as Hitoshi Sameshima. It had been seventy years since he had been on the USC campus, but he made the trip back, such was the importance of the ceremony. The occasion was bittersweet, and not simply because of his own experience. His wife died in March 2012, days after he received the news he would receive his diploma. His daughter, who herself had attended USC, had died a year earlier. Of their absence, he said "we were going to go as a family. My daughter would have had her camera and everything."[50] Sameshima also lamented that many of his peers would not receive recognition, since USC agreed only to award honorary degrees to the living and continues to deny recognition for deceased prisoners.[51] The afterlife of wartime injustice is fragile, and not simply because of continued right-wing attempts to recast the mistreatment of Nikkei North Americans. Dependent on empathetic agency, it persists only so long as those agents are active, either directly or, as in the case of the Fred Korematsu Institute, indirectly. With each death of someone who was incarcerated after the bombing of Pearl Harbor, the purchase of that afterlife on American and Canadian cultures grows more tenuous.

Time is of the essence, and not only for those who might receive retro-active diplomas but also for the work they hope to achieve. Roy Oshiro, one of the UBC degree recipients, explained that work in a series of interviews after the 2012 ceremony. The details of Oshiro's incarceration narrative and postwar descriptions reveal a turn away from intellectual or political ap-proaches to incarceration and toward a more spiritual framework for com-prehending such events. Born in Manitoba in 1921, he traveled to Okinawa with his family, who early on found Canada inhospitable, both economi-cally and politically. By 1932, however, they returned to British Columbia, where Oshiro attended Templeton Junior High School, Britannia High School, and, for one year until his forced removal from Vancouver, UBC.[52] With each new affliction from 1941 onward (forced removal to Calgary, fragmentation of the family, confiscation and eventual involuntary sale of the family business, BC Wood and Coal), Oshiro's father would resignedly ask, *Dou shiyou?* ("What should we do?").[53] Moved by the kindness shown to him during the difficult war years by a handful of Canadians and fel-low Nikkei, the younger Oshiro devoted his postwar life to religious work. In 1955, he traveled as a missionary to Okinawa, but he returned often to Canada, his primary residence. Consequently, he has rightly called himself "a living symbol of those whose life trajectories spanned the East China Sea across the Pacific to Canada."[54]

Oshiro's account of his removal from UBC and then the retroactive diploma ceremony decades later is instructive, because it embodies both functions of the ceremony, shedding light on a past wrong and, simul-taneously, spurring contemporary political engagement. Of the ceremony itself, Oshiro said it "was just like being in heaven," but he was at a loss for how to express the full extent of the "joy" he had felt since learning that he might receive a retroactive diploma.[55] As the ceremony neared, he had begun to wonder how many of the Nikkei students evicted from UBC had withstood their mistreatment when they had no means to express the "shock" they felt. Hence the emotional importance of the ceremony: it meant that wartime Nikkei could finally "tell the world" what they could not have said in 1942, that they were going to "enjoy the fact that we are Canadians or Americans."[56]

Oshiro also emphasized that the next generation had a responsibility to continue to retell the stories of wartime Nikkei "for the sake of others."[57] Receiving his diploma was thus not only palliative but also preventative.

This lends a second sort of urgency to awarding retroactive diplomas; as Oshiro remarked, such work is never really done, for to suggest the contrary would mean that history only needs to be told once.[58] For him, ceremonies of this sort give contemporary onlookers a chance "to hear it [the history of wartime incarceration], to see it, to think about it."[59] The ceremony was an opportunity to get people to stop and think about this wartime moment, and for some to learn about it for the first time. He also realized the importance of his physical presence in enacting such change. Thus, while Oshiro expressed gratitude for the chance to give new personal meaning to UBC through this graduation ceremony, he also realized that his attendance, the very sight of him, was precisely what gave the ceremony its significance, both in the present and for the future. He and his fellow recipients aimed to help enact not just a new policy, but a new mentality that would both preserve that history and help prevent its repetition.

Oshiro described that enactment as necessarily ongoing. Noting the opportunity to engage contemporary observers, he tempered his optimism with the suggestion, "It's going to take time."[60] The mention of taking time reminds us that change happens slowly, but time is of the essence. As mentioned earlier, not all were able to attend the UBC graduation ceremony. One such person was Ted Aoki, former wartime student who eventually returned to UBC as a professor of secondary education. Although he had planned to attend the May 2012 graduation ceremony along with his brother, musician Harry Aoki, both were in poor health. Consequently, only Harry was able to attend, which he did in order to represent his family. Ted Aoki died that following autumn, on September 2; Harry died shortly after, on January 24, 2013; he was 91. Of his wartime eviction from British Columbia, Harry had said that he "didn't like the idea of being kicked out" of a place he had called home and, as a result, bought his own ticket to head east.[61] The death of both brothers punctuated the fact that the ceremony, four years in the making, was the last chance for this sort of public enactment of history at UBC. But, in enacting history, the recipients of retroactive diplomas would also be creating a new generation of people for whom wartime incarceration was more than a historical footnote. They would be initiating another phase of empathetic agency that would help move contemporary observers toward a more measured, less complacent view of freedoms and their relationship to being fully human.

Placing a Value on Education

What exactly is the value of a diploma? As noted early in this chapter, for Nikkei students who had been removed from UBC and other schools after the bombing of Pearl Harbor it could not have been in any way material. Take, for instance, the case of Teiso Edward Uyeno, who also attended Britannia High School before entering UBC in 1940.[62] In 1942, Uyeno was ordered to a prison camp in New Denver, in the interior of British Columbia.[63] In addition, he was ordered to help build part of the prison.[64] Plus, during the spring of 1943, the British Columbia Security Commission (the provincial body managing Japanese Canadian incarceration) tasked him with teaching science to incarcerated elementary school children. In addition, he taught physical education for boys in the fourth through sixth grades. During the fall of the same year, Uyeno was transferred to teach at Kaslo, another prison camp in British Columbia.[65] During the war years, Uyeno recalled feeling "in between," belonging neither to Japan nor to Canada.[66] Although he had never known any country but Canada, he recognized that Canadians had not accepted him. He experienced "severe discrimination" at the time, recalling that even Japanese Canadians with a UBC degree were not hired in a professional capacity.[67]

A positive outcome of Uyeno's wartime experience, however, was that he discovered his passion for teaching. As a result, when he was able to resume his studies in 1944 at the University of Toronto, he took up psychology, earning a BA in 1947, which he financed by working as a dishwasher and short order cook. He then took time to earn more money for graduate study by teaching at a school for young girls in Northern Ontario. After two years, he returned to the University of Toronto, earning an MA in psychology and statistics (1952) and a PhD in experimental psychology and education (1958).[68] Then Uyeno moved to the United States, where more funding was available for his work.[69] In 1961, got a job as a research associate in psychology at Stanford University, where he remained until his retirement in 1994.[70]

Uyeno's 2012 degree from UBC would obviously have no material impact on his career or his finances. So, why make the journey? Because doing so would go a long way toward recuperating the society in which he had for decades occupied a marginal position. To some extent, that recuperation would be personal, as these and other former students were welcomed back to a campus that had ejected them in 1942. The 2012 ceremony represented a change of heart by UBC and its administration, and Uyeno, like so many others, recognized that by attending he would help enact that change visibly and incontrovertibly.[71]

Doing so was meant to impart the past to present generations, revivifying it so that others could extend the memory of it into the future. Walking across the dais at UBC, for instance, nonagenarian Roy Oshiro aimed to move history out of books and articles and into the lives of the other students and their families; to make his experience theirs, if only to a limited extent; to let them see him as living history, to experience the afterlife he both lived and caused, and to think about that afterlife in the future.[72] He aimed, in short, to teach by example. And he knew full well that that example would be marked as much by its urgency (in view of his age and the ages of his fellow recipients) as by its justness.

It is useful to think of retroactive diplomas as another instance of civil religion for Nikkei North Americans, both in Canada and in the United States. Diplomas have no economic or material value for people like Oshiro and Uyeno, let alone Kitagawa and Furutani. And yet, in each case these people have tenaciously pursued or embraced retroactive diplomas. As this chapter has noted, that comes from a recognition that the effects of wartime incarceration continue for those who suffered under it decades after the last camp closed. But as this chapter has also noted, the mass imprisonment of Japanese Americans and Japanese Canadians continues to influence the present precisely because its effects never reach an end. To some extent, that influence has manifested itself in educational projects, whether retroactive diploma ceremonies or public-education initiatives. To some extent, though, it also has manifested itself daily in a thousand other ways. And that may be the most noteworthy thing about the work of people like Furutani and Kitagawa: that their watershed actions are only the most publicly visible expressions of an underlying drive to continue making history live. Their actions in this regard are akin to the February 14 Annual Women's Memorial March, which commemorates the nearly three thousand women who have disappeared or been murdered in Canada since the 1970s. Although marching will not bring these women back, nor have any immediate material impact on their killers, it provides a space in the social fabric for the dead and the disappeared, whose stories may then linger in the minds of onlookers.[73] In much the same way as Renee C. Romano has suggested in her important work on the murders of blacks during the 1950s and 1960s, a proper reckoning with the histories of racism must necessarily move beyond basic legal or legislative action to include other modes of cultural production.[74]

The retroactive diploma campaigns in the United States and Canada demonstrate the extent to which the afterlife of wartime injustice has continued to dog societies on either side of the border by reverberating spatially, temporally, and psychologically across arbitrary governmental boundaries. As Kitagawa's years of public campaigns illustrate, she could not draw on the help of influential Asian Canadian elected officials, as was the case in California (e.g., Assemblyman Furutani). Ceremonies in both countries had similar aims: to retake old territory and change educational and university policies, emphasizing collaborations that were already in the making. Finally, the need for these ceremonies over seventy years later illustrates a point that Roy Oshiro, Mary Kitagawa, Warren Furutani, and others know well: the past may be a foreign country, but it is one with which we live and interact daily.

FIGURE 2   Members of the Uchida family at Tule Lake in 1943. *Clockwise from left*: Jeanette Kiyoko (later Inouye), George, Marian, Richard, Prentiss, and Ellen.

Epilogue

A few years ago I was driving the 250-mile stretch from Saint Louis to Bloomington with my family. Somewhere west of the Indiana border we pulled off to use a gas station restroom. As my daughter and I went to wash up, we noticed a woman with wet hair scrubbing her daughter's hair in the neighboring sink. I smiled at the woman, one mother to another, hoping to ease the embarrassment betrayed by her facial expression. Perhaps the woman hoped to return the favor by taking an interest in my daughter, who was clinging tightly to my shirt, having never experienced the sight of people bathing in a gas station sink. Looking from my daughter to me, the woman smiled and asked: "How do you say 'wash your hands?'" I could feel my daughter pressing even closer, as if to push bodily through me and out the door. I dried my hands, smiled, and replied: "Wash your hands." The woman paused to rephrase the question, thinking I had misunderstood its substance. Politely, somewhat pityingly, she tried again, "No, how do you say 'wash your hands' in *your* language?" I repeated, echoing the woman's now more methodical cadence, "Wash your hands." The woman smiled warmly, even though she was clearly frustrated and puzzled by my apparent lack of comprehension. I smiled back and moved casually toward the door, knowing my daughter was absorbing every detail of our interaction.

I've often thought back to that interaction. I've also thought about my daughter's fear and confusion in relation to the fear and confusion my grandmother must have felt upon arriving in the filthy barracks at Tule Lake, her six children and various relatives in tow. More recently, as I write the final draft of this book, I've imagined the three of us—me, my grand-mother, and that woman in southern Illinois—standing at those sinks and talking about our paths to and through motherhood. A conversation like that would have turned out very differently; my grandmother, ever social and generous, would have found bridges through motherhood and all the filthy sinks of her own past.

As this book went to press, I was struggling with how to end a class I teach on the history of race, gender, and labor. The fatal shooting of seventeen-year-old Laquan McDonald was on my mind because of the Thanksgiving protests in Chicago, just days before. Haunted by images of black men knocked to the ground, I abandoned my dry outline of comparative statistics. Instead, I asked the students to read an essay by my colleague here at Indiana, Ross Gay, and to listen to a recording of him reading an abbreviated version of the piece. I don't know Ross well, despite the many years we've spent sharing an office wall, but I've always been impressed by the consistently long line of eager students waiting in the hall during (and frequently outside of) his office hours.

The essay, "Some Thoughts on Mercy," is a meditation on the emotions he experienced during and after being pulled over by local police after a late night working on his tenure dossier.[1] The experience dogged him in ways that he found surprising and painful, but it ultimately produced an essay the likes of which I hadn't read in a long time. I was particularly struck by the open-endedness of what he wrote, the way that it allows readers to identify simultaneously with two parties that stand in a tense, poten-tially deadly—but also potentially beautiful—relationship to one another. Leaving class that day, one student, who had often been absent for military training, asked for the link to Ross's recitation of the essay.[2] Drained from the final push of the semester and working from habit, I replied tiredly, "It won't be on the final exam." The student smiled, perhaps frustrated and puzzled by my apparent lack of comprehension, and said: "Actually, I want my friend to listen to it." And in that moment, I became more fully human.

Reference Matter

Notes

INTRODUCTION

1. This study refers to incarceration and, occasionally, imprisonment, rather than "internment" for the simple reason that over 120,000 Nikkei North Americans were in fact prisoners. It also refers to "camps," for two very specific reasons. First, the term is used here as an abbreviation of the longer and more accurate, if loaded, term, "concentration camps." (No less an authority than Franklin Delano Roosevelt found the word applicable.) Second, and more importantly, it also is the term most Nikkei have used, including in the author's family. It therefore seems like a fitting term to her, insofar as it carries complex and frequently ironic implications that became familiar and, eventually, clear to her only over decades of use. On the importance of terminology, see Roger Daniels, "Words Do Matter: A Note on Inappropriate Terminology and the Incarceration of the Japanese Americans," in Louis Fiset and Gail Nomura, eds., *Nikkei in the Pacific Northwest: Japanese Americans and Japanese Canadians in the Twentieth Century* (Seattle: Center for the Study of the Pacific Northwest, 2005): 183–207. Daniels (ibid., 201) also discusses Roosevelt's apparently unreflective admission. With respect to Canada, see Mona Oikawa, *Cartographies of Violence: Japanese Canadian Women, Memory, and the Subjects of the Internment* (Toronto: University of Toronto Press, 2012): 23–25 and 39–43.

2. On Korematsu's case, as well as those of others who resisted incarceration, see Peter Irons, *The Courage of Their Convictions* (New York: Penguin, 1988); idem, *Justice at War: The Story of the Japanese American Internment Cases* (Berkeley: University of California Press, 1993); Roger Daniels, *The Japanese American Cases: The Rule of Law in Time of War* (Lawrence: University Press of Kansas, 2013); Lorraine K. Bannai, "Taking the Stand: The Lessons of Three Men Who Took the Japanese American Internment to Court," *Seattle Journal for Social Justice* 4:1 (2005): 1–57;

idem, *Enduring Conviction: Fred Korematsu and His Quest for Justice* (Seattle: University of Washington Press, 2015); Patrick O. Gudridge, "The Constitution Glimpsed from Tule Lake," in Eric L. Muller, ed., "Judgments Judged and Wrongs Remembered: Examining the Japanese American Civil Liberties Cases on Their Sixtieth Anniversary," a special issue of *Law and Contemporary Problems* 68:2 (2005): 81–118; idem, "Remember 'Endo'?," *Harvard Law Review* 116:7 (2003): 1933–1970; Eugene R. Gressman, "Korematsu: A Mélange of Military Imperatives," in Muller ed., "Judgments Judged and Wrongs Remembered," 15–27. See also Stephanie Bangarth, *Voices Raised in Protest: Defending North American Citizens of Japanese Ancestry, 1942–1949* (Vancouver: University of British Columbia Press, 2008); Masumi Izumi, "Japanese American Internment and the Emergency Detention Act (Title II of the Internal Security Act of 1950), 1941–1971: Balancing Internal Security and Civil Liberties in the United States" (PhD diss., Doshisha University, 2003), esp. chap. 1; and idem, "Alienable Citizenship: Race, Loyalty and the Law in the Age of 'American Concentration Camps,' 1941–1971," *Asian American Law Journal* 13:1 (2006): 1–30. On Nikkei draft resisters, see Eric L. Muller, *Free to Die for Their Country: The Story of the Japanese American Draft Resisters in World War II* (Chicago: University of Chicago Press, 2001); idem, "A Penny for Their Thoughts: Draft Resistance at the Poston Relocation Center," in Muller, ed., "Judgments Judged and Wrongs Remembered," 119–157.

3. Karen Korematsu-Haigh, interview by Neal Conan, January 31, 2012, http://www.npr.org/2012/01/31/146149345/the-legacy-of-civil-rights-leader-fred-korematsu (accessed June 6, 2014). For the text in question, see Roger Daniels, *Concentration Camps USA: Japanese Americans and World War II* (New York: Holt, Rinehart and Winston, 1971). On the obliviation of wartime imprisonment in schools, particularly with respect to women, see Oikawa, *Cartographies of Violence*, 267–302.

4. Harry H. L. Kitano, *Japanese Americans: Evolution of a Subculture* (Englewood Cliffs, NJ: Prentice-Hall, 1969); Yasuko I. Takezawa, *Breaking the Silence: Redress and Japanese American Ethnicity* (Ithaca, NY: Cornell University Press, 1995).

5. Korematsu-Haigh, interview.

6. Kitano, *Japanese Americans,* remains the classic source; Takezawa, *Breaking the Silence,* provides a wealth of case studies. See also Bill Hosokawa, *Nisei: The Quiet Americans,* rev. ed. (Boulder: University of Colorado Press, 2002), which was first published the same year as Kitano's study.

7. See Chapters Two and Three.

8. As Korematsu-Haigh pointed out in her interview with Neal Conan, Korematsu's felony conviction barred him from many kinds of work.

9. See Irons, *The Courage of Their Convictions.*

10. See Korematsu's comments on the profiling of Arab Americans and Muslims in the wake of 9/11 in the documentary by Eric Paul Fournier, *Civil Wrongs*

and Rights: The Fred Korematsu Story (San Francisco: National Asian American Telecommunications Association, 2001). On the relationship between wartime incarceration and post-9/11 policy, see Jerry Kang, "Denying Prejudice: Internment, Redress, and Denial," *UCLA Law Review* 51 (2004): 933–1013; idem, "Watching the Watchers: Enemy Combatants in the Internment's Shadow," in Muller, ed., "Judgments Judged and Wrongs Remembered," 255–283; Eric L. Muller, "12/7 and 9/11: War, Liberties, and the Lessons of History," *West Virginia Law Review* 104:3 (2002): 571–592; idem, "Inference or Impact? Racial Profiling and the Interment's True Legacy," *Ohio State Journal of Criminal Law* 103 (2003): 103–131; Greg Robinson and Toni Robinson, "*Korematsu* and Beyond: Japanese Americans and the Origins of Strict Scrutiny," in Muller, ed., "Judgments Judged and Wrongs Remembered," 29–55; A. Wallace Tashima, "Play It Again, Uncle Sam," in Muller, ed., "Judgments Judged and Wrongs Remembered," 7–14.

11. See, for instance, Saidiya Hartman, *Lose Your Mother: A Journey along the Atlantic Slave Route* (New York: Farrar, Straus and Giroux, 2007).

12. On more radical Asian American approaches to the civil rights movement, see Yuri Kochiyama, *Passing It On: A Memoir* (Los Angeles: UCLA Asian American Studies Center Press, 2004); Diane C. Fujino, *Samurai among Panthers: Richard Aoki on Race, Resistance, and a Paradoxical Life* (Minneapolis: University of Minnesota Press, 2012); idem, *Heartbeat of Struggle: The Revolutionary Life of Yuri Kochiyama* (Minneapolis: University of Minnesota Press, 2005). On radicalism in Asia, see Judy Tzu-Chun Wu, *Radicals on the Road: Internationalism, Orientalism, and Feminism during the Vietnam Era* (Ithaca, NY: Cornell University Press, 2013).

13. For an in-depth discussion of Roosevelt's decision to incarcerate Nikkei, see most recently Greg Robinson, *By Order of the President: FDR and the Internment of Japanese Americans* (Cambridge, MA: Harvard University Press, 2003), esp. 73–124; Roger Daniels, *Prisoners Without Trial: Japanese Americans in World War II*, rev. ed. (New York: Hill and Wang, 2004); Brian Masaru Hayashi, *Democratizing the Enemy: The Japanese American Internment* (Princeton, NJ: Princeton University Press, 2008).

14. On non-Nikkei inmates of these camps, see Paul R. Spickard, "Injustice Compounded: Amerasians and Non-Japanese Americans in World War II Concentration Camps," *Journal of American Ethnic History* 5:2 (1986): 5–22.

15. In addition to Daniels, *Prisoners Without Trial*, see also Jeffrey Burton, Mary Farrell, Florence Lord, and Richard Lord, *Confinement and Ethnicity: An Overview of World War II Japanese American Relocation Sites* (Tucson, AZ: Western Archeological and Conservation Center, National Park Service, 1999), on the physical circumstances of wartime incarceration.

16. Yamato Ichihashi, *Japanese in the United States: A Critical Study of the Problems of the Japanese Immigrants and Their Children* (Stanford, CA: Stanford

University Press, 1932), 364: "The history of Japanese immigration to the United States ended with the exclusion law of 1924, and with it hostile sentiment even in the historic anti-Japanese district began to moderate, and subsequently there has been little hostility to the Japanese. This tendency is said to be due to the fact that those who were interested in bringing about exclusion consider it as the definitive settlement of the Japanese question." On Nikkei in the United States before imprisonment, see Yuji Ichioka, *The Issei: The World of the First Generation Japanese Immigrants, 1885–1924* (New York: Collier Macmillan, 1988); Paul Spickard, *Japanese Americans: The Formation and Transformations of an Ethnic Group*, rev. ed. (New York, Twayne, 1996), esp. chaps. 1–5; and Jere Takahashi, *Nisei/Sansei: Shifting Japanese American Identities and Politics* (Philadelphia: Temple University Press, 1997), chap. 1.

17. See Roger Daniels, *Prisoners Without Trial*; idem, *The Politics of Prejudice: The Anti-Japanese Movement in California and the Struggle for Japanese Exclusion*, rev. ed. (Berkeley: University of California Press, 1977). Daniels documents how the growing success of Nikkei in agriculture (and thus competition for white farmers), combined with general anti-Asian sentiment, provided the impetus for their wartime removal. Even though the U.S. government investigated Nikkei to see if it could find evidence of traitorous activity and found none (as determined by the Munson Report), widespread racial hysteria and hatred fueled the removal of Nikkei from the West Coast. See also Hayashi, *Democratizing the Enemy*. For earlier discussions of the motivation behind incarceration, see Morton Grodzins, *Americans Betrayed* (Chicago: University of Chicago Press, 1949); and Jacobus tenBroek, Edward N. Barnhart, and Floyd W. Matson, *Prejudice, War, and the Constitution: Causes and Consequences of the Evacuation of the Japanese Americans in World War II* (Berkeley: University of California Press, 1954).

18. See Ken Adachi, *The Enemy That Never Was: An Account of the Deplorable Treatment Inflicted on Japanese Canadians during World War Two* (Toronto: McClelland and Stewart, 1976); Audrey Kobayashi, "The Historical Context of Japanese-Canadian Uprooting," in Ludger Müller-Wille, ed., *Social Change and Space: Indigenous Nations and Ethnic Communities* (Montreal: McGill University, 1989), 69–82; Ann Gomer Sunahara, *The Politics of Racism: The Uprooting of Japanese Canadians during the Second World War* (Toronto: Lorimer, 1981). Sunahara's book is now available online: http://www.japanesecanadianhistory.ca/. For a comparative account of North American policies and their outcomes on either side of the U.S.-Canadian border, see Greg Robinson, *A Tragedy of Democracy: Japanese Confinement in North America* (New York: Columbia University Press, 2009).

19. This paragraph depends on the analysis in Adachi, *The Enemy That Never Was*, esp. 189–216. On Franklin Delano Roosevelt's approach to Nikkei in the United States, see Greg Robinson, *By Order of the President*.

20. See, for instance, Priscilla Wegars, *Imprisoned in Paradise: Japanese Internee Road Workers at the World War II Kooskia Internment Camp* (Moscow, ID: Asian American Comparative Collective/University of Idaho, 2010).

21. Ibid., 199–224. In some instances, local authorities seem to have recognized the potential economic benefits of having a new influx of residents (ibid., 254).

22. Roy Miki and Cassandra Kobayashi, *Justice in Our Time: The Japanese Canadian Redress Settlement* (Vancouver, BC: Talonbooks, 1991), 47. On the experience of these people, see Tatsuo Kage, *Uprooted Again: Japanese Canadians Move to Japan after World War II*, trans. by Kathleen Chisato Merken (Victoria, BC: Ti-Jean Press, 2012).

23. Quoted in Adachi, *The Enemy That Never Was*, 335. This book, in particular chapter 14, remains the standard source on the postwar treatment of Nikkei in Canada. However, see also Robinson, *A Tragedy of Democracy*, esp. 262–274; and Roy Miki, *Redress: Inside the Japanese Canadian Call for Justice* (Vancouver, BC: Raincoast Books, 2005), esp. chaps. 4 and 5.

24. On Leighton's work in Poston, see Karen M. Inouye, "Changing History: Competing Notions of Japanese American Experience, 1942–2006" (PhD diss., Brown University, 2008), chap. 2.

25. Avery F. Gordon, *Ghostly Matters: Haunting and the Sociological Imagination* (Minneapolis: University of Minnesota Press, 1997), xvi.

26. See in particular Kandice Chuh, who draws on Gordon's formulation for the title of her book, *Imagine Otherwise: On Asian Americanist Critique* (Durham, NC: Duke University Press, 2003), esp. 58–84. See also Avery F. Gordon, *Keeping Good Time: Reflections on Knowledge, Power, and People* (Boulder, CO: Paradigm, 2004).

27. On the political invisibility of Nikkei in the years after the war, see Caroline Chung Simpson, *An Absent Presence: Japanese Americans in Postwar American Culture, 1945–1960* (Durham, NC: Duke University Press, 2002).

28. See Fujino, *Samurai among Panthers*, and idem, *Heartbeat of Struggle*.

29. S. I. Hayakawa, who strongly opposed redress, provides an example of the first instance; Mary Kitagawa, who figures prominently in Chapter Five, exemplifies the second.

30. See, for instance, Amy I. Mass, "The Psychological Effects of the Camps on Japanese Americans," in Roger Daniels, Sandra C. Taylor, and Harry H. L. Kitano, eds., *Japanese Americans: From Relocation to Redress*, rev. ed. (Seattle: University of Washington Press, 2013), 159–162; idem, "Psychological Effects of Internment," in Mike Mackey, ed., *A Matter of Conscience: Essays on the World War II Heart Mountain Draft Resistance Movement* (Powell, WY: Western History Publications, 2002), 145–152; Donna K. Nagata, *Legacy of Injustice: Exploring the Cross-Generational Impact of the Japanese American Internment* (New York: Plenum Press, 1993); Donna K. Nagata and Yuzuru J. Takeshita, "Coping and Resilience across Gen-

erations: Japanese Americans and the World War II Internment," *Psychoanalytic Review* 85 (1998): 587–613; and Inouye, "Changing History."

31. Cf. Hartman, *Lose Your Mother*, 6. See also Kirsten Emiko McAllister, "Stories of Escape: Family Photographs from World War Two Internment Camps," in Annette Kuhn and Kirsten Emiko McAllister, eds., *Locating Memory: Photographic Acts* (Oxford: Berghahn, 2006), 81–110; idem, *Terrain of Memory: A Japanese Canadian Memorial Project* (Vancouver: University of British Columbia Press, 2010).

32. I follow the definition of civil society offered by Jürgen Habermas: a "sphere of private autonomy" that articulates its needs via political organs in the public sphere. According to this definition, wartime incarceration was a failure on the part of government, but it also on the part of those government serves. See Jürgen Habermas, *The Structural Transformation of the Public Sphere: An Inquiry into a Category of Bourgeois Society*, trans. Thomas Burger with Frederick Lawrence (Cambridge, MA: Harvard University Press, 1989), 73. On the intertwining of public and private, particularly as they bear on economic concerns, see Grodzins, *Americans Betrayed*. See also Eric K. Yamamoto, "White (House) Lies: Why the Public Must Compel the Courts to Hold the President Accountable for National Security Abuses," in Muller, ed., "Judgments Judged and Wrongs Remembered," 285–339.

33. This is not to suggest that such strategies are unique to Japanese American and Japanese Canadian activisms.

34. I use the term "contagious" specifically to repurpose it. On historical discourses of Asian bodies in relationship to their supposedly white counterparts, see Nayan Shah, *Contagious Divides: Epidemics and Race in San Francisco's Chinatown* (Berkeley: University of California Press, 2001), and Warwick Anderson, *Colonial Pathologies: American Tropical Medicine, Race, and Hygiene in the Philippines* (Durham, NC: Duke University Press, 2006).

35. My model of empathy derives from that in Karl F. Morrison, *I Am You: The Hermeneutics of Empathy in Western Literature, Theology, and Art* (Princeton, NJ: Princeton University Press, 1988). Cf. Fritz Breithaupt, *Kulturen der Empathie* (Berlin: Suhrkamp/Insel, 2009), and idem, "A Three-Person Model of Empathy," *Emotion Review* 4:1 (2012): 84–91. On empathy and wartime incarceration, see Kirsten Emiko McAllister, "Memoryscapes of Postwar British Columbia: A Look of Recognition," in Ashok Mathur, Jonathan Dewar, and Mike DeGagné, eds., *Cultivating Canada: Reconciliation through the Lens of Cultural Diversity, Aboriginal Healing Foundation*, vol. 3 (Ottawa, ON: Aboriginal Healing Foundation, 2011), 419–444, esp. 440–441.

36. It is important to emphasize, however, the importance of work by Peter Irons and Aiko Herzig-Yoshinaga, who turned up evidence of government misbehavior and, thus, greatly increased the chances of legal victory for Korematsu and his fellow resisters of Executive Order 9066.

37. Chuh, *Imagine Otherwise*, 83.

38. Alice Yang Murray, *Historical Memories of the Japanese American Internment and the Struggle for Redress* (Stanford, CA: Stanford University Press, 2008), 13.

39. Renee C. Romano, *Racial Reckoning: Prosecuting America's Civil Rights Murders* (Cambridge, MA: Harvard University Press, 2014); Patricia Hill Collins, *Black Feminist Thought: Knowledge, Consciousness, and the Politics of Empowerment* (Boston: Routledge, 1990); Orlando Patterson, *Slavery and Social Death: A Comparative Study* (Cambridge, MA: Harvard University Press, 1985); Lisa Cacho, *Social Death: Racialized Rightlessness and the Criminalization of the Unprotected* (New York: New York University Press, 2012).

40. Publications associated with JERS include Dorothy Swaine Thomas and Richard S. Nishimoto, *The Spoilage* (Berkeley: University of California Press, 1946); Dorothy Swaine Thomas, *The Salvage* (Berkeley: University of California Press, 1952); and tenBroek et al., *Prejudice, War, and the Constitution*. Grodzins's *Americans Betrayed* grew out of his work for JERS, but a falling out with Thomas led to this text standing apart from the others. See Peter Suzuki, "For the Sake of Inter-University Comity: The Attempted Suppression by the University of California of Morton Grodzins' *Americans Betrayed*," in Ichioka, ed., *Views from Within*, 95–123; Stephen O. Murray, "The Rights of Research Assistants and the Rhetoric of Political Suppression: Morton Grodzins and the University of California Japanese-American Evacuation and Resettlement Study," *Journal of the History of the Behavioral Sciences* 27:2 (1991): 130–156.

41. On Canada, see Adachi, *The Enemy That Never Was*; Sunahara, *The Politics of Racism*. On the United States (and, in some cases, also Canada), see Roger Daniels, *Concentration Camps USA*; idem, *Concentration Camps, North America: Japanese in the United States and Canada during World War II* (Malabar, FL: Kreiger, 1993); idem, *Prisoners Without Trial*; Greg Robinson, *After Camp: Portraits in Midcentury Japanese American Life and Politics* (Berkeley: University of California Press, 2012); idem, *By Order of the President*; idem, *A Tragedy of Democracy*; Michi Weglyn, *Years of Infamy: The Untold Story of America's Concentration Camps* (New York: Morrow, 1976). See also the report of the U.S. Commission on Wartime Relocation and Internment of Civilians, *Personal Justice Denied: Report of the Commission on Wartime Relocation and Internment of Civilians* (Washington, D.C.: Government Publications Office, 1982).

42. See Bangarth, *Voices Raised in Protest*; Daniels, *Japanese American Cases*; Irons, *The Courage of Their Convictions*; idem, *Justice at War*.

43. See Leslie T. Hatamiya, *Righting a Wrong: Japanese Americans and the Passage of the Civil Liberties Act of 1988* (Stanford, CA: Stanford University Press, 1993); Bill Hosokawa, *JACL in Quest of Justice: The History of the Japanese American Citizens League* (New York: Morrow, 1982); William Minoru Hohri, *Repairing America: An Account of the Movement for Japanese-American Redress* (Pullman: Washington

State University Press, 1988); Mitchell T. Maki, Harry H. L. Kitano, and S. Megan Berthold, *Achieving the Impossible Dream: How Japanese Americans Obtained Redress* (Urbana: University of Illinois Press, 1999); Miki, *Redress*; Maryka Omatsu, *Bittersweet Passage: Redress and the Japanese Canadian Experience* (Toronto: Between the Lines, 1992); and Yang Murray, *Historical Memories*.

44. See Chuh, *Imagine Otherwise*, esp. chap. 2; Iyko Day, "Alien Intimacies: The Coloniality of Japanese Incarceration in Australia, Canada, and the U.S.," *Amerasia Journal* 36:2 (2010): 107–124.

45. Iyko Day, "Lost in Transnation: Uncovering Asian Canada," *Amerasia Journal* 33:2 (2007): 69–86; Donald Goellnicht, "Asian Kanadian, Eh?," *Canadian Literature* 199 (2008): 71–99; Christopher Lee, "The Lateness of Asian Canadian Studies," *Amerasia Journal* 33:2 (2007): 1–17; Roy Miki, "Altered States: Global Currents, the Spectral Nation, and the Production of 'Asian Canadian,'" *Journal of Canadian Studies/Revue d'études canadiennes* 35:3 (2000): 43–72; idem, "Asiancy: Making Space for Asian Canadian Writing," in Gary Y. Okihiro, Marilyn Alquizola, Dorothy Fujita Rony, and K. Scott Wong, eds., *Privileging Positions: The Sites of Asian American Studies* (Pullman: Washington State University Press, 1995): 135–151; and Eleanor Ty and Donald Goellnicht, "Introduction," in Eleanor Ty and Donald Goellnicht, eds., *Asian North American Identities: Beyond the Hyphen* (Bloomington: Indiana University Press, 2004), 1–14. See also a roundtable discussion featuring Guy Beauregard, Iyko Day, Glenn Deer, Donald Goellnicht, Christopher Lee, Marie Lo, Roy Miki, Rita Wong, and Henry Yu: "Epilogue: A Conversation on Unfinished Projects," *Canadian Literature* 199 (2008): 208–211.

CHAPTER ONE

1. October 30, 1943, letter from Tamotsu Shibutani to Dorothy Swaine Thomas, Japanese American Evacuation and Resettlement Records, BANCMSS 67/14c, reel 91: 551.

2. Some of my early thoughts about the material covered in this chapter appeared as "Japanese American Wartime Experience: Tamotsu Shibutani and Methodological Innovation, 1942–1978," *Journal of the History of the Behavioral Sciences* 48:4 (2012): 318–338.

3. Thomas and her husband, the sociologist W. I. Thomas, helped JERS workers navigate various legal, financial, and familial challenges. On the complicated nature of these relationships, see Henry Yu, *Thinking Orientals: Migration, Contact, and Exoticism in Modern America* (Oxford: Oxford University Press, 2001), and Gary Y. Okihiro, *Storied Lives: Japanese American Students and World War II* (Seattle: University of Washington Press, 1999).

4. Ellen Herman, *The Romance of American Psychology: Political Culture in the Age of Experts* (Berkeley: University of California Press, 1995); James Capshew, *Psy-*

chologists on the March: Science, Practice, and Professional Identity in America, 1929–1969 (Cambridge: Cambridge University Press, 1999). See also James M. Sakoda, "Reminiscences of a Participant Observer," in Yuji Ichioka, ed., *Views from Within: The Japanese American Evacuation and Resettlement Study* (Los Angeles: UCLA Asian American Studies Center, 1989), 222–224; and James M. Sakoda, interview by Arthur A. Hansen, in idem, ed., *Japanese American World War II Evacuation Oral History Project* (Munich: K.G. Sauer, 1991–1995), 431.

5. For example, some inmates felt they should protest their imprisonment while others thought doing so would only cause more trouble. Such rifts exacerbated the difficulties that participant observers—as such researchers were called—faced in their work.

6. See, for example, Peter Suzuki, "Anthropologists in the Wartime Camps for Japanese Americans: A Documentary Study," *Dialectical Anthropology* 6:1 (1981): 23–60; idem, "University of California Japanese Evacuation and Resettlement Study: A Prolegomenon," *Dialectical Anthropology* 10:3 (1986): 189–213; Ichioka, ed., *Views from Within*; Lane Hirabayashi, *The Politics of Fieldwork: Research in an American Concentration Camps* (Tucson: University of Arizona Press, 1999); Yu, *Thinking Orientals*.

7. While several other Japanese Americans served as participant observers, few other than these three went on to pursue academic careers that circled back to their time in camp and its impact on Nikkei identity in the United States. See Karen M. Inouye, "Changing History: Competing Notions of Japanese American Experience, 1942–2006" (PhD diss., Brown University, 2008).

8. Peter Irons, *The Courage of Their Convictions* (New York: Penguin, 1988); idem, *Justice at War: The Story of the Japanese American Internment Cases* (Berkeley: University of California Press, 1993); Roger Daniels, *The Japanese American Cases: The Rule of Law in Time of War* (Lawrence: University Press of Kansas, 2013); Lorraine K. Bannai, "Taking the Stand: The Lessons of Three Men Who Took the Japanese American Internment to Court," *Seattle Journal for Social Justice* 4:1 (2005): 1–57. See also Stephanie Bangarth, *Voices Raised in Protest: Defending North American Citizens of Japanese Ancestry, 1942–1949* (Vancouver: University of British Columbia Press, 2008).

9. Ken Adachi, *The Enemy That Never Was: An Account of the Deplorable Treatment Inflicted on Japanese Canadians during World War Two* (Toronto: McClelland and Stewart, 1976), 265–266. On the treatment of Japanese Americans, see Allan W. Austin, *From Concentration Camps to Campus: Japanese American Students and World War II* (Urbana: University of Illinois Press, 2004).

10. In fact, one notable exception to that relative lack, Gordon Hirabayashi, was born, raised, and trained in the United States; he moved to the University of Alberta in 1959.

11. The BSR was brought to Poston in order to identify the causes of a November 1942 deadlock between inmates and the administration. That deadlock, eventually known as the Poston Strike, occurred after a series of disruptions. First, tensions were already running high among inmates as well as between inmates and camp staff. Second, though autumn had arrived and winter was just around the corner, barracks were not yet heated consistently or properly, so prisoners had to stand in front of open-air fires to warm themselves. This provided them with a visible rallying point around which to gather and voice their collective discontent. Third, on November 14, 1942, an inmate suspected of providing surveillance to camp administrators was attacked while sleeping. The resulting investigation made matters worse, as fifty suspects were summarily rounded up and interviewed by the chief of internal security and by the reports officer. The reports officer exacerbated the situation by suggesting there was a "pro-Axis" gang involved in the incident and that the beating was evidence that it was gaining more control of the Nikkei community. Tensions continued to escalate until work ground to a halt on November 19. The camp had become, Leighton suggested, defunct, akin to an automobile "with its motor still turning over, but no longer pulling." Though the BSR's work was strongly psychological in orientation, the text that resulted was almost entirely administrative in focus. See Alexander Leighton, *The Governing of Men: General Principles and Recommendations Based on Experience at a Japanese Relocation Camp* (Princeton, NJ: Princeton University Press, 1946). For more on the psychosocial interests of Leighton and his staff, see Inouye, "Changing History," chap. 2.

12. For a list of publications associated with JERS, see Introduction, note 40. Another study was conducted by the War Relocation Authority, but both its methods and its output were almost exclusively administrative rather than psychological or sociological (Ichioka, ed., *Views from Within*, 3).

13. On Sakoda and Miyamoto, see Inouye, "Changing History," esp. chaps. 1 and 3. On Shibutani, see idem, "Japanese American Wartime Experience." Aside from his contributions to *The Salvage*, most of Sakoda's work was psychological.

14. On Sakoda's interest in social psychology rather than sociology, see Hansen, ed., *Oral History Project*, 367–368.

15. "Reminiscences of a Participant Observer" (219–245) and "The 'Residue': The Unresettled Minidokans, 1943–1945" (247–281), both in Ichioka, ed., *Views from Within.*

16. Miyamoto also explicitly discussed wartime incarceration as well as his work for JERS in three contributions to Ichioka, ed., *Views from Within*, but the majority of his writing about Nikkei in North America took a broader view. This is the case, for instance, even in his early publications, such as "Immigrants and Citizens of Japanese Origin," *Annals of the American Academy of Political and Social Science* 223 (1942): 107–113. This is also the case in his mid-career work, such as

"The Japanese Minority in the Pacific Northwest," *Pacific Northwest Quarterly* 54:4 (1963): 143–149; and in later collaborative work, such as Stephen S. Fugita, S. Frank Miyamoto, and Tetsuden Kashima, "Interpersonal Style and Japanese American Organizational Involvement," *Behaviormetrika* 29:2 (2002): 185–202.

17. Hansen, ed., *Oral History Project*, 376.

18. Ibid., 372.

19. Ibid., 371.

20. John D. Baldwin, "Advancing the Chicago School of Pragmatic Sociology: The Life and Work of Tamotsu Shibutani," *Sociological Inquiry* 60:2 (2001): 115. See also idem, "Shibutani and Pragmatism," *Symbolic Interaction* 28:4 (2005): 487–504.

21. Baldwin, "Advancing the Chicago School of Pragmatic Sociology," 116.

22. Ibid., 117.

23. Ibid.

24. Ibid.

25. Ibid.

26. Ibid., 121.

27. Ibid.

28. Ichioka, ed., *Views from Within*, 5.

29. Ibid.

30. Ibid., 3.

31. Leighton, *The Governing of Men*, 48–52.

32. See note 11 above.

33. See Inouye, "Changing History," chap. 2.

34. Jacobus tenBroek, Edward N. Barnhart, and Floyd W. Matson, *Prejudice, War and the Constitution: Causes and Consequences of the Evacuation of the Japanese Americans in World War II* (Berkeley: University of California Press, 1954); Roger Daniels, *Prisoners Without Trial: Japanese Americans in World War II*, rev. ed. (New York: Hill and Wang, 2004).

35. Dorothy Swaine Thomas and Richard S. Nishimoto, *The Spoilage* (Berkeley: University of California Press, 1946), 58–72. On the complexities of assessing loyalty among Nikkei, see Eric L. Muller, *American Inquisition: The Hunt for Japanese American Disloyalty in World War II* (Chapel Hill: University of North Carolina Press, 2007).

36. Thomas, among others, visited several times.

37. June 24, 1942, letter from Shibutani to Thomas, Japanese American Evacuation and Resettlement Records, BANCMSS 67/14c, reel 182: 549.

38. July 21, 1943, journal entry by Shibutani, Japanese American Evacuation and Resettlement Records, BANCMSS 67/14c, reel 183: 149. Brian Masaru Hayashi, *Democratizing the Enemy: The Japanese American Internment* (Princeton, NJ: Princeton University Press, 2008), 125–127. James Sakoda later remarked, in an interview

with Arthur A. Hansen, that "Tom [Shibutani] and Frank [Miyamoto] felt that their lives were in danger; they just felt they couldn't stay [in Tule Lake, and thus were eventually transferred in 1943]." He then added that "I imagine that if they had stayed it would have blown over," going on to attribute the situation to a combination of misinformation about the Loyalty Questionnaire and the specific bunkhouse in which Shibutani and Miyamoto lived. See Hansen, ed., *Oral History Project*, Part III: 349ff.

39. During the first part of the twentieth century, many famous studies associated with the so-called Chicago school of sociology had used participant observation. Examples include Nels Anderson's *The Hobo: Sociology of the Homeless Man* (Chicago: University of Chicago Press, 1923); Clifford Shaw's *The Jack Roller: A Delinquent Boy's Own Story* (Chicago: University of Chicago Press, 1930); and William F. Whyte's *Street Corner Society: The Social Structure of an Italian Slum* (Chicago: University of Chicago Press, 1943).

For more on the history of participant observation, see Phyllis Kaberry, "Malinowski's Contribution to Fieldwork Methods and the Writing of Ethnography," in Raymond Firth, ed., *Man and Culture* (London: Routledge, 1935), 71–91; Fred Mathews, *Quest for an American Sociology: Robert E. Park and the Chicago School* (Montreal: McGill-Queen's University Press, 1977), 88–89; Lewis Coser, ed., *Masters of Sociological Thought: Ideas in Historical and Social Context*, rev. ed. (New York: Waveland Press, 1977); Yu, *Thinking Orientals*.

40. Thomas and Nishimoto, *The Spoilage*, viii.

41. Ibid., vii.

42. Ichioka, ed., *Views from Within*, 7–8.

43. As Peter Suzuki, Henry Yu, and others have demonstrated, however, the power dynamic was fraught and weighed heavily upon them as well. Thus, it is all the more noteworthy that Shibutani was willing to challenge his academic mentor despite his simultaneous role as student and inmate. (See note 6 above.)

44. Much of W. I. Thomas's influence derived from the foundational text he coauthored with Florian Znaniecki, *The Polish Peasant in Europe and America* (Chicago: University of Chicago Press, 1918). The book has been cited as the first to use biographical information collected from immigrants themselves to understand migration and culture.

45. See, for instance, Shibutani's journal entries from 1943, Japanese American Evacuation and Resettlement Records, BANCMSS 67/14c, reels 88–92.

46. Ichioka, ed., *Views from Within*, 10. See also, S. Frank Miyamoto, "Dorothy Swaine Thomas as Director of JERS: Some Personal Observations," in Ichioka, ed., *Views from Within*, 31–64.

47. October 30, 1943, letter from Shibutani to Thomas, Japanese American Evacuation and Resettlement Records, BANCMSS 67/14c, reel 91: 551.

48. Ichioka, ed., *Views from Within*, 11–12.

49. October 1943 memo from Thomas to the JERS researchers, Japanese American Evacuation and Resettlement Records, BANCMSS 67/14c, reel 182: 549.

50. Ibid.

51. Ibid.

52. Ibid.

53. Shibutani shared this concern with others. S. Frank Miyamoto, another of Thomas's main researchers, recalled that many of the JERS workers were frustrated by Thomas's lack of explicit direction and theoretical orientation. Concerning this matter, Miyamoto wrote to Thomas in October 1943: "I am inclined to insist that to have our feet on the ground we've got to start with at least a minimum of ground to stand on, and if we're trying to get anywhere, we should have some hunches as to how to get there" (Japanese American Evacuation and Resettlement Records, BANCMSS 67/14c, reel 90: 218). A few of Thomas's white research assistants also shared this concern. In a November 6, 1943, letter to Shibutani, Morton Grodzins declared: "I had the definite impression that I was in the dog-house around here for at least several days that followed my lengthy discussion with Dorothy about matters methodological." He added, "In any case, let it be known that I served as the punch-bag for Dorothy's warm-up. I did this cheerfully, but I came out pretty limp in the end" (Japanese American Evacuation and Resettlement Records, BANCMSS 67/14c, reel 91: 552). Sakoda, for his part, noted that Thomas's considerable generosity was the flipside of her equally considerable toughness: "when she got angry, she got real nasty" (quoted in Hansen, ed., *Oral History Project*, Part III: 372). See also Miyamoto, "Thomas as Director," in Ichioka, ed., *Views from Within*, esp. 39–40; see also Ichioka's introductory remarks in the same work (9).

54. Ichioka, ed., *Views from Within*, 12.

55. Avery F. Gordon, *Ghostly Matters: Haunting and the Sociological Imagination* (Minneapolis: University of Minnesota Press, 1997).

56. Thomas and Nishimoto, *The Spoilage*, xii.

57. Dorothy Swaine Thomas, *The Salvage* (Berkeley: University of California Press, 1952), 15.

58. Robert C. Bannister, "Dorothy Swaine Thomas: The Hard Way in the Profession," http://www.swarthmore.edu/SocSci/rbannis1/DST.html. Published originally as "Dorothy Swain Thomas: Soziologischer Objectivismus: Der harte Weg in die Profession," in Claudia Honegger und Teresa Wobbe, eds., *Frauen in der Soziologie*, 226–257 (Munich: C.H. Beck, 1998).

59. Cf., for example, Thomas and Znaniecki, *The Polish Peasant*.

60. Bannister, "Dorothy Swaine Thomas." For more on Charles Kikuchi, see Matthew M. Briones, *Jim and Jap Crow: A Cultural History of 1940s Interracial America* (Princeton, NJ: Princeton University Press, 2013).

61. Thomas, *The Salvage*, 146–147.

62. Mae M. Ngai, "'An Ironic Testimony to the Value of American Democracy':

Assimilationism and the World War II Internment of Japanese Americans," in Manisha Sinha and Penny von Eschen, eds., *Contested Democracy: Freedom, Race, and Power in American History* (New York: Columbia University Press, 2007), 249. See also Mae M. Ngai, *Impossible Subjects: Illegal Aliens and the Making of Modern America* (Princeton, NJ: Princeton University Press, 2004), 175–201.

63. Dorothy Swaine Thomas, "Statistics in Social Research," *American Journal of Sociology* 35:1 (1929): 13. Compare this with a similar declaration by her mentor, William F. Ogburn, in "The Folkways of a Scientific Sociology," Presidential address to the American Sociological Society annual meeting in 1929; reprinted in *Publication of the American Sociological Society* 24 (May 1930): "The happy ending for a scientific sociology will be its achievement. It will be necessary to crush out emotion and to discipline the mind so strongly that the fanciful pleasures of intellectuality will have to be eschewed in the verification process" (10).

64. Ichioka, ed., *Views from Within*, 13.

65. As quoted in Stephen O. Murray, "The Rights of Research Assistants and the Rhetoric of Political Suppression: Morton Grodzins and the University of California Japanese-American Evacuation and Resettlement Study," *Journal of the History of the Behavioral Sciences* 27:2 (1991): 151n17.

66. Hansen, ed., *Oral History Project*, Part III: 376.

67. Baldwin, "Advancing the Chicago School," 119.

68. Herbert Blumer, "Sociological Implications of the Thought of George Herbert Mead," *American Journal of Sociology* 71 (1966): 536.

69. Gil Richard Musof, "The Chicago School," in Larry J. Reynolds and Nancy Herman-Kinney, eds., *Handbook of Symbolic Interactionism* (Walnut Creek, CA: AltaMira Press, 2003), 102–106. See also Herbert Blumer, *Symbolic Interactionism: Perspective and Method* (Englewood Cliffs, NJ: Prentice-Hall, 1969); Martyn Hammersly, *The Dilemma of Qualitative Method: Herbert Blumer and the Chicago Tradition* (London: Routledge, 1989).

70. November 8, 1943, letter from Shibutani to Thomas, Japanese American Evacuation and Resettlement Records, BANCMSS 67/14c, reel 91: 553.

71. January 19, 1944, letter from Shibutani to Thomas, Japanese American Evacuation and Resettlement Records, BANCMSS 67/14c, reel 91: 564.

72. Baldwin, "Advancing the Chicago School," 119.

73. Tamotsu Shibutani, *Improvised News: A Sociological Study of Rumor* (Indianapolis: Bobbs-Merrill, 1966), v–vi.

74. Ibid., vii.

75. Ibid.

76. Shibutani served in the army from 1944 to 1946 and was part of Company K. See Gordon Hirabayashi, Review of *The Derelicts of Company K, Pacific Affairs* 52:2 (1979): 347.

77. Ibid.

78. The very subject of his book, rumor, was itself a similar rejoinder to Thomas's refusal to deal with what she felt was unquantifiable.

79. Shibutani, *Improvised News*, 127–128.

80. Shibutani journal entry, July 11, 1942, Japanese American Evacuation and Resettlement Records, BANCMSS 67/14c, reel 182: 560.

81. July 21, 1943, report by Shibutani, Japanese American Evacuation and Resettlement Records, BANCMSS 67/14c, reel 183: 138.

82. Shibutani, *Improvised News*, 65ff.

83. Ibid., 132.

84. Ibid., 38. The emphasis is that of Shibutani, who paraphrases John Dewey, *The Public and Its Problems: An Essay in Political Inquiry* (New York: H. Holt, 1927).

85. Shibutani, *Improvised News*, 67.

86. Ibid.

87. Ibid., 68.

88. Ibid., 132–134.

89. Ibid., 56.

90. Ibid., 133–134.

91. Ibid., 134.

92. Ibid., 50–52.

93. Ibid., v.

94. May 5, 1942, journal entry by Shibutani, Japanese American Evacuation and Resettlement Records, BANCMSS 67/14c, reel 182: 515; Inouye, "Japanese American Wartime Experience," 326–328.

95. Shibutani, *Improvised News*, v–vi.

96. Tamotsu Shibutani, *The Derelicts of Company K: A Sociological Study of Demoralization* (Berkeley: University of California Press, 1978), 44.

97. Ibid., 48.

98. June 29, 1942, journal entry by Shibutani, Japanese American Evacuation and Resettlement Records, BANCMSS 67/14c, reel 182: 551. On those who resisted the draft, see Eric L. Muller, *Free to Die for Their Country: The Story of the Japanese American Draft Resisters in World War II* (Chicago: University of Chicago Press, 2001).

99. Shibutani, *Derelicts of Company K*, 50.

100. Ibid.

101. Ibid., 58.

102. Ibid., 65.

103. Ibid., 78.

104. Ibid., vii, 3.

105. Ibid., vii.

106. Ibid., 69. On circumstances in the United States, see Madeline Y. Hsu, *The Good Immigrants: How the Yellow Peril Became the Model Minority* (Princeton, NJ: Princeton University Press, 2015); Erin Khuê Ninh, "The Model Minority: Asian American Immigrant Families and Intimate Harm," *Kalfou* 1:2 (2014): 168–173; Keith Osajima, "Asian Americans as the Model Minority: An Analysis of the Popular Press Image in the 1960s and 1980s," in Gary Y. Okihiro, ed., *Reflections on Shattered Windows: Promises and Prospects for Asian American Studies* (Pullman: Washington State University Press, 1988), 165–174; Ellen Wu, *The Color of Success: Asian Americans and the Origins of the Model Minority* (Princeton, NJ: Princeton University Press, 2013); and Christine So, *Economic Citizens: A Narrative of Asian American Visibility* (Philadelphia: Temple University Press, 2007). On Canadian discourses, see Naoko Hawkins, "Becoming a Model Minority: The Depiction of Japanese Canadians in the *Globe and Mail*, 1946–2000," *Canadian Ethnic Studies* 41:1–2 (2009): 137–154; Marie Lo, "Model Minority, Models of Resistance: Native Figures in Asian Canadian Literature," Canadian Literature 196 (2008): 96–112.

107. Shibutani, *Derelicts of Company K*, ix.

108. Ibid., vii.

109. Ibid., ix.

110. Ibid., x–xi. Years later Shibutani would still continue to find the subject of wartime incarceration fraught. A former graduate student of his, William L. Shay, remarked on this in an article celebrating Shibutani's legacy: "Reflections on Tamotsu Shibutani: On a Biography and Sociology of America," *Symbolic Interaction* 28:4 (2005): 521–523. In the article, Shay remarked that "even decades later Tom was not comfortable speaking directly about his personal experience. In his graduate research methodology practicum, he shared that he was on safer ground emotionally and thus intellectually in treating his published works remotely, as objects of inquiry" (522).

111. Shibutani, *Derelicts of Company K*, 18.

112. May 13, 1942, journal entry by Shibutani, Japanese American Evacuation and Resettlement Records, BANCMSS 67/14c, reel 182: 524.

113. Tamotsu Shibutani, *Society and Personality: An Interactionist Approach to Social Psychology* (Englewood Cliffs, NJ: Prentice-Hall, 1961): 6–7.

114. Ibid., 4.

115. Ibid.

CHAPTER TWO

1. Mineta's liberalism reveals an idea of society similar to that laid out in Jürgen Habermas, *The Structural Transformation of the Public Sphere: An Inquiry into a Category of Bourgeois Society*, trans. Thomas Burger with Frederick Lawrence (Cambridge, MA: Harvard University Press, 1989). See also John Ehrenberg, *Civil*

Society: The Critical History of an Idea (New York: New York University Press, 1999); Nancy Fraser, "Rethinking the Public Sphere: A Contribution to the Critique of Actually Existing Democracy," *Social Text* 25/26 (1990): 56–80. The failure was not purely governmental, but also social and economic. See Roger Daniels, *The Politics of Prejudice: The Anti-Japanese Movement in California and the Struggle for Japanese Exclusion*, rev. ed. (Berkeley: University of California Press, 1977); Morton Grodzins, *Americans Betrayed* (Chicago: University of Chicago Press, 1949).

2. Mineta's fellow Nikkei legislators included Senator Spark Matsunaga (D-HI), Representative Robert Matsui (D-CA), and Senator Daniel Inouye (D-HI).

3. Harry H. L. Kitano, *Japanese Americans: Evolution of a Subculture* (Englewood Cliffs, NJ: Prentice-Hall, 1969).

4. Yasuko I. Takezawa, *Breaking the Silence: Redress and Japanese American Ethnicity* (Ithaca, NY: Cornell University Press, 1995).

5. "A Time to Look across the Pacific," remarks by Norman Mineta at the Commencement of the University of California, Berkeley, Asian Studies, May 23, 1987: 2 (Norman Mineta Papers, San Jose University Special Collections and Archives, box 101).

6. Peckham apparently did this on a fairly large scale, having used the same mechanism for Chinese and Filipinos, in addition to Nikkei. In the case of the Mineta family, this arrangement wound up being advantageous. As Mineta recounted in a June 3, 2006, interview, "Fortunately, many of our properties were not escheated by the government in 1942, just because of what Mr. Peckham had done in the '20s and '30s. So when we got our evacuation orders, we rented our home to a professor at San Jose State. . . . She and her mother lived in the home for the duration of World War II, and our properties were saved" (June 3, 2006, interview for the Academy of Achievement, http://www.achievement.org/autodoc/page/minoint-3).

7. Ibid. As Mineta pointed out, the FBI targeted community leaders, claiming that they would be in a particularly good position to aid any enemy activity.

8. Ibid.

9. Norman Mineta, interview by Tom Ikeda, July 4, 2008, Denshō Archive, Norman Mineta Collection, segment 1.

10. On that distaste for attracting attention, see Kitano, *Japanese Americans*.

11. "Mineta Named to Council," *San Jose News* 168:146 (July 11, 1967), 4, column 1.

12. An example is Wayne Kanemoto, who was the first Nisei in Northern California to be named to the bench. Kanemoto not only believed he represented other Japanese Americans but also credited them for "making it possible" for him to become a judge. He believed it was the collective attitude and conduct (i.e., "industry," "self-respect," "honesty," "responsibility") of Nikkei that helped him achieve his

post. He added that the Nikkei community impressed upon its members that it was "disgraceful" to be lacking these qualities. At the same time, when Kanemoto was sworn in 1961 he adopted a "forgive and forget" attitude toward wartime incarceration. This was an ironic development for someone whose wrongful imprisonment forced him to receive his law degree in absentia in 1942 and take the bar exam under guard in 1943. Furthermore, Kanemoto characterized Nikkei postwar attitudes as "without bitterness or rancor, neither vengeful nor anti-social." That attitude, he suggested, was pragmatic rather than performative: "We conducted ourselves in a manner showing willingness to forgive and forget, and to move on to the building of a new and better future for ourselves, and to move on to the building of a new and better community as good Americans, whether by birth or naturalization." "An American Story with Japanese Beginnings: New Judge Credits Fellow Nisei," *San Jose Mercury*, November 16, 1961 (Norman Mineta Papers, box 45).

13. For contemporaneous analysis of the decision, see Donna M. Murasky, "*James v. Valtierra*: Housing Discrimination by Referendum?," *University of Chicago Law Review* 39:1 (1971): 115–142. See also the report of the U.S. Commission on Civil Rights, *Equal Opportunity in Suburbia* (Washington, D.C.: Government Publications Office, 1974).

14. Statement of Norman Y. Mineta, mayor-elect of San Jose, California, before the U.S. Commission on Civil Rights, Washington, D.C., June 15, 1971: 7 (Norman Mineta Papers, box 101).

15. Ibid., 5–6.

16. Ibid., 4. Mineta refers here to the findings of Lyndon Johnson's Commission on Urban Housing, which was chaired by Henry Kaiser.

17. Ibid., 6.

18. Mineta, interview by Ikeda, segment 3.

19. Other Japanese American officials have been elected from Hawaii, which has a significant Japanese American population, including Daniel Inouye (elected in 1959), Patsy (Matsu Takemoto) Mink (1965), and Spark Masayuki Matsunaga (1977).

20. For another view of afterlife, personal testimony, and redress, see A. Naomi Paik, *Rightlessness: Testimony and Redress in U.S. Prison Camps since World War II* (Chapel Hill: University of North Carolina Press, 2016), esp. 19–83.

21. Commission on Wartime Relocation and Internment of Civilians, *Personal Justice Denied: Report of the Commission on Wartime Relocation and Internment of Civilians* (Washington, D.C.: Government Publications Office, 1982); and idem, *Personal Justice Denied, Part II: Recommendations* (Washington, D.C.: Government Publications Office, 1983). On the history of redress in the United States, see Alice Yang Murray, *Historical Memories of the Japanese American Internment and the Struggle for Redress* (Stanford, CA: Stanford University Press, 2008).

22. The term "model minority" appears in William Peterson, "Success Story, Japanese American Style," *New York Times Magazine*, January 6, 1966. For more on the concept with respect mainly to the United States, see Madeline Y. Hsu, *The Good Immigrants: How the Yellow Peril Became the Model Minority* (Princeton, NJ: Princeton University Press, 2015); Erin Khuê Ninh, "The Model Minority: Asian American Immigrant Families and Intimate Harm," *Kalfou* 1:2 (2014): 168–173; Keith Osajima, "Asian Americans as the Model Minority: An Analysis of the Popular Press Image in the 1960s and 1980s," in Gary Y. Okihiro, ed., *Reflections on Shattered Windows: Promises and Prospects for Asian American Studies* (Pullman: Washington State University Press, 1988), 165–174; Ellen Wu, *The Color of Success: Asian Americans and the Origins of the Model Minority* (Princeton, NJ: Princeton University Press, 2013); and Christine So, *Economic Citizens: A Narrative of Asian American Visibility* (Philadelphia: Temple University Press, 2007). Regarding Canada, see Naoko Hawkins, "Becoming a Model Minority: The Depiction of Japanese Canadians in the *Globe and Mail*, 1946–2000," *Canadian Ethnic Studies* 41:1–2 (2009): 137–154; Marie Lo, "Model Minority, Models of Resistance: Native Figures in Asian Canadian Literature," Canadian Literature 196 (2008): 96–112.

23. Think, for instance, of "working through" as described in Dominick LaCapra, *Writing History, Writing Trauma* (Baltimore: Johns Hopkins University Press, 2000).

24. Unless otherwise noted, the information in this section comes from Betty Cuniberti, "Internment: Personal Voices, Powerful Choices," *Los Angeles Times*, October 4, 1987, Part VI: 1, 10–12.

25. Mineta reiterated this story, and many others, in print in order to gather public support for redress. See, for instance, Norman Y. Mineta, "An American Tragedy, and Reparations," *San Jose Mercury News*, June 26, 1983, Section C: 1 and 4.

26. On the terms referring to the treatment of Japanese Americans and their family members, see Roger Daniels, "Words Do Matter: A Note on Inappropriate Terminology and the Incarceration of the Japanese Americans," in Louis Fiset and Gail Nomura, eds., *Nikkei in the Pacific Northwest: Japanese Americans and Japanese Canadians in the Twentieth Century* (Seattle: Center for the Study of the Pacific Northwest, 2005), 183–207.

27. As Mineta recounted, "We'd have a dry run to see how much we could carry, and how much we could pack into a suitcase. There was a list of contraband articles: regular AM radios, irons, cameras, knives, scissors in excess of four inches or so. The only special thing I took with me was a baseball mitt I had gotten as an Easter gift in 1941. You couldn't take a bat because that was a deadly weapon." Quoted in Cuniberti, "Internment," Part VI: 1.

28. Arthur Zich, "Japanese Americans: Home at Last," *National Geographic* 169:4 (1986): 528. Mineta is mentioned in this article about the postwar history of Japanese Americans, in which one of the main points is that "they have risen so

high and so fast, in fact, that they have been called a model minority—an epithet they deplore as simplistic, condescending, and forgetful of their traumatic history in the United States" (512). For more on that epithet, see note 22 above.

29. Irvin Molotsky, "The Heat of War Welds a Bond That Endures Across Aisles and Years," *New York Times*, April 26, 1988, A22.

30. Cuniberti, "Internment," Part VI: 11.

31. *Japanese American and Aleutian Wartime Relocation: Hearings before the Subcommittee on Administrative Law and Governmental Relations of the Committee on the Judiciary, House of Representatives, 98th Congress, Second Session on H.R. 3387, H.R. 4110, and H.R. 4322, June 20, 21, 27, and September 12, 1984* (Washington, D.C.: Government Publication Office, 1985): 75.

32. Testimony by Norman Y. Mineta before the House Committee on the Judiciary Subcommittee on Administrative Law and Governmental Relations, Washington, D.C., June 20, 1984: 3 (Norman Mineta Papers, box 101).

33. Ibid. The FBI had sent Hinoki to a camp near Bismarck, North Dakota.

34. Ibid. Mineta recounted this episode after noting that "one thousand, eight hundred and sixty two internees died while in camp, a figure which does not include people like my father-in-law." On social death, see Orlando Patterson, *Slavery and Social Death: A Comparative Study* (Cambridge, MA: Harvard University Press, 1985). See also Lisa Cacho, *Social Death: Racialized Rightlessness and the Criminalization of the Unprotected* (New York: New York University Press, 2012).

35. Testimony by Norman Y. Mineta before the House Committee on the Judiciary Subcommittee on Administrative Law and Governmental Relations, Washington, D.C., June 20, 1984, 11. In such moments, Mineta was providing an emotional counterpoint to his discussion of liquidating damages. A similar engagement also characterized discourses of redress in Canada. For more, see Jennifer Matsunaga, "Publics in the Making: A Genealogical Inquiry into the Discursive Publics of Japanese Canadian Redress" (MA thesis, Carleton University, 2011).

36. Testimony by Norman Y. Mineta before the House Committee on the Judiciary Subcommittee on Administrative Law and Governmental Relations, Washington, D.C., June 20, 1984.

37. Mineta expanded on this point by suggesting that "these payments are an essential element of the legislative package, and . . . any step short of compensation would be an empty gesture" (ibid., 4). Failure to provide liquidating damages would avoid making any kind of substantive attempt to rectify past wrongs and, thus, neutralize any verbal acknowledgment of wrongdoing.

38. Ibid., 4.

39. Ibid., 6.

40. Kandice Chuh, *Imagine Otherwise: On Asian Americanist Critique* (Durham, NC: Duke University Press, 2003), esp. chap. 2.

41. Testimony by Norman Y. Mineta before the House Committee on the Judiciary Subcommittee on Administrative Law and Governmental Relations, Washington, D.C., June 20, 1984: 7 (Norman Mineta Papers, box 101). For more on the reticence of Nikkei citizens to address wartime incarceration vocally, see Kitano, *Japanese Americans.*

42. Testimony by Norman Y. Mineta before the House Committee on the Judiciary Subcommittee on Administrative Law and Governmental Relations, Washington, D.C., June 20, 1984: 6 (Norman Mineta Papers, box 101).

43. Ibid.

44. See note 25 above.

45. Norman Y. Mineta, "Striving for Equality," presented at the "Division of Cultural Pluralism Colloquium," April 6, 1988, at San Jose State University: 6 (Norman Mineta Papers, box 101).

46. Testimony by Norman Y. Mineta before the House Committee on the Judiciary Subcommittee on Administrative Law and Governmental Relations, Washington, D.C., June 20, 1984: 5.

47. Mineta, interview by Ikeda, segment 4.

48. Ibid.

49. Ibid. On the relationship between redress and intergenerational tensions within both the JACL and the Japanese American community, see Greg Robinson, *A Tragedy of Democracy: Japanese Confinement in North America* (New York: Columbia University Press, 2009), 288–304; Leslie T. Hatamiya, *Righting a Wrong: Japanese Americans and the Passage of the Civil Liberties Act of 1988* (Stanford, CA: Stanford University Press, 1993).

50. On the Hawaiian Native claims bill, see Linda S. Parker, *Native American Estate: The Struggle over Indian and Hawaiian Lands* (Honolulu: University of Hawai'i Press, 1989), 135–137, which includes additional sources.

51. Commission on Wartime Relocation and Internment of Civilians, *Personal Justice Denied*; idem, *Personal Justice Denied, Part II.*

52. Norman Y. Mineta, testimony in support of the Civil Liberties Act of 1983 (H.R. 4110 and S. 2116) before the U.S. Senate Committee on Governmental Affairs Subcommittee on Civil Service, Post Office and General Government, Los Angeles, August 16, 1984: 3 (Norman Mineta Papers, box 101).

53. Norman Y. Mineta, "Redress: Triumph Awaits," remarks to the National Coalition for Redress/Reparations, June 27, 1987, San Francisco: 1 (Norman Mineta Papers, box 101).

54. Norman Y. Mineta, "Changing Times," remarks delivered at the Japanese American Art Memorial and Cultural Preservation Benefit Dinner, Fairmont Hotel, San Jose, CA, Sunday, February 7, 1988: 3 (Norman Mineta Papers, box 101).

55. Ibid., 4.

56. Mineta, interview by Ikeda, segment 4.

57. Ibid.

58. Ibid. The "Lost Battalion" was a unit in the 36th Infantry Division trapped by German soldiers in the Vosges Mountains in October 1944.

59. See Yang Murray, *Historical Memories*; and the *Robert Matsui Legacy Project: Road to Redress and Reparations*, California State History, Sacramento, Digital Collections, http://digital.lib.csus.edu/cdm/landingpage/collection/mats.

60. Mineta, interview by Ikeda, segment 5.

61. Ibid.

62. Ibid. According to Mineta, proposed legislation expires every two years, so he had to drop the bill in at the right time every two years to make sure it was numbered 442. It took eight years to get the bill passed.

63. Molotsky, "The Heat of War," A22.

64. Ibid.

65. Mineta, interview by Ikeda, segment 9.

66. The Clinton administration adopted several of the commission's recommendations regarding the Federal Aviation Administration.

67. William J. Clinton, "Remarks Announcing the Nomination of Norman Y. Mineta to Be Secretary of Commerce and Exchange With Reporters," *Weekly Compilation of Presidential Documents 36:26* (2000): 1540.

68. George W. Bush, "Remarks at the Swearing-In Ceremony for Norman Y. Mineta as Secretary of Transportation," *Weekly Compilation of Presidential Documents* 37:6 (2001): 273. Though its analysis pertains specifically to Canada, for another approach to the hazards of representation, see Kirsten Emiko McAllister, "Narrating Japanese Canadians in and out of the Canadian Nation: A Critique of Realist Forms of Representation," *Canadian Journal of Communication* 24:1 (1999), http://cjc-online.ca/index.php/journal/article/view/1083/989.

69. Norman Y. Mineta, "Mentoring Our Youth in Aviation," *Executive Speeches* 16:2 (2001): 28.

70. Ibid, 29.

71. This is not to suggest, however, that there were not missed opportunities. See, for example, Greg Robinson, *After Camp: Portraits in Midcentury Japanese American Life and Politics* (Berkeley: University of California Press, 2012), which discusses the possibility, during the redress movement, for building a coalition with other marginalized groups.

72. Mineta, "Striving for Equality," 7–8. On the model minority, see note 22 above. See also Mona Oikawa, *Cartographies of Violence: Japanese Canadian Women, Memory, and the Subjects of the Internment* (Toronto: University of Toronto Press, 2012), 50–54.

73. Mineta, "Mentoring Our Youth," 12.

74. Ibid., 16.

75. Ibid., 12.

76. "Bill to Compensate Japanese-Americans Nears Passage," *San Jose Mercury News*, September 12, 1987: 24A (Norman Mineta Papers, box 87b). For more on this dynamic, see Takezawa, *Breaking the Silence*; idem, "Children of Inmates: The Effects of the Redress Movement among Third Generation Japanese Americans," *Qualitative Sociology* 14:1 (1991): 39–56.

77. Mineta, interview by Ikeda, segment 10.

78. Mineta, "An American Tragedy," Section C: 4.

79. Mineta, interview by Ikeda, segment 10.

80. See, among others, Grodzins, *Americans Betrayed*; Jacobus tenBroek, Edward N. Barnhart, and Floyd W. Matson, *Prejudice, War, and the Constitution: Causes and Consequences of the Evacuation of the Japanese Americans in World War II* (Berkeley: University of California Press, 1954); and Brian Masaru Hayashi, *Democratizing the Enemy: The Japanese American Internment* (Princeton, NJ: Princeton University Press, 2008).

81. Norman Y. Mineta, "Facing the Tests of History," *Executive Speeches* 16:3 (December, 2001): 36.

82. Ibid., 34.

83. Ibid.

84. Ibid., 35.

85. Mineta made this statement during his presentation at the August 2011 dedication ceremony for the Heart Mountain Interpretive Center. A recording of Mineta's speech is available at http://www.c-span.org/video/?301340-1/heart-mountain-dedication-ceremony. On the relationship between past and present at Heart Mountain, see also Eric L. Muller, "Apologies or Apologists? Remembering the Japanese American Internment in Wyoming," *Wyoming Law Review* 1:2 (2001): 473–495; idem, "All the Themes But One," *University of Chicago Law Review* 66:4 (1999): 1395–1433.

86. Ibid.

CHAPTER THREE

1. As transcribed in Cassandra Kobayashi and Roy Miki, eds., *Spirit of Redress: Japanese Canadians in Conference* (Vancouver, BC: National Association of Japanese Canadians/Japanese Canadian Studies Society, 1989), 34.

2. Ann Gomer Sunahara, *The Politics of Racism: The Uprooting of Japanese Canadians during the Second World War* (Toronto, Lorimer, 1981), 7.

3. Roy Miki, *Redress: Inside the Japanese Canadian Call for Justice* (Vancouver, BC: Raincoast Books, 2005), 272–301; Roy Miki and Cassandra Kobayashi, *Justice in Our Time: The Japanese Canadian Redress Settlement* (Vancouver, BC: Talonbooks, 1991), 74–88.

4. Tokawa went on to point out that "there probably would have been such a protest that it still might not have gone through" even if voted up by the Parks Board (Kobayashi and Miki, *Spirit of Redress*, 34).

5. Kornel Chang, *Pacific Connections: The Making of the U.S.-Canadian Borderlands* (Berkeley: University of California Press, 2012).

6. For an in-depth discussion of redress in the United States, see Alice Yang Murray, *Historical Memories of the Japanese American Internment and the Struggle for Redress* (Stanford, CA: Stanford University Press, 2008). See also Mitchell T. Maki, Harry H. L Kitano, and S. Megan Berthold, *Achieving the Impossible Dream: How Japanese Americans Obtained Redress* (Urbana: University of Illinois Press, 1999); William Minoru Hohri, *Repairing America: An Account of the Movement for Japanese-American Redress* (Pullman: Washington State University Press, 1988); Commission on Wartime Relocation and Internment of Civilians, *Personal Justice Denied: Report of the Commission on Wartime Relocation and Internment of Civilians* (Washington, D.C.: Government Publications Office, 1982); and idem, *Personal Justice Denied, Part II: Recommendations* (Washington, D.C.: Government Publications Office, 1983).

7. See, for example, Yang Murray, *Historical Memories,* and Hohri, *Repairing America.*

8. Yang Murray, *Historical Memories.* At the same time, however, it must be noted that resistance to redress came not only from outside of Nikkei communities but also from within, particularly among older members who had lived through incarceration. Of particular concern for those wary of redress was the possibility of political reprisal. This is an understandable worry, given historical precedent. For more on intergenerational dynamics surrounding redress, see Miki, *Redress,* 63–168. On other factors that likely contributed to this resistance, Harry H. L. Kitano, *Japanese Americans: The Evolution of a Subculture,* rev. ed. (Englewood Cliffs, NJ: Prentice-Hall, 1969); Yasuko I. Takezawa, *Breaking the Silence: Redress and Japanese American Ethnicity* (Ithaca, NY: Cornell University Press, 1995). For another account of the evolution of Nikkei identity in the United States, see Paul Spickard, *Japanese Americans: The Formation and Transformations of an Ethnic Group* (New York: Twayne, 1996).

9. Miki, *Redress*; Maryka Omatsu, *Bittersweet Passage: Redress and the Japanese Canadian Experience* (Toronto: Between the Lines, 1992). Both authors attend to various differences between American and Canadian reparations, including how the viciousness of postwar dispersal policies in Canada was used to justify slightly higher financial compensation ($21,000 for Japanese Canadians, compared with the $20,000 that American Nikkei received). See also Arthur K. Miki, *The Japanese Canadian Redress Legacy: A Community Revitalized* (Winnipeg: National Association of Japanese Canadians, 2003); Kobayashi and Miki, *Spirit of Redress*; Miki and Kobayashi, *Justice in Our Time.*

10. Stanley Meisler, "Japanese Canadians Still Keep Low Profile after Evacuation Trauma," *New Canadian*, 47:22 (March 22, 1983): 1–3. For more on the place of Japanese Canadians in Vancouver, see Masumi Izumi, "Reclaiming and Reinventing 'Powell Street': Reconstruction of the Japanese-Canadian Community in Post–World War II Vancouver," in Louis Fiset and Gail Nomura, eds., *Nikkei in the Pacific Northwest: Japanese Americans and Japanese Canadians in the Twentieth Century* (Seattle: Center for the Study of the Pacific Northwest, 2005), 308–333; Patricia Roy, "The Re-Creation of Vancouver's Japanese Community, 1945–2008," *Journal of the Canadian Historical Association/Revue de la Société historique du Canada* 19:2 (2008): 127–154.

11. Miki, *Redress*, 164. Roy Miki is the brother of Arthur Miki, who, as president of the NAJC from 1984 to 1992, was a key figure in negotiating a settlement with the Canadian government.

12. The tag line with which the editors sold space promised "the best results from the J.C. Community."

13. On the economics of incarceration in Canada, see Mona Oikawa, *Cartographies of Violence: Japanese Canadian Women, Memory, and the Subjects of the Internment* (Toronto: University of Toronto Press, 2012), 167–202. See also Iyko Day, *Alien Capital: Asian Racialization and the Logic of Settler Colonial Capitalism* (Durham, NC: Duke University Press, 2016).

14. See Ken Adachi, *The Enemy That Never Was: An Account of the Deplorable Treatment Inflicted on Japanese Canadians during World War Two* (Toronto: McClelland and Stewart, 1976); Stephanie Bangarth, *Voices Raised in Protest: Defending North American Citizens of Japanese Ancestry, 1941–1949* (Vancouver: University of British Columbia Press, 2008); and, earlier, Sunahara, *The Politics of Racism*.

15. That fight had not only gained momentum, but also become a source of strife within the community itself. See Miki, *Redress*.

16. Stanley Meisler, "Japanese—Low Profile in Canada," *Los Angeles Times*, February 26, 1983: A1; *New Canadian*, March 22, 1983: 1.

17. I am following the suggestion of Christopher Lee that "the role of Asian Canadian Studies is to illuminate and unravel the complex interplay between socioeconomic power and personal experience" ("The Lateness of Asian Canadian Studies," in Henry Yu and Guy Beauregard, eds., "Pacific Canada: Beyond the 49th Parallel," special issue of *Amerasia Journal* 33:2 [2007]: 3).

18. The *Los Angeles Times* article depended in part on Meisler's interviews with Japanese Canadian activists. On the interviews and on the place of Meisler's article in debates about redress, see Miki, *Redress*, 148–150.

19. Iyko Day, "Lost in Transnation: Uncovering Asian Canada," in Yu and Beauregard, eds., "Pacific Canada," 73. Cf. Kandice Chuh, *Imagine Otherwise: On Asian Americanist Critique* (Durham, NC: Duke University Press, 2003), 33. Cat-

egorization even within relatively localized groups is fraught, a situation Sylvia J. Yanagisako summed up elegantly in the introduction to her study, *Transforming the Past: Tradition and Kinship among Japanese Americans* (Stanford, CA: Stanford University Press, 1985). She noted that, despite the generational and geographical differences between her and her subjects (Seattle-based Nikkei), "the people I interviewed frequently voiced their assumption that as 'Japanese Americans' we shared experiences, knowledge, attitudes, and vocabularies. At times we did" (9). For another approach to transnationality, see Micol Seigel, *Uneven Encounters: Making Race and Nation in Brazil and the United States* (Durham, NC: Duke University Press, 2009).

20. See, for instance, Lisa Lowe, *Immigrant Acts: On Asian American Cultural Politics* (Durham, NC: Duke University Press, 1996), 60–83 and 97–127; Roy Miki, "Altered States: Global Currents, The Spectral Nation, and the Production of 'Asian Canadian,'" *Journal of Canadian Studies/Revue d'études canadiennes* 35:3 (2000): 43–72; idem, "Unclassified Subjects: Question Marking 'Japanese Canadian' Identity," in Roy Miki, ed., *Broken Entries: Race, Subjectivity, Writing* (Toronto: Mercury Press, 1998), 181–204.

21. Miki, "Altered States," 53. An example of such action might be Kirsten Emiko McAllister, "Memoryscapes of Postwar British Columbia: A Look of Recognition," in Ashok Mathur, Jonathan Dewar, and Mike DeGagné, eds., *Cultivating Canada: Reconciliation Through the Lens of Cultural Diversity, Aboriginal Healing Foundation*, vol. 3 (Ottawa: Aboriginal Healing Foundation, 2011), 419–444. See also Donald Goellnicht's suggestion about the concept of a specifically Asian Canadian literature that "the term has validity only if it can be made to work for the benefit of Asian Canadians by performing as a sign under which forces fighting racism, classism, sexism, and colonialism can find some form of solidarity for the purposes of resistance to the dominant hegemony" (Donald Goellnicht, "A Long Labour: The Protracted Birth of Asian Canadian Literature," *Essays on Canadian Writing* 72 [Winter 2000]: 37). For an early analysis of the potential of Japanese Canadian redress, particularly with respect to formal "multicultural" initiatives, see Audrey Kobayashi, "The Japanese-Canadian Redress Settlement and Its Implications for 'Race Relations,'" *Canadian Ethnic Studies* 24:1 (1992): 1–19. On the interplay of Asian Canadian and Asian American in literature, see Marie Lo, "Fields of Recognition: Reading Asian Canadian Literature in Asian America" (PhD diss., University of California, Berkeley, 2001).

22. Miki had made a similar point in 1995, when he wrote that "Asian Canadian writers . . . have begun to interrogate and undermine representations of their communities manufactured by outsiders, often liberal and sympathetic white writers, artists, and film-makers whose intentions may be sincere but who fail to account for differences based on subjectivity, language, and the problematics of ap-

propriation." See Roy Miki, "Asiancy: Making Space for Asian Canadian Writing," in Gary Y. Okihiro, Marilyn Alquizola, Dorothy Fujita Rony, and K. Scott Wong, eds., *Privileging Positions: The Sites of Asian American Studies* (Pullman: Washington State University Press, 1995), 136. In some respects, his comment echoes Rey Chow's suggestion that "difference rather than sameness now becomes the key to a radicalized way of thinking about identity . . . so that (the experience of) dislocation per se, as it were, often becomes valorized and idealized—as what is different, mobile, contingent, indeterminable, and so on." Quoted in Christopher Lee's discussion of the post-identity turn in literature, *The Semblance of Identity: Aesthetic Mediation in Asian American Literature* (Stanford, CA: Stanford University Press, 2012), 4.

23. Miki, "Altered States," 56. Cf. Day's observation regarding the United States ("Lost in Transnation," 73) that "there are real life referents of the term 'Asian American,' which include its hard-won role as a state-recognized minority category for civil rights monitoring and its more negative existence in U.S. society as an undifferentiated 'foreign' population subject to racial hostilities."

24. Chuh, *Imagine Otherwise*, 83 (emphasis in the original). One thinks of Miki's observation in the introduction to *Redress* (vi) that, "In Canada, redress for abuses in the residential schools set up for aboriginal children has yet to be settled, and earlier redress calls for the head tax levied on Chinese Canadians and for the internment of Ukrainian Canadians during World War I have been denied—at least so far—by the federal government." Cf. note 22 above.

25. Miki, *Redress*, xiii.

26. Henry Yu, "Towards a Pacific History of the Americas," in Yu and Beauregard, eds., "Pacific Canada," xvii–xviii.

27. Miki, "Asiancy," 138.

28. Chuh, *Imagine Otherwise*, 62.

29. Before the bombing of Pearl Harbor the government of Prime Minister Mackenzie King used passport and visa controls to restrict the influx of immigrants, even as he also trumpeted his decision to open a legation in Tokyo. See John Price, *Orienting Canada: Race, Empire, and the Transpacific* (Vancouver: University of British Columbia Press, 2011), esp. 17, 31, and 138.

30. Russell C. Leong, "Parallel Pacifics," in Yu and Beauregard, eds., "Pacific Canada," iii.

31. On the complexities of Japanese American transnationality, see the work of Yuji Ichioka, in particular *Before Internment: Essays in Prewar Japanese American History*, eds. Gordon H. Chang and Eiichiro Azuma (Stanford, CA: Stanford University Press, 2006), as well as a special issue of *Amerasia Journal* Ichioka edited, "Beyond National Boundaries: The Complexity of Japanese-American History," 23:3 (1997–1998).

32. Chuh, *Imagine Otherwise*, 63–70.

33. Muriel Kitagawa, *This Is My Own: Letters to Wes and Other Writings on Japanese Canadians, 1941–1948*, ed. Roy Miki (Vancouver, BC: Talonbooks, 1985), 74.

34. *New Canadian*, April 8, 1983: 1. As the article went on to point out, Hayakawa "never faced internment because he was a native of Canada and lived in Chicago during the war." On the coercive circumstances of that "absorption," see Mae M. Ngai, *Impossible Subjects: Illegal Aliens and the Making of Modern America* (Princeton, NJ: Princeton University Press, 2004), 175–201.

35. The silences within many Nikkei families ultimately galvanized younger members to uncover the past, and to pursue new modes of Nikkei existence at odds with what Hayakawa considered a properly American way of being.

36. In early 1984, for instance, the NAJC established as one of its primary goals "review and amendment of the War Measures Act and relevant sections of the Charter of Rights and Freedoms so that no Canadian will ever again be subjected to the wrongs committed against Japanese Canadians during World War II" (quoted in Miki and Kobayashi, *Justice in Our Time*, 72). See also Sunahara, *The Politics of Racism*, 150–151.

37. Omatsu, *Bittersweet Passage*, 96.

38. Ibid., 95–96. On earlier manifestations of Nikkei activism in Canada, see Masumi Izumi, "The Japanese Canadian Movement: Migration and Activism before and after World War II," *Amerasia Journal* 33:2 (2007): 49–66.

39. Tamio Wakayama credits Sakata with initiating the project. See *Japanese Canadian Centennial Project Committee, A Dream of Riches: The Japanese Canadians, 1877–1977* (Vancouver/Toronto: Japanese Canadian Centennial Project/Dreadnaught, 1978), 3–4, which also includes Sakata's recollection regarding the man in question.

40. Izumi, "The Japanese Canadian Movement," 58.

41. Omatsu, *Bittersweet Passage*, 96. For a discussion of intergenerational dynamics south of the 49th parallel, see Yasuko I. Takezawa, "Children of Inmates: The Effects of the Redress Movement among Third Generation Japanese Americans," *Qualitative Sociology* 14:1 (1991): 39–56. Though much of what both Miki and Omatsu describe pertains to legal and economic issues, insofar as they "bear witness" to the suffering caused by wartime injustice, passages such as the one quoted here also exemplify the "subjectivism" of the 1980s redress discourse identified in Jennifer Matsunaga, "Publics in the Making: A Genealogical Inquiry into the Discursive Publics of Japanese Canadian Redress" (MA thesis, Carleton University, 2011), chap. 4.

42. Miki, *Redress*, esp. 144–150.

43. "Sodan Kai Next J.C. Redress [meeting] is Listed for Oct. 23 at JCC Centre," *New Canadian*, September 20, 1983: 1.

44. Roger Obata, quoted in Miki, *Redress*, 146.

45. On redress in the United States, see Alice Yang Murray, *Historical Memories of the Japanese American Internment and the Struggle for Redress* (Stanford, CA: Stanford University Press, 2008), which includes an extensive bibliography.

46. Miki, *Redress*, 145.

47. Miki defines *sodan-kai* as "arriving at a mutual decision through quiet group discussion" (*Redress*, 154n2). See also Omatsu, *Bittersweet Passage*. In autumn 1983 both the Sodan-kai and the JCCP Redress Committee came under fire from members of the Nikkei community who accused them of bias and of deviating from protocol in handling redress meetings.

48. A less benign version of this idea involved the Canadian government making a blanket apology and then establishing a fund for all Canadians, not just those whose families had been incarcerated. This initiative helped prompt the JCCP Redress Committee to organize community meetings in conjunction with a letter-writing campaign in favor of individual compensation. See Miki, *Redress*, 144–161, which also lists JCCP Redress Committee members (145n1).

49. Ibid., 113–126.

50. See ibid.; Omatsu, *Bittersweet Passage*.

51. Even the *New Canadian* quoted Wilson on this point (March 25, 1983: 1).

52. Quoted in Miki and Kobayashi, *Justice in Our Time*, 73.

53. Ibid., 79–84.

54. Miki, *Redress*, 153.

55. See, for instance, ibid., 303–307.

56. May 13, 1942, journal entry by Tamotsu Shibutani, Japanese American Evacuation and Resettlement Records, BANCMSS 67/14c, reel 182: 524. For a more recent approach to this idea, see Mae M. Ngai, "'An Ironic Testimony to the Value of American Democracy': Assimilationism and the World War II Internment of Japanese Americans," in Manisha Sinha and Penny von Eschen, eds., *Contested Democracy: Freedom, Race, and Power in American History* (New York: Columbia University Press, 2007), 237–257; idem, *Impossible Subjects*, 175–201. For more first-person accounts of incarceration, see the work of Arthur A. Hansen, especially his *Japanese American World War II Evacuation Oral History Project* (Munich: K.G. Sauer, 1991–1995).

57. May 13, 1942, journal entry by Tamotsu Shibutani, Japanese American Evacuation and Resettlement Records, BANCMSS 67/14c, reel 182: 524.

58. On the disenfranchisement of Nikkei in Canada, see Price, *Orienting Canada*, 17, 113.

59. Kitagawa was on the staff of the *New Canadian*, where she published extensively before and during incarceration. For her biography, see Kitagawa, *This Is My Own*, esp. 20–32.

60. Kitagawa, *This Is My Own*, 74.

61. Meisler, "Japanese," 16 (*Los Angeles Times*); 2 (*New Canadian*).

62. Benedict Anderson, *Imagined Communities: Reflections on the Origin and Spread of Nationalism*, rev. ed. (London: Verso, 1991).

63. Mark Suzuki, "Questions and Answers on J.C. Redress by National Association," *New Canadian*, July 19, 1983: 1.

64. Ibid.

65. Ibid. In this respect, the article is a prime example of how a community imagines itself.

66. Ibid.

67. The internal conflicts roiling the Japanese Canadian community also had a formative effect on it. Several newspaper articles and editorials from that period suggest as much, particularly in their frequent call for greater unity of purpose, a review of the NAJC leadership, and the like.

68. Meisler, "Japanese," A1 (*Los Angeles Times*); 1 (*New Canadian*).

69. Ibid.

70. "$20,000 to Each Survivor of Nikkei Concentration Camp Says US Federal Study Group," *New Canadian*, June 28, 1983: 1.

71. Brian Power, "When It Was a Crime to Be Canadian of Japanese Descent," *New Canadian*, June 28, 1983: 3. On the NCJAR and its relationship to the JACL, see Yang Murray, *Historical Memories*, 301ff.

72. Vic Ogura, "Would You Support These Fellow Canadians?," *New Canadian*, September 6, 1983: 1.

73. Maryka Omatsu, "Redress Options," *New Canadian*, May 6, 1983: 1.

74. Ibid.

75. See, for instance, Miki, *Redress*, 154–185.

76. Frank Moritsugu, "Redress Becoming Everybody's Business," *New Canadian*, October 18, 1983: 2.

77. Susan Phillips, "A Life in the Day of Gordon Kadota," *New Canadian*, March 25, 1983: 2. On the relationship between economic conditions and anti-Asian sentiment, see also Alexander Saxton, *The Indispensable Enemy: Labor and the Anti-Chinese Movement in California* (Berkeley: University of California Press, 1971).

78. Kadota went on to talk about his own experience of the war, which broke up the Kadota family in an unusual way: he, three (of six other) siblings, and their mother went to Japan before the bombing of Pearl Harbor. On returning to Canada in 1952, he and his brothers had to sponsor his father, who had relinquished his citizenship and returned to Japan in 1943 in order to rejoin his wife and children there (Phillips, "A Life in the Day of Gordon Kadota," 2).

79. For a different account of what it meant to be Japanese Canadian in 1983, see Sally Ito, "Sansei Looks at Canadian 'Biculturalism,'" *New Canadian*, September 20, 1983: 1–2.

80. Roland Kawano, "Reflections on Redress in the Japanese Community," *New Canadian*, September 30, 1983: 1.

81. Thanks to Christopher Lee for helping me formulate this idea. See also

Chang, *Pacific Connections*; and Lisa Rose Mar, *Brokering Belonging: Chinese in Canada's Exclusion Era, 1885–1945* (Oxford: Oxford University Press, 2010).

82. Tom Shoyama, who had held several appointed governmental positions, spoke of this sense as a major obstacle to seeking redress. See Miki, *Redress*, 247.

83. On the postwar dispersal of Nikkei in Canada and its place in the contemporaneous discourses of race, see Price, *Orienting Canada*, 112, 128–147.

84. "M.P. Ian Waddell Asks Measures to Offset J.C. Evacuation Treatment in House of Commons on Jan. 21," *New Canadian*, February 11, 1983: 1.

85. Trudeau had, perversely, already made an apology during a visit to Japan, as M.P. Waddell pointed out (ibid.).

86. Ibid.

87. "Redress Compensation by 'Moral and Ethical Routes Rather Than through Courts,' Says Nikkei Prof. Roy Miki," *New Canadian*, April 22, 1983: 1.

88. Ibid., 2.

89. Ibid., 1.

90. Ibid.

91. Frank Moritsugu, "All Those Books about Us JCs," *New Canadian*, July 29, 1983: 1–2.

92. He was echoing a sentiment Bill Hosokawa had expressed in a 1980 editorial in the *New Canadian* that "Japanese Americans these days have been poked, probed, weighed, biopsied, analyzed, x-rayed and dissected as thoroughly as any American group." Bill Hosokawa, "Haji vs. Emotional Vulnerability," *New Canadian*, November 14, 1980: 4.

93. See, for instance, Bill Hosokawa, "Dr. Harry Kitano's Book 'Japanese Americans,'" *New Canadian*, May 11, 1976: 1–2. Interestingly, here too Hosokawa suggested that "we must be one of the most studied, most investigated, most written-about minorities in the country" (1).

94. Bill Marutani, "Inter-Racial Marriages," *New Canadian*, March 11, 1983: 1–2. Cf. Audrey Kobayashi, "Intermarriage among Japanese Canadians: Cultural Rejection or Intercultural Tolerance?," *Horizons Interculturels* 26 (1992): 6–18.

95. Ronald Tanaka, "The Paradox of Identity," *New Canadian*, June 3, 1983: 1–4. Tanaka's article originally appeared in *State of the Arts*, a publication of the California Arts Council. Patty Wada, "Nikkei Culture Facing Extinction? 'No Way, Jose!' Says Nikkei Writer," *New Canadian*, July 15, 1983: 1–2.

96. Tanaka, "Paradox of Identity," 1.

97. Ibid., 3.

98. I owe Christopher Lee a debt of gratitude for bringing this fact to my attention.

99. Wada, "Nikkei Culture Facing Extinction?," 1.

100. The terms come from Tanaka, "Paradox of Identity," 2. Wada talked at

length of the arts scene in San Francisco and Los Angeles (1) and pointed out the importance of playwright Lane Nishikawa and the jazz bassist Mark Izu (2), both of whom are based in California. She also was careful to point out how close San Francisco's Nikkei cultural resources were to Sacramento, where Tanaka lived and worked.

101. Tanaka, "Paradox of Identity," 3.

102. Ibid., 4: "Most Nisei were and still are intensely loyal to their people. But the war, the evacuation and other factors like discrimination, demography and sheer economic survival tilted the scale towards Americanization."

103. Teresa Watanabe, editorial reprinted in *New Canadian*, June 3, 1983: 1–2.

104. Ibid., 2 (emphasis in the original).

105. Chang, *Pacific Connections*.

106. George Imai, "Canadians Urged to Attend 1st Pan-Am Nikkei Confab Slated July 22–29," *New Canadian*, June 16, 1981: 1. On the complexities of Nikkei identity, see Lane Ryo Hirabayashi, Akemi Kikumura-Yano, and James A. Hirabayashi, eds., *New Worlds, New Lives: Globalization and People of Japanese Descent in the Americas and from Latin America in Japan* (Stanford, CA: Stanford University Press, 2002). See also Akemi Kikumura-Yano, ed., *Encyclopedia of Japanese Descendants in the Americas: An Illustrated History* (Walnut Creek, CA: AltaMira Press, 2002).

107. Roy Kiyooka, "We Asian North Americanos: An Unhistorical 'Take' on Growing Up Yellow in a White World," *West Coast Line* 24:3 (1990): 118.

108. Gordon Hirabayashi, "Can the Second World War Tragedy Happen Again?," *New Canadian*, July 8, 1983: 1.

109. Ibid., 2. The NAJC has demonstrated a similarly expansive approach to its political undertakings. See Masumi Izumi, "Lessons from History: Japanese Canadians and Civil Liberties in Canada," *Journal of American and Canadian Studies* 17 (1999): 1–24.

110. Hirabayashi was articulating a widespread recognition of common interests. The editorial by Roland Kawano, for instance, observed that "the Jewish experience and the Japanese experience are full of great anguish, of individuals and families suffering great privation," despite profound differences of historical circumstance (Kawano, "Reflections," 2). That sense of shared anguish, he suggested, was part of the reason Jews had been vigorous supporters of Nikkei redress. On the complexities of interethnic and interracial political engagement, see Greg Robinson, *After Camp: Portraits in Midcentury Japanese American Life and Politics* (Berkeley: University of California Press, 2012), esp. chaps. 6–12.

CHAPTER FOUR

1. "Bill to Compensate Japanese-Americans Nears Passage," *San Jose Mercury News*, September 12, 1987: 24A (Norman Mineta Papers, San Jose University Special Collections and Archives, box 87b). On the intergenerational reverberation

of wartime injustice among Canadians of Japanese ancestry, see Mona Oikawa, *Cartographies of Violence: Japanese Canadian Women, Memory, and the Subjects of the Internment* (Toronto: University of Toronto Press, 2012), 226–266; Yasuko I. Takezawa, *Breaking the Silence: Redress and Japanese American Ethnicity* (Ithaca, NY: Cornell University Press, 1995); idem, "Children of Inmates: The Effects of the Redress Movement among Third Generation Japanese Americans," *Qualitative Sociology* 14:1 (1991): 39–56. See also Audrey Kobayashi, "Learning Their Place: Japanese/Canadian Workers/Mothers," in idem, ed., *Women, Work and Place* (Montreal: McGill-Queen's University Press, 1994), 45–72.

2. On this dynamic and its relationship to postmemory, see Marianne Hirsch, "Past Lives: Postmemories in Exile," *Poetics Today* 17:4 (1996): 659–686; Yến Lê Espiritu, *Body Counts: The Vietnam War and Militarized Refugees* (Berkeley: University of California Press, 2014), esp. chap. 6.

3. From Warren Furutani's presentation at "Community Builders: Japanese American Activism 1960–1980, Part I," October 8, 2011, Japanese American National Museum, Los Angeles. A video recording of part of Furutani's speech is available on the Manzanar Committee's YouTube channel. See http://www.youtube.com/watch?v=65smkPI4AYs. Cf. the account provided by Alice Yang Murray, *Historical Memories of the Japanese American Internment and the Struggle for Redress* (Stanford, CA: Stanford University Press, 2008), 207–208.

4. Mary Douglas, *Natural Symbols: Explorations in Cosmology* (New York: Vintage Books, 1973), chap. 5.

5. Avery F. Gordon, *Ghostly Matters: Haunting and the Sociological Imagination* (Minneapolis: University of Minnesota Press, 1997).

6. Warren Furutani, interview by Karen M. Inouye, Sacramento, CA, June 26, 2012. For more on that dynamic, see Takezawa, *Breaking the Silence, and idem,* "Children of Inmates."

7. Furutani Sr. returned from active duty earlier than expected. According to Furutani, his father claimed that it was when Hitler found out Furutani Sr. "was coming that he [Hitler] gave up." Furutani, interview.

8. Ibid.

9. Ibid.

10. Ibid.

11. Ibid.

12. Ibid.

13. Ibid.

14. Ibid.

15. Stokely Carmichael, "Black Power," October 29, 1966, Berkeley, California, http://voicesofdemocracy.umd.edu/carmichael-black-power-speech-text/. Cf. the engagements of Richard Aoki and Yuri Kochiyama as described in Yuri Kochiyama,

Passing It On: A Memoir (Los Angeles: UCLA Asian American Studies Center Press, 2004); Diane C. Fujino, *Samurai among Panthers: Richard Aoki on Race, Resistance, and a Paradoxical Life* (Minneapolis: University of Minnesota Press, 2012); idem, *Heartbeat of Struggle: The Revolutionary Life of Yuri Kochiyama* (Minneapolis: University of Minnesota Press, 2005).

16. Furutani, interview.

17. Ibid.

18. *Amerasia* staff, "An Interview with Warren Furutani," *Amerasia Journal* 1:1 (1971): 74. On Asian American activisms in general, see Karen L. Ishizuka, *Serve the People: Making Asian America in the Long Sixties* (New York: Verso, 2016).

19. The matter remains fraught. See Kirsten Emiko McAllister, "Narrating Japanese Canadians in and out of the Canadian Nation: A Critique of Realist Forms of Representation," *Canadian Journal of Communication* 24:1 (1999), http://cjc-online .ca/index.php/journal/article/view/1083/989.

20. *Amerasia* staff, "Interview," 73.

21. Yang Murray, *Historical Memories*, 206–207.

22. Former inmates had been returning annually to Manzanar ever since it was vacated, but the 1969 gathering was the first formal pilgrimage for friends and family members who had been interned there (or even elsewhere). See Joanne Doi, "Bridge to Compassion: Theological Pilgrimage to Tule Lake and Manzanar" (PhD diss., Graduate Theological Union, Berkeley, 2007); idem, "Tule Lake Pilgrimage: Dissonant Memories, Sacred Journey," in Jane Naomi Iwamura and Paul Spickard, eds., *Revealing the Sacred in Asian and Pacific America* (London: Routledge, 2003), 273–290.

23. Furutani, interview.

24. On the relationship between voice and history in Canada, see Roy Miki, "Asiancy: Making Space for Asian Canadian Writing," in Gary Y. Okihiro, Marilyn Alquizola, Dorothy Fujita Rony, and K. Scott Wong, eds., *Privileging Positions: The Sites of Asian American Studies* (Pullman: Washington State University Press, 1995), 135–151; and Oikawa, *Cartographies of Violence*, esp. 17–18, 56–78.

25. Roy Kiyooka, "We Asian North Americanos: An Unhistorical 'Take' on Growing Up Yellow in a White World," *West Coast Line* 24:3 (1990): 117. Kiyooka dates this text to 1975; he read it at the 1981 Japanese Canadian/Japanese American Symposium in Seattle.

26. Other Japanese Americans were also making the connection between black voices, black activism, and the need for analogous work by Nikkei. Reflecting on the 1960s, Donald Hata, professor emeritus of history at California State University, Dominguez Hills, said in a lecture to the Albany Civil Rights Institute: "I think it's time for Japanese Americans to say 'thank you' to African Americans because of the example they set for us during the Civil Rights Movement." He added: "A great deal has changed since the Civil Rights Movement. We owe a lot to

the Movement." Hata was referring to the inspiration the movement provided for Nikkei to fight for redress. Like Furutani when he heard Carmichael's speech, Hata considered the civil rights movement, and black leaders in particular, as models for criticizing injustice and seeking redress: "The Movement gave us inspiration for our own redress of crimes committed against us." See Terry Lewis, "Historian Pays Tribute to Civil Rights Movement," *Albany Herald*, December 17, 2010, reprinted in the San Francisco-based *Nichi Bei Weekly*, January 6–12, 2011. 3. See also Donald Hata and Nadine Hata, *Japanese Americans and World War II: Mass Removal, Imprisonment and Redress* (Wheeling, IL: Harlan Davidson, 1995). During Furutani's own period of reflection during the 1960s, he became convinced that Nikkei needed to return to their memories of wartime incarceration more than once in order to more fully integrate them. During the 1940s and well into the 1960s, "camp" was not talked about in the Japanese American community even though it was an ever-present echo in the lives of most Nikkei (Furutani, interview).

27. Furutani, interview.

28. Karen Piper, *Left in the Dust: How Race and Politics Created a Human and Environmental Tragedy in L.A.* (New York: Palgrave Macmillan, 2006), chap. 4.

29. See most recently, for instance, Eric L. Muller, ed., *Colors of Confinement: Rare Kodachrome Photographs of Japanese American Incarceration in World War II* (Chapel Hill: University of North Carolina Press, 2012); Jasmine Alinder, *Moving Images: Photography and the Japanese American Incarceration* (Urbana: University of Illinois Press, 2009). Kirsten Emiko McAllister has written eloquently about the problematics of representing the sites of wartime incarceration. See, e.g., *Terrain of Memory: A Japanese Canadian Memorial Project* (Vancouver: University of British Columbia Press, 2010), as well as "Archive and Myth: The Changing Memoryscape of Japanese Canadian Internment Camps," in James Opp and John C. Walsh, eds., *Placing Memory and Remembering Place in Canada* (Vancouver: University of British Columbia Press, 2010), 215–246; and "Photographs of a Japanese Canadian Internment Camp: Mourning Loss and Invoking a Future," *Visual Studies* 21:2 (2006): 133–156. On memory and the necessity of judgment, see Eric L. Muller, "Apologies or Apologists? Remembering the Japanese American Internment in Wyoming," *Wyoming Law Review* 1:2 (2001): 473–495.

30. Furutani, presentation at "Community Builders."

31. As quoted in Gann Matsuda, "Manzanar Committee Statement on the Passing of Victor H. Shibata, One of the Founding Members of the Manzanar Pilgrimage," http://blog.manzanarcommittee.org/2012/04/19/manzanar-committee -statement-on-the-passing-of-victor-h-shibata-one-of-the-founders-of-the-manza nar-pilgrimage/. Cf. Oikawa, *Cartographies of Violence*, 251–254.

32. This paragraph depends on the narrative recounted in Yang Murray, *Historical Memories*, 208–210.

33. Cf. more global efforts documented in Judy Tzu-Chun Wu, *Radicals on the Road: Internationalism, Orientalism, and Feminism during the Vietnam Era* (Ithaca, NY: Cornell University Press, 2013).

34. Ibid. Regarding how learning about camp through the redress movement affected younger Nikkei—particularly their ideas of assimilation, silence, and keeping a generally low cultural profile—see Takezawa, *Breaking the Silence*, and idem, "Children of Inmates." For Embrey's account of the pilgrimages, see Sue Kunitomi-Embrey, "From Manzanar to the Present: A Personal Journey," in Erica Harth, ed., *Last Witnesses: Reflections on the Wartime Internment of Japanese Americans* (New York: Palgrave, 2001), 167–185.

35. Furutani, presentation at "Community Builders."

36. More recently the pilgrimage has become more historically minded and self-consciously instructional.

37. On the religious implications of the Manzanar pilgrimages, see Doi, "Bridge to Compassion"; idem, "Tule Lake Pilgrimage"; Jane Naomi Iwamura, "Critical Faith: Japanese Americans and the Birth of a New Civil Religion," *American Quarterly* 59:3 (2007): 937–968. Although the weather was far from ideal for travel, in retrospect Shibata (like Furutani) felt that it gave the travelers a chance to more accurately experience the harshness of their parents' living conditions. See Matsuda, "Manzanar Committee Statement."

38. Unsurprisingly, some Japanese Americans resisted the pilgrimage. Many Nisei wondered why Furutani was digging up the past. They thought it was better left buried (Furutani, interview).

39. In addition to being one of the first of her generation who later spoke out against the wartime treatment of Nikkei, Embrey was the main organizer of the pilgrimage for the next thirty-seven years. http://www.nps.gov/history/museum/exhibits/manz/pilgrimage.html.

40. Approximately 150 people died in Manzanar. Most were cremated; some were buried in a makeshift cemetery. Manzanar Exhibit, National Park Service, http://www.nps.gov/history/museum/exhibits/manz/cemetery.html.

41. Because Wakahiro and Maeda spoke only Japanese, Furutani and Shibata brought along an interpreter. Furutani, interview.

42. Ibid.

43. Ibid.

44. Cf. the intergenerational impact of redress as discussed by Takezawa, "Children of Inmates," 49–50; Takezawa, *Breaking the Silence*.

45. Takezawa, "Children of Inmates," 54.

46. On the most notable of those silences, see Caroline Chung Simpson, *An Absent Presence: Japanese Americans in Postwar American Culture, 1945–1960* (Durham, NC: Duke University Press, 2002).

47. As quoted on the Manzanar Committee website, http://www.manzanarcom mittee.org/The_Manzanar_Committee/About_Us.html.

48. Yang Murray, *Historical Memories*, 268–270, 497–498n120.

49. Bill Hosokawa, *JACL in Quest of Justice: The History of the Japanese American Citizens League* (New York: Morrow, 1982), 325–330; Lon Kurashige, *Japanese American Celebration and Conflict: A History of Ethnic Identity and Festival, 1934–1990* (Berkeley: University of California Press, 2002), 160–163.

50. Michi Weglyn, *Years of Infamy: The Untold Story of America's Concentration Camps* (New York: Morrow, 1976), 278.

51. Embrey, "From Manzanar to the Present," 177.

52. On other aspects of these efforts, see Masumi Izumi, "Japanese American Internment and the Emergency Detention Act (Title II of the Internal Security Act of 1950), 1941–1971: Balancing Internal Security and Civil Liberties in the United States" (PhD diss., Doshisha University, 2003); idem, "Prohibiting 'American Concentration Camps': Repeal of the Emergency Detention Act and the Public Historical Memory of the Japanese American Internment," *Pacific Historical Review* 74:2 (2005): 165–193; and idem, "Rumors of 'American Concentration Camps': The Emergency Detention Act and the Public Fear of Political Repression, 1966–1971," *Doshisha Studies in Language and Culture* 4:4 (2002): 737–766.

53. Cindy I-Fen Cheng, *Citizens of Asian America: Democracy and Race during the Cold War* (New York: New York University Press, 2013), chap. 4.

54. Quoted in Yang Murray, *Historical Memories*, 268.

55. The classic counterexample is Richard Serra's *Tilted Arc*. Although Serra's object was not a memorial per se, the fate of his object demonstrates how strong triumphalist and aestheticist ideals can be even in relatively unproblematic places. *Tilted Arc* ultimately was destroyed because it failed to adhere to colloquial ideas about public art. See Sherrill Jordan, *Public Art, Public Controversy: The Tilted Arc on Trial* (New York: American Council for the Arts, 1987); Clara Weyergraf-Serra and Martha Buskirk, eds., *The Destruction of Tilted Arc* (Cambridge, MA: MIT Press, 1991).

56. Cf. Roy Miki's similar observation about the apology by Prime Minister Mulroney in 1988: "Redress was a thing in the future. When it was done, there was a loss because that history then got absorbed into the official history of Canada. And that official history, of course, to a certain extent is mediated and managed by the state." See Guy Beauregard, "After Redress: A Conversation with Roy Miki," *Canadian Literature* 201 (2009): 73.

57. Embrey, "From Manzanar to the Present," 179.

58. Yang Murray, *Historical Memories*, 269–275.

59. Quoted on the California State Parks Service website, http://ohp.parks.ca .gov/?page_id=21422.

60. Sue Kunitomi Embrey has recalled significant resistance, particularly among Nisei, to the publicity that pilgrimages might attract. See Yang Murray, *Historical Memories*, 212.

61. California Assembly Bill No. 1775 (filed September 24, 2010), http://www .leginfo.ca.gov/pub/09-10/bill/asm/ab_1751-1800/ab_1775_bill_20100924_chaptered .html.

62. Korematsu tells of visiting the local recruitment office in the company of white friends and being rejected on explicitly racial grounds.

63. Boston University Public Interest Law Journal Staff, "Japanese American Internment: An Interview with Fred Korematsu," *Boston University Public Interest Law Journal* 99:3 (1993): 100.

64. For an in-depth discussion of the 1983 reversal and related cases, see Peter Irons, *The Courage of Their Convictions* (New York: Penguin, 1988); idem, *Justice at War: The Story of the Japanese American Internment Cases* (Berkeley: University of California Press, 1993); Lorraine K. Bannai, *Enduring Conviction: Fred Korematsu and His Quest for Justice* (Seattle: University of Washington Press, 2015); idem, "Taking the Stand: The Lessons of Three Men Who Took the Japanese American Internment to Court," *Seattle Journal for Social Justice* 4:1 (2005): 1–57; Roger Daniels, *The Japanese American Cases: The Rule of Law in Time of War* (Lawrence: University Press of Kansas, 2013).

65. They operated in tandem with two other teams, each located in the city where their clients lived: Seattle, Washington, and Portland, Oregon. See Irons, *Justice at War*. On the legal issues at stake, see Marc Hideo Iyeki, "The Japanese American Coram Nobis Cases: Exposing the Myth of Disloyalty," *New York University Review of Law and Social Change* 13 (1984–1985): 199–221.

66. *Korematsu v. United States*, 584 F. Supp. 1406, 16 Fed. R. Evid. Serv. 1231 (N.D. Cal. April 19, 1984). For a recent discussion of Patel's decision in historical context, see Natsu Taylor Saito, "Interning the 'Non-Alien' Other: The Illusory Protections of Citizenship," in Eric L. Muller, ed., "Judgments Judged and Wrongs Remembered: Examining the Japanese American Civil Liberties Cases on Their Sixtieth Anniversary," a special issue of *Law and Contemporary Problems* 68:2 (2005): 173–213.

67. However, it did little to undo the profound economic difficulties Korematsu had faced as a result of his wartime conviction.

68. Simpson, *An Absent Presence*.

69. Karl F. Morrison, *I Am You: The Hermeneutics of Empathy in Western Literature, Theology, and Art* (Princeton, NJ: Princeton University Press, 1988). See also Kirsten Emiko McAllister, "Memoryscapes of Postwar British Columbia: A Look of Recognition," in Ashok Mathur, Jonathan Dewar, and Mike DeGagné, eds., *Cultivating Canada: Reconciliation Through the Lens of Cultural Diversity, Aboriginal Healing Foundation*, vol. 3 (Ottawa: Aboriginal Healing Foundation, 2011), 440–441.

70. Korematsu, as quoted in Bannai, "Taking the Stand,"33.

71. Korematsu, as quoted in ibid., 34.

72. From a presentation by Fred Korematsu at the Japanese American National Museum conference "Judgments Judged and Wrongs Remembered: Examining the Japanese American Civil Liberties Cases of World War II on Their 60th Anniversary," Los Angeles, November 5–6, 2004, as quoted in Bannai, "Taking the Stand," 12. Elsewhere, Korematsu said that his fellow inmates "knew about me and they kept away from me. They figured I was a troublemaker. Because they were already interned, they feared for their lives. They were also concerned about their parents' safety. They were afraid of what harm would come to them. So they wanted to be good Americans by going along with the internment—with what the government wanted, with what America wanted. They didn't like what I was doing" (Boston University Public Interest Law Journal Staff, "An Interview with Fred Korematsu," 102).

73. Quoted in Bannai, "Taking the Stand," 12.

74. Clifford Geertz, "Common Sense as a Cultural System," *Antioch Review* 33 (1975): 47–53.

75. Quoted in Bannai, "Taking the Stand," 15.

76. Boston University Public Interest Law Journal Staff, "An Interview with Fred Korematsu," 100.

77. http://www.korematsuinstitute.org.

78. http://korematsuinstitute.org/fredkorematsuday/curriculum/.

CHAPTER FIVE

1. Portions of this chapter appeared in Karen M. Inouye, "Eternal Present: Retroactive Diplomas in Canada and the US," *Journal of Asian American Studies* 17:3 (2014): 339–366.

2. On literature, see Joy Kogawa's *Obasan* (Boston: D.R. Godine, 1981), and John Okada's *No-No Boy* (Rutland, VT: Tuttle, 1957); on the visual arts, see the work of Miné Okubo (e.g., *Citizen 13660*), and films such as *The Cats of Mirikitani* (Hattendorf, 2006). On visual expression in the camps, see most recently Delphine Hirasuna, *The Art of Gaman: Arts and Crafts from the Japanese American Internment Camps 1942–1946* (Berkeley: Ten Speed Press, 2005), which includes a bibliography on the topic.

3. On the benefits and drawbacks of such an approach, see Kandice Chuh, *Imagine Otherwise: On Asian Americanist Critique* (Durham, NC: Duke University Press, 2003); Iyko Day, "Lost in Transnation: Uncovering Asian Canada," in Henry Yu and Guy Beauregard, eds., "Pacific Canada: Beyond the 49th Parallel," special issue of *Amerasia Journal* 33:2 (2007): 69–86; Roy Kiyooka, "We Asian North Americanos: An Unhistorical 'Take' on Growing Up Yellow in a White World," *West Coast Line* 24:3 (1990): 116–118; Lisa Lowe, *Immigrant Acts: On Asian American Cultural Politics* (Durham, NC: Duke University Press, 1996), 60–83, 97–127; Roy

Miki, "Altered States: Global Currents, the Spectral Nation, and the Production of 'Asian Canadian,'" *Journal of Canadian Studies/Revue d'études canadiennes* 35:3 (2000): 43–72.

4. John H. Provinse, "Relocation of Japanese-American College Students: Acceptance of a Challenge," *Higher Education* 1:8 (April 16, 1945): 1–4. On the topic more generally, see Allan W. Austin, *From Concentration Camp to Campus: Japanese American Students and World War II* (Urbana: University of Illinois Press, 2004), which provides a detailed account of the NJASRC and its efforts to relocate Nisei college students.

5. For more on the number of students affected by Executive Order 9066, where some of these students had gone, and where the remainder might go, see Provinse, "Relocation." See also Margaret Cosgrove, "Relocation of American-Japanese Students," *Journal of the American Association of Collegiate Registrars* 18:3 (1943): 221–226; Forrest E. La Violette, "The American-Born Japanese and the World Crisis," *Canadian Journal of Economics and Political Science* 7:4 (1941): 517–552; National Japanese American Student Relocation Council, *From Camp to College: The Story of Japanese American Student Relocation* (Philadelphia: National Japanese American Student Relocation Council, 1945); idem, *How to Help Japanese American Student Relocation* (Philadelphia: National Japanese American Student Relocation Council, 1944); Robert W. O'Brien, "The Changing Role of the College Nisei during the Crisis Period: 1931–1945" (PhD diss., University of Washington, 1945); and Provinse, "Relocation of Japanese-American College Students." See also Gary Y. Okihiro, *Storied Lives: Japanese American Students and World War II* (Seattle: University of Washington Press, 1999).

6. See, for example, his correspondence with the dean of the UW Law School, http://www.lib.washington.edu/exhibits/harmony/interrupted_lives/text/law.jpg.

7. Quoted in "Relocating Japanese American Students," *Education for Victory* 1:14 (1942): 24, https://www.lib.washington.edu/exhibits/harmony/interrupted_lives/text/ev.pdf.

8. Ibid., 2.

9. Ibid.

10. On the relocation of Nikkei students, see Austin, *From Concentration Camp to Campus.*

11. Ibid., 77.

12. On Nikkei resettlement, see Greg Robinson, *A Tragedy of Democracy: Japanese Confinement in North America* (New York: Columbia University Press, 2009), esp. chap. 6. On Japanese American experience after the war, see idem, *After Camp: Portraits in Midcentury Japanese American Life and Politics* (Berkeley: University of California Press, 2012).

13. On cultural factors that also bear on the pursuit of redress, see Harry H. L.

Kitano, *Japanese Americans: Evolution of a Subculture* (Englewood Cliffs, NJ: Prentice-Hall, 1969); Yasuko I. Takezawa, *Breaking the Silence: Redress and Japanese American Ethnicity* (Ithaca, NY: Cornell University Press, 1995); and idem, "Children of Inmates: The Effects of the Redress Movement among Third Generation Japanese Americans," *Qualitative Sociology* 14:1 (1991): 39–56.

14. On the events leading up to the Civil Liberties Act of 1988, see Alice Yang Murray, *Historical Memories of the Japanese American Internment and the Struggle for Redress* (Stanford, CA: Stanford University Press, 2008).

15. The act itself notes the need to "provide for a public education fund to finance efforts to inform the public about the internment of such individuals [i.e., citizens and resident aliens of Japanese ancestry] so as to prevent the reoccurrence of any similar event" (Public Law 100–383, August 10, 1988). In addition to pursuing other operations, the California Civil Liberties Public Education Act has issued 135 grants totaling over 3 million dollars in over twenty states. Projects have covered a range of topics aimed at a wide variety of audiences, with each receiving financial support of up to $100,000. See http://www.momomedia.com/CLPEF/backgrnd.html#Link to History.

16. Warren Furutani, interview by Karen M. Inouye, Sacramento, CA, June 26, 2012.

17. Whether they reflected fully on that enactment is another matter.

18. Jane Naomi Iwamura, "Critical Faith: Japanese Americans and the Birth of a New Civil Religion," *American Quarterly* 59:3 (2007): 957. Though it has a long history, the term "civil religion" comes from Robert N. Bellah, "Civil Religion in America," *Daedalus* 96:1 (1967): 1–21. On the religious implications of Japanese American historical engagement, see Joanne Doi, "Bridge to Compassion: Theological Pilgrimage to Tule Lake and Manzanar" (PhD diss., Graduate Theological Union, 2007); idem, "Tule Lake Pilgrimage: Dissonant Memories, Sacred Journey," in Jane Naomi Iwamura and Paul Spickard, eds., *Revealing the Sacred in Asian and Pacific America* (London: Routledge, 2003), 273–290; Jane Naomi Iwamura, "Critical Faith: Japanese Americans and the Birth of a New Civil Religion," *American Quarterly* 59:3 (2007): 937–968; and Masumi Izumi, "Seeking the Truth, Spiritual and Political: Japanese American Community Building through Engaged Ethnic Buddhism," *Peace and Change* 35:1 (2010): 39–67. See also Kirsten Emiko McAllister, *Terrain of Memory: A Japanese Canadian Memorial Project* (Vancouver: University of British Columbia Press, 2010).

19. Aiko Herzig-Yoshinaga, a prominent activist and historian of internment (and Furutani's mother-in-law), was among the recipients.

20. http://leginfo.legislature.ca.gov/faces/billNavClient.xhtml?bill_id=2003 20040AB781&search_keywords=.

21. The findings of the Commission on Wartime Relocation and Internment of

Civilians (CWRIC), for instance, proved definitively and at a national level that Executive Order 9066 was based not on military necessity but racism. The Civil Liberties Act that derived from CWRIC's findings demonstrated that the government itself recognized that fact.

22. Tetsuden Kashima, interview by Karen M. Inouye, Seattle, April 19, 2013.

23. For more on the response to the UW ceremony, see Molly Rosbauch, "UW to Give Honorary Degrees to Japanese-American Former Students," *Daily*, February 28, 2008, which also includes a reprinted March 4, 1942, *Daily* article on how Executive Order 9066 would affect students at the university (http://dailyuw .com/archive/2008/02/28/imported/uw-give-honorary-degrees-japanese-american -former-students#.U15asMftR8Q).

24. Citation given to graduates and signed by Stanley Barer, chair of the Board of Regents, and Mark Emmert, president of the University of Washington, May 18, 2008. http://www.washington.edu/ceremony/files/2012/10/Nikkei-Insert-compiled .pdf.

25. Iwamura, "Civil Religion," 957. On the concept of social death, see Orlando Patterson, *Slavery and Social Death: A Comparative Study* (Cambridge, MA: Harvard University Press, 1985).

26. Iwamura, "Civil Religion," reformulates the phrase: "*Shikata ga nai*. There is nothing I can do to change the past. *Shikata ga nai*. But there is something I can and must do now" (961). On the phrase as a form of negotiation, see Mona Oikawa, *Cartographies of Violence: Japanese Canadian Women, Memory, and the Subjects of the Internment* (Toronto: University of Toronto Press, 2012), 51.

27. Governor Arnold Schwarzenegger signed the bill into law on October 11, 2009. For the text of AB37, see http://leginfo.legislature.ca.gov/faces/billNavClient .xhtml?bill_id=200920100AB37&search_keywords=.

28. Ibid.

29. Furutani, interview.

30. At UBC, for example, Professors Henry Angus (Economics) and E. H. Morrow (Commerce) helped their students complete pending academic work and transfer to schools in Ottawa and points east. Primary documents relating to Dr. Angus are in the library of the University of British Columbia. Dr. Morrow's correspondence can be found mainly in the collection of the Nikkei National Museum and Cultural Center (Burnaby, BC); additional documents, including articles about his work on behalf of Japanese Canadian students, are in the library of the University of British Columbia.

31. Maryka Omatsu, *Bittersweet Passage: Redress and the Japanese Canadian Experience* (Toronto: Between the Lines, 1992), provides a detailed account of how Japanese Canadians struggled with their painful wartime history and how they came to terms with it. On the silence of older generations, see Kitano, *Japanese Americans*.

32. In addition to the ceremony, UBC also allocated resources (money, staff, and space) to record and preserve the history of its Nikkei students. See http:// japanese-canadian-student-tribute.ubc.ca/the-people/.

33. Kitagawa has noted that Clarence Moriwaki and Tetsuden Kashima were particularly helpful regarding educational and political initiatives in Washington State. Mary Kitagawa, interview by Karen M. Inouye, Vancouver, BC, May 30, 2012; correspondence with Mary Kitagawa, March 29, 2014.

34. The title of the conference was *"Honouring Our People: Stories of the Internment"* and included a presentation by Harry Aoki, whose brother Ted was a former UBC student who would receive his diploma from that institution in the May 2012 ceremony.

35. Kitagawa, interview.

36. Ibid.

37. Ibid.

38. Ibid.

39. Ibid.

40. Ibid.

41. In Canada, the War Measures Act, invoked by Prime Minister Mackenzie King, authorized the removal of Nikkei from the coast and mostly into prisons. Ken Adachi, *The Enemy That Never Was: An Account of the Deplorable Treatment Inflicted on Japanese Canadians during World War Two* (Toronto: McClelland and Stewart, 1976), 220–221.

42. Roy Miki, *Redress: Inside the Japanese Canadian Call for Justice* (Vancouver, BC: Raincoast Books, 2005), 272.

43. Matt James, "Scaling Memory: Reparation Displacement and the Case of BC," *Canadian Journal of Political Science* 42:2 (2009): 363. Roy Miki, Grace Thomson, and Ann Sunahara wrote the report in question, "Taking Responsibility: A Submission to the Canadian Government on the Misrepresentation of Japanese Canadians and Their History," which the National Association of Japanese Canadians issued as a white paper.

44. British Columbia Ministry of Education, *Internment and Redress: The Japanese Canadian Experience* (Vancouver: Queen's Printer for British Columbia, 2005). On the politics of teaching that history, see Alexandra L. Wood, "Challenging History: Public Education and Reluctance to Remember the Japanese Canadian Experience in British Columbia," *Historical Studies in Education/Revue d'histoire de l'éducation* 25:2 (2013): 65–85.

45. Correspondence with Mary Kitagawa, March 28, 2014.

46. Adachi, *The Enemy That Never Was*, provides background on the forms of exclusion that Japanese Canadians endured.

47. John Price, *Orienting Canada: Race, Empire, and the Transpacific* (Vancouver: University of British Columbia Press, 2011), 20, 328.

48. Kitagawa, interview.

49. Ibid.

50. Matt Stevens, "U.S.C. to Award Degrees to Japanese Interned During WWII," *Los Angeles Times*, May 11, 2012, http://articles.latimes.com/2012/may/11/local/la-me-usc-degrees-20120511.

51. Ibid. Others were angered because the university is the only institution that has not yet apologized for withholding transcripts during the war. In both cases, the source of the problem is USC's reluctance to acknowledge any but the most visible of the people it wronged.

52. Ubyssey staff, *Return: A Commemorative Yearbook in Honour of the Japanese Canadian Students of 1942* (Vancouver: University of British Columbia, 2012), 62.

53. Roy Oshiro, interview by Karen M. Inouye, Vancouver, BC, May 31, 2012. In this respect, Oshiro was echoing the sentiment conveyed by *Shikata ga nai*. Soon after, the Canadian government provided an earnest answer to his ironic question by mandating the mass removal of all Japanese Canadians. For additional interviews with Oshiro, see https://circle.ubc.ca/handle/2429/46030.

54. Ibid.

55. Ibid.

56. Ibid.

57. Ibid.

58. Ibid.

59. Ibid.

60. Ibid.

61. In addition to being a musician, Harry was also a ski instructor, a systems analyst for B.C. Electric, a logger, and a timber cruiser. John Endo Greenaway, "Harry Aoki: A Life of Music," *Bulletin: A Journal of Japanese Canadian History and Culture*, July 5, 2008, http://jccabulletin-geppo.ca/harry-aoki-a-life-of-music/.

62. Teiso Edward Uyeno, interview by Karen M. Inouye, Vancouver, BC, May 30, 2012.

63. Ibid.

64. Ibid.

65. Ibid.

66. Ibid.

67. Ibid.

68. Ibid.

69. Ibid.

70. Ibid.

71. Ibid.

72. Cf. Karen L. Ishizuka, *Lost & Found: Reclaiming the Japanese American Incarceration* (Urbana: University of Illinois Press, 2006), esp. 39–56.

73. Similar actions abound in the United States as well. See, for instance, the discussion of "restorative justice" in Renee C. Romano, *Racial Reckoning: Prosecuting America's Civil Rights Murders* (Cambridge, MA: Harvard University Press, 2014), e.g., concerning the establishment of a truth and reconciliation committee in Greensboro, North Carolina (182–183).

74. Ibid.

EPILOGUE

1. Ross Gay, "Some Thoughts on Mercy," *Sun* 451 (2013), http://thesunmagazine .org/issues/451/some_thoughts_on_mercy.

2. https://beta.prx.org/stories/141747.

Bibliography

Adachi, Ken. *The Enemy That Never Was: An Account of the Deplorable Treatment Inflicted on Japanese Canadians during World War Two*. Toronto: McClelland and Stewart, 1976.

Alinder, Jasmine. *Moving Images: Photography and the Japanese American Incarceration*. Urbana: University of Illinois Press, 2009.

Amerasia staff. "An Interview with Warren Furutani." *Amerasia Journal* 1:1 (1971): 70–76.

"An American Story with Japanese Beginnings: New Judge Credits Fellow Nisei." *San Jose Mercury*, November 16, 1961.

Anderson, Benedict. *Imagined Communities: Reflections on the Origin and Spread of Nationalism*, rev. ed. London: Verso, 1991.

Anderson, Warwick. *Colonial Pathologies: American Tropical Medicine, Race, and Hygiene in the Philippines*. Durham, NC: Duke University Press, 2006.

Austin, Allan W. *From Concentration Camps to Campus: Japanese American Students and World War II*. Urbana: University of Illinois Press, 2004.

Baldwin, John D. "Advancing the Chicago School of Pragmatic Sociology: The Life and Work of Tamotsu Shibutani." *Sociological Inquiry* 60:2 (2001): 115–126.

———. "Shibutani and Pragmatism." *Symbolic Interaction* 28:4 (2005): 487–504.

Bangarth, Stephanie. *Voices Raised in Protest: Defending North American Citizens of Japanese Ancestry, 1942–1949*. Vancouver: University of British Columbia Press, 2008.

Bannai, Lorraine K. *Enduring Conviction: Fred Korematsu and His Quest for Justice*. Seattle: University of Washington Press, 2015.

———. "Taking the Stand: The Lessons of Three Men Who Took the Japanese American Internment to Court." *Seattle Journal for Social Justice* 4:1 (2005): 1–57.

Bannister, Robert C. "Dorothy Swaine Thomas: The Hard Way in the Profession." http://www.swarthmore.edu/SocSci/rbannis1/DST.html. Published originally as "Dorothy Swain Thomas: Soziologischer Objectivismus: Der harte Weg in die Profession," in Claudia Honegger and Theresa Wobbe, eds., *Frauen in der Soziologie*, 226–257. Munich: C.H. Beck, 1998.

Beauregard, Guy. "After Redress: A Conversation with Roy Miki." *Canadian Literature* 201 (2009): 71–86.

———. "Asian American Studies, Asian Canadian Questions." In Yu and Beauregard, eds., "Pacific Canada," xxi–xxviii.

———. "Asian Canadian Studies: Unfinished Projects." *Canadian Literature* 199 (2008): 6–27.

Beauregard, Guy, Iyko Day, Glenn Deer, Donald Goellnicht, Christopher Lee, Marie Lo, Roy Miki, Rita Wong, and Henry Yu. "Epilogue: A Conversation on Unfinished Projects." *Canadian Literature* 199 (2008): 208–211.

Bellah, Robert N. "Civil Religion in America." *Daedalus* 96:1 (1967): 1–21.

Blumer, Herbert. "Sociological Implications of the Thought of George Herbert Mead." *American Journal of Sociology* 71 (1966): 535–544.

———. *Symbolic Interactionism: Perspective and Method*. Englewood Cliffs, NJ: Prentice-Hall, 1969.

Boston University Public Interest Law Journal staff. "Japanese American Internment: An Interview with Fred Korematsu." *Boston University Public Interest Law Journal* 3:1 (1993): 99–104.

Breithaupt, Fritz A. *Kulturen der Empathie*. Berlin: Suhrkamp/Insel, 2009.

———. "A Three-Person Model of Empathy." *Emotion Review* 4:1 (2012): 84–91.

British Columbia Ministry of Education. *Internment and Redress: The Japanese Canadian Experience*. Vancouver: Queen's Printer for British Columbia, 2005.

Briones, Matthew M. *Jim and Jap Crow: A Cultural History of 1940s Interracial America*. Princeton, NJ: Princeton University Press, 2013.

Bureau of Sociological Research Reports. Rare and Manuscript Collections, Carl A. Kroch Library, Cornell University.

Burton, Jeffrey, Mary Farrell, Florence Lord, and Richard Lord. *Confinement and Ethnicity: An Overview of World War II Japanese American Relocation Sites*. Tucson, AZ: Western Archeological and Conservation Center, National Park Service, 1999.

Cacho, Lisa. *Social Death: Racialized Rightlessness and the Criminalization of the Unprotected*. New York: New York University Press, 2012.

Capshew, James. *Psychologists on the March: Science, Practice, and Professional Identity in America, 1929–1969*. Cambridge: Cambridge University Press, 1999.

Chang, Kornel. *Pacific Connections: The Making of the U.S.-Canadian Borderlands*. Berkeley: University of California Press, 2012.

Cheng, Cindy I-Fen. *Citizens of Asian America: Democracy and Race during the Cold War.* New York: New York University Press, 2013.

Chuh, Kandice. *Imagine Otherwise: On Asian Americanist Critique.* Durham, NC: Duke University Press, 2003.

Clinton, William J. "Remarks Announcing the Nomination of Norman Y. Mineta to Be Secretary of Commerce and Exchange with Reporters." *Weekly Compilation of Presidential Documents* 36:26 (2000): 1540–1543.

Collins, Patricia Hill. *Black Feminist Thought: Knowledge, Consciousness, and the Politics of Empowerment.* Boston: Routledge, 1990.

Coser, Lewis, ed. *Masters of Sociological Thought: Ideas in Historical and Social Context.* Rev. ed. New York: Waveland Press, 1977.

Cosgrove, Margaret. "Relocation of American-Japanese Students." *Journal of the American Association of Collegiate Registrars* 18:3 (1943): 221–226.

Cuniberti, Betty. "Internment: Personal Voices, Powerful Choices." *Los Angeles Times,* October 4, 1987, Part VI: 1, 10–12.

Daniels, Roger. *Concentration Camps, North America: Japanese in the United States and Canada during World War II.* Malabar, FL: Krieger, 1993.

———. *Concentration Camps USA: Japanese Americans and World War II.* New York: Holt, Rinehart and Winston, 1971.

———. *The Japanese American Cases: The Rule of Law in Time of War.* Lawrence: University Press of Kansas, 2013.

———. *The Politics of Prejudice: The Anti-Japanese Movement in California and the Struggle for Japanese Exclusion.* Rev. ed. Berkeley: University of California Press, 1977.

———. *Prisoners Without Trial: Japanese Americans in World War II.* Rev. ed. New York: Hill and Wang, 2004.

———. "Words Do Matter: A Note on Inappropriate Terminology and the Incarceration of the Japanese Americans." In Fiset and Nomura, eds., *Nikkei in the Pacific Northwest,* 183–207.

Daniels, Roger, Sandra C. Taylor, and Harry H. L. Kitano, eds. *Japanese Americans: From Relocation to Redress.* Rev. ed. Seattle: University of Washington Press, 2013.

Day, Iyko. *Alien Capital: Asian Racialization and the Logic of Settler Colonial Capitalism.* Durham, NC: Duke University Press, 2016.

———. "Alien Intimacies: The Coloniality of Japanese Incarceration in Australia, Canada, and the U.S." *Amerasia Journal* 36:2 (2010): 107–124.

———. "Lost in Transnation: Uncovering Asian Canada." In Yu and Beauregard, eds., "Pacific Canada," 69–86.

Dewey, John. *The Public and Its Problems: An Essay in Political Inquiry.* New York: H. Holt, 1927.

Doi, Joanne. "Bridge to Compassion: Theological Pilgrimage to Tule Lake and Manzanar." PhD diss., Graduate Theological Union, Berkeley, CA, 2007.

———. "Tule Lake Pilgrimage: Dissonant Memories, Sacred Journey." In Jane Naomi Iwamura and Paul Spickard, eds., *Revealing the Sacred in Asian and Pacific America*, 273–290. London: Routledge, 2003.

Douglas, Mary. *Natural Symbols: Explorations in Cosmology.* New York: Vintage Books, 1973.

Ehrenberg, John. *Civil Society: The Critical History of an Idea.* New York: New York University Press, 1999.

Embrey, Sue Kunitomi. "From Manzanar to the Present: A Personal Journey." In Erica Harth, ed., *Last Witnesses: Reflections on the Wartime Internment of Japanese Americans*, 167–185. New York: Palgrave, 2001.

Espiritu, Yến Lê. *Body Counts: The Vietnam War and Militarized Refugees.* Berkeley: University of California Press, 2014.

———. "Toward a Critical Refugee Study: The Vietnamese Refugee Subject in US Scholarship." *Journal of Vietnamese Studies* 1:1–2 (2006): 410–432.

Fiset, Louis, and Gail Nomura, eds. *Nikkei in the Pacific Northwest: Japanese Americans and Japanese Canadians in the Twentieth Century.* Seattle, WA: Center for the Study of the Pacific Northwest, 2005.

Fournier, Eric Paul, dir. *Civil Wrongs and Rights: The Fred Korematsu Story.* Documentary. San Francisco: National Asian American Telecommunications Association, 2001.

Fraser, Nancy. "Rethinking the Public Sphere: A Contribution to the Critique of Actually Existing Democracy." *Social Text* 25/26 (1990): 56–80.

Fugita, Stephen S., S. Frank Miyamoto, and Tetsuden Kashima. "Interpersonal Style and Japanese American Organizational Involvement." *Behaviormetrika* 29:2 (2002): 185–202.

Fujino, Diane C. *Heartbeat of Struggle: The Revolutionary Life of Yuri Kochiyama.* Minneapolis: University of Minnesota Press, 2005.

———. *Samurai among Panthers: Richard Aoki on Race, Resistance, and a Paradoxical Life.* Minneapolis: University of Minnesota Press, 2012.

Gay, Ross. "Some Thoughts on Mercy." *Sun* 451 (2013). http://thesunmagazine.org/issues/451/some_thoughts_on_mercy.

Geertz, Clifford. "Common Sense as a Cultural System." *Antioch Review* 33 (1975): 47–53.

Goellnicht, Donald. "Asian Kanadian, Eh?" *Canadian Literature* 199 (2008): 71–99.

———. "A Long Labour: The Protracted Birth of Asian Canadian Literature." *Essays on Canadian Writing* 72 (Winter 2000): 1–41.

Gordon, Avery F. *Ghostly Matters: Haunting and the Sociological Imagination.* Minneapolis: University of Minnesota Press, 1997.

———. *Keeping Good Time: Reflections on Knowledge, Power, and People*. Boulder, CO: Paradigm, 2004.

Gressman, Eugene R. "Korematsu: A Mélange of Military Imperatives." In Muller, ed., "Judgments Judged and Wrongs Remembered," 15–27.

Grodzins, Morton. *Americans Betrayed*. Chicago: University of Chicago Press, 1949.

Gudridge, Patrick O. "The Constitution Glimpsed from Tule Lake." In Muller, ed., "Judgments Judged and Wrongs Remembered," 81–118.

———. "Remember 'Endo'?" *Harvard Law Review* 116:7 (2003): 1933–1970.

Habermas, Jürgen. *The Structural Transformation of the Public Sphere: An Inquiry into a Category of Bourgeois Society*. Translated by Thomas Burger with Frederick Lawrence. Cambridge, MA: Harvard University Press, 1989.

Hammersly, Martyn. *The Dilemma of Qualitative Method: Herbert Blumer and the Chicago Tradition*. London: Routledge, 1989.

Hansen, Arthur A., ed. *Japanese American World War II Evacuation Oral History Project*. Munich: K.G. Sauer, 1991–1995.

Hartman, Saidiya. *Lose Your Mother: A Journey along the Atlantic Slave Route*. New York: Farrar, Straus and Giroux, 2007.

Hata, Donald, and Nadine Hata. *Japanese Americans and World War II: Mass Removal, Imprisonment and Redress*. Wheeling, IL: Harlan Davidson, 1995.

Hatamiya, Leslie T. *Righting a Wrong: Japanese Americans and the Passage of the Civil Liberties Act of 1988*. Stanford, CA: Stanford University Press, 1993.

Hattendorf, Linda, dir. *The Cats of Mirikitani*. Documentary. New York: Lucid Dreaming, 2006.

Hawkins, Naoko. "Becoming a Model Minority: The Depiction of Japanese Canadians in the *Globe and Mail*, 1946–2000." *Canadian Ethnic Studies* 41:1–2 (2009): 137–154.

Hayashi, Brian Masaru. *Democratizing the Enemy: The Japanese American Internment*. Princeton, NJ: Princeton University Press, 2008.

Herman, Ellen. *The Romance of American Psychology: Political Culture in the Age of Experts*. Berkeley: University of California Press, 1995.

Hirabayashi, Gordon. Review of *The Derelicts of Company K*. *Pacific Affairs* 52:2 (1979): 346–347.

Hirabayashi, Lane Ryo. *The Politics of Fieldwork: Research in an American Concentration Camp*. Tucson: University of Arizona Press, 1999.

Hirabayashi, Lane Ryo, Akemi Kikumura-Yano, and James A. Hirabayashi, eds. *New Worlds, New Lives: Globalization and People of Japanese Descent in the Americas and from Latin America in Japan*. Stanford, CA: Stanford University Press, 2002.

Hirasuna, Delphine. *The Art of Gaman: Arts and Crafts from the Japanese American Internment Camps 1942–1946*. Berkeley: Ten Speed Press, 2005.

Hirsch, Marianne. "Past Lives: Postmemories in Exile." *Poetics Today* 17:4 (1996): 659–686.

Hohri, William Minoru. *Repairing America: An Account of the Movement for Japanese-American Redress.* Pullman: Washington State University Press, 1988.

Hosokawa, Bill. *JACL in Quest of Justice: The History of the Japanese American Citizens League.* New York: Morrow, 1982.

———. *Nisei: The Quiet Americans.* Rev. ed. Boulder: University of Colorado Press, 2002.

Hsu, Madeline Y. *The Good Immigrants: How the Yellow Peril Became the Model Minority.* Princeton, NJ: Princeton University Press, 2015.

Ichihashi, Yamato. *Japanese in the United States: A Critical Study of the Problems of the Japanese Immigrants and Their Children.* Stanford, CA: Stanford University Press, 1932.

Ichioka, Yuji. *Before Internment: Essays in Prewar Japanese American History.* Edited by Gordon H. Chang and Eiichiro Azuma. Stanford, CA: Stanford University Press, 2006.

———, ed. "Beyond National Boundaries: The Complexity of Japanese-American History." Special issue of *Amerasia Journal* 23:3 (1997–1998).

———. *The Issei: The World of the First Generation Japanese Immigrants, 1885–1924.* New York: Collier Macmillan, 1988.

———. "JERS Revisited: Introduction." In Ichioka, ed. *Views from Within,* 3–23.

———. "Nikkei in the Western Hemisphere." *Amerasia Journal* 15:2 (1989): 175–177.

———, ed. *Views from Within: The Japanese American Evacuation and Resettlement Study.* Los Angeles: UCLA Asian American Studies Center, 1989.

Ina, Satsuki, dir. *Children of the Camps.* Documentary. San Francisco: Asian American Media.

Inouye, Karen M. "Changing History: Competing Notions of Japanese American Experience, 1942–2006." PhD diss., Brown University, 2008.

———. "Eternal Present: Retroactive Diplomas in Canada and the U.S." *Journal of Asian American Studies* 17:3 (2014): 337–365.

———. "Japanese American Wartime Experience, Tamotsu Shibutani and Methodological Innovation, 1942–1978." *Journal of the History of the Behavioral Sciences* 48:4 (2012): 318–338.

Irons, Peter. *The Courage of Their Convictions.* New York: Penguin, 1988.

———. *Justice at War: The Story of the Japanese American Internment Cases.* Berkeley: University of California Press, 1993.

Ishizuka, Karen L. *Lost & Found: Reclaiming the Japanese American Incarceration.* Urbana: University of Illinois Press, 2006.

————. *Serve the People: Making Asian America in the Long Sixties.* New York: Verso, 2016.

Iwamura, Jane Naomi. "Critical Faith: Japanese Americans and the Birth of a New Civil Religion." *American Quarterly* 59:3 (2007): 937–968.

Iyeki, Marc Hideo. "The Japanese American Coram Nobis Cases: Exposing the Myth of Disloyalty." *New York University Review of Law and Social Change* 13 (1984–1985): 199–221.

Izumi, Masumi. "Alienable Citizenship: Race, Loyalty and the Law in the Age of 'American Concentration Camps,' 1941–1971." *Asian American Law Journal* 13:1 (2006): 1–30.

————. "Japanese American Internment and the Emergency Detention Act (Title II of the Internal Security Act of 1950), 1941–1971: Balancing Internal Security and Civil Liberties in the United States." PhD diss., Doshisha University, 2003.

————. "The Japanese Canadian Movement: Migration and Activism before and after World War II." *Amerasia Journal* 33:2 (2007): 49–66.

————. "Lessons from History: Japanese Canadians and Civil Liberties in Canada." *Journal of American and Canadian Studies* 17 (1999): 1–24.

————. "Prohibiting 'American Concentration Camps': Repeal of the Emergency Detention Act and the Public Historical Memory of the Japanese American Internment." *Pacific Historical Review* 74:2 (2005): 165–193.

————. "Reclaiming and Reinventing 'Powell Street': Reconstruction of the Japanese-Canadian Community in Post–World War II Vancouver." In Fiset and Nomura, eds., *Nikkei in the Pacific Northwest*, 308–333.

————. "Rumors of 'American Concentration Camps': The Emergency Detention Act and the Public Fear of Political Repression, 1966–1971." *Doshisha Studies in Language and Culture* 4:4 (2002): 737–766.

————. "Seeking the Truth, Spiritual and Political: Japanese American Community Building through Engaged Ethnic Buddhism." *Peace and Change* 35:1 (2010): 39–67.

James, Matt. "Scaling Memory: Reparation Displacement and the Case of BC." *Canadian Journal of Political Science* 42:2 (2009): 363–386.

Japanese American and Aleutian Wartime Relocation: Hearings before the Subcommittee on Administrative Law and Governmental Relations of the Committee on the Judiciary, House of Representatives, 98th Congress, Second Session on H.R. 3387, H.R. 4110, and H.R. 4322, June 20, 21, 27, and September 12, 1984. Washington, D.C.: Government Publications Office, 1985.

Japanese American Evacuation and Resettlement Records. Bancroft Library, University of California, Berkeley.

Japanese Canadian Centennial Project Committee. *A Dream of Riches: The Japa-*

nese Canadians, 1877–1977. Vancouver/Toronto: Japanese Canadian Centennial Project/Dreadnaught, 1978.

Jordan, Sherrill. *Public Art, Public Controversy: The Tilted Arc on Trial.* New York: American Council for the Arts, 1987.

Kaberry, Phyllis. "Malinowski's Contribution to Fieldwork Methods and the Writing of Ethnography." In Raymond Firth, ed., *Man and Culture,* 71–91. London: Routledge, 1935.

Kage, Tatsuo. *Uprooted Again: Japanese Canadians Move to Japan after World War II.* Translated by Kathleen Chisato Merken. Victoria, BC: Ti-Jean Press, 2012.

Kang, Jerry. "Denying Prejudice: Internment, Redress, and Denial." *UCLA Law Review* 51 (2004): 933–1013.

———. "Watching the Watchers: Enemy Combattants in the Internment's Shadow." In Muller, ed., "Judgments Judged and Wrongs Remembered," 255–283.

Kikumura-Yano, Akemi, ed. *Encyclopedia of Japanese Descendants in the Americas: An Illustrated History.* Walnut Creek, CA: AltaMira Press, 2002.

Kitagawa, Muriel. *This Is My Own: Letters to Wes and Other Writings on Japanese Canadians, 1941–1948.* Edited by Roy Miki. Vancouver, BC: Talonbooks, 1985.

Kitano, Harry H. L. *Japanese Americans: Evolution of a Subculture.* Englewood Cliffs, NJ: Prentice-Hall, 1969.

Kiyooka, Roy. "We Asian North Americanos: An Unhistorical 'Take' on Growing Up Yellow in a White World." *West Coast Line* 24:3 (1990): 116–118.

Kobayashi, Audrey. "The Historical Context of Japanese-Canadian Uprooting." In Ludger Müller-Wille, ed., *Social Change and Space: Indigenous Nations and Ethnic Communities,* 69–82. Montreal: McGill University, 1989.

———. "Intermarriage among Japanese Canadians: Cultural Rejection or Intercultural Tolerance?" *Horizons Interculturels* 26 (1992): 6–18.

———. "The Japanese-Canadian Redress Settlement and Its Implications for 'Race Relations.'" *Canadian Ethnic Studies* 24:1 (1992): 1–19.

———. "Learning Their Place: Japanese/Canadian Workers/Mothers." In Audrey Kobayashi, ed., *Women, Work and Place,* 45–72. Montreal: McGill-Queen's University Press, 1994.

Kobayashi, Cassandra, and Roy Miki, eds. *Spirit of Redress: Japanese Canadians in Conference.* Vancouver, BC: National Association of Japanese Canadians/Japanese Canadian Studies Society, 1989.

Kochiyama, Yuri. *Passing It On: A Memoir.* Los Angeles: UCLA Asian American Studies Center Press, 2004.

Kogawa, Joy. *Obasan.* Boston: D.R. Godine, 1981.

Kurashige, Lon. *Japanese American Celebration and Conflict: A History of Ethnic Identity and Festival, 1934–1990.* Berkeley: University of California Press, 2002.

LaCapra, Dominick. *Writing History, Writing Trauma.* Baltimore: Johns Hopkins University Press, 2000.

La Violette, Forrest E. "The American-Born Japanese and the World Crisis." *Canadian Journal of Economics and Political Science* 7:4 (1941): 517–552.

Lee, Christopher. "The Lateness of Asian Canadian Studies." In Yu and Beauregard, eds., "Pacific Canada," 1–17.

———. *The Semblance of Identity: Aesthetic Mediation in Asian American Literature.* Stanford, CA: Stanford University Press, 2012.

Leighton, Alexander. *The Governing of Men: General Principles and Recommendations Based on Experience at a Japanese Relocation Camp.* Princeton, NJ: Princeton University Press, 1946.

Leong, Russell C. "Parallel Pacifics." In Yu and Beauregard, eds., "Pacific Canada," iii–xix.

Lo, Marie. "Fields of Recognition: Reading Asian Canadian Literature in Asian America." PhD diss., University of California, Berkeley, 2001.

———. "Model Minority, Models of Resistance: Native Figures in Asian Canadian Literature." *Canadian Literature* 196 (2008): 96–112.

Lowe, Lisa. *Immigrant Acts: On Asian American Cultural Politics.* Durham, NC: Duke University Press, 1996.

Maki, Mitchell T., Harry H. L. Kitano, and S. Megan Berthold. *Achieving the Impossible Dream: How Japanese Americans Obtained Redress.* Urbana: University of Illinois Press, 1999.

Mar, Lisa Rose. *Brokering Belonging: Chinese in Canada's Exclusion Era, 1885–1945.* Oxford: Oxford University Press, 2010.

Mass, Amy Iwasaki. "The Psychological Effects of the Camps on Japanese Americans." In Daniels, Taylor, and Kitano, eds., *Japanese Americans*, 159–162.

———. "Psychological Effects of Internment." In Mike Mackey, ed., *A Matter of Conscience: Essays on the World War II Heart Mountain Draft Resistance Movement*, 145–152. Powell, WY: Western History Publications, 2002.

Mathews, Fred. *Quest for an American Sociology: Robert E. Park and the Chicago School.* Montreal: McGill-Queen's University Press, 1977.

Matsunaga, Jennifer. "Publics in the Making: A Genealogical Inquiry into the Discursive Publics of Japanese Canadian Redress." MA thesis, Carleton University, 2011.

McAllister, Kirsten Emiko. "Archive and Myth: The Changing Memoryscape of Japanese Canadian Internment Camps." In James Opp and John C. Walsh, eds., *Placing Memory and Remembering Place in Canada*, 215–246. Vancouver: University of British Columbia Press, 2010.

———. "Memoryscapes of Postwar British Columbia: A Look of Recognition." In Ashok Mathur, Jonathan Dewar, and Mike DeGagné, eds., *Cultivating Canada:*

Reconciliation through the Lens of Cultural Diversity, Aboriginal Healing Founda-tion, vol. 3: 419–444. Ottawa: Aboriginal Healing Foundation, 2011.

———. "Narrating Japanese Canadians in and out of the Canadian Nation: A Critique of Realist Forms of Representation." *Canadian Journal of Communica-tion* 24:1 (1999). http://cjc-online.ca/index.php/journal/article/view/1083/989.

———. "Photographs of a Japanese Canadian Internment Camp: Mourning Loss and Invoking a Future." *Visual Studies* 21:2 (2006): 133–156.

———. "Stories of Escape: Family Photographs from World War Two Intern-ment Camps." In Annette Kuhn and Kirsten Emiko McAllister, eds., *Locating Memory: Photographic Acts*, 81–110. Oxford: Berghahn, 2006.

———. *Terrain of Memory: A Japanese Canadian Memorial Project*. Vancouver: University of British Columbia Press, 2010.

Miki, Arthur K. *The Japanese Canadian Redress Legacy: A Community Revitalized.* Winnipeg: National Association of Japanese Canadians, 2003.

Miki, Roy. "Altered States: Global Currents, the Spectral Nation, and the Produc-tion of 'Asian Canadian.'" *Journal of Canadian Studies/Revue d'études canadiennes* 35:3 (2000): 43–72.

———. "Asiancy: Making Space for Asian Canadian Writing." In Gary Y. Okihiro, Marilyn Alquizola, Dorothy Fujita Rony, and K. Scott Wong, eds., *Privileging Positions: The Sites of Asian American Studies*, 135–151. Pullman: Washington State University Press, 1995.

———. *Redress: Inside the Japanese Canadian Call for Justice*. Vancouver, BC: Rain-coast Books, 2005.

———. "Unclassified Subjects: Question Marking 'Japanese Canadian' Identity." In Roy Miki, ed., *Broken Entries: Race, Subjectivity, Writing*, 181–204. Toronto: Mercury Press, 1998.

Miki, Roy, and Cassandra Kobayashi. *Justice in Our Time: The Japanese Canadian Redress Settlement*. Vancouver, BC: Talonbooks, 1991.

"Mineta Named to Council." *San Jose News* 168:146 (July 11, 1967): 1 and 4.

Mineta, Norman Y. "An American Tragedy, and Reparations." *San Jose Mercury News*, June 26, 1983, Section C: 1 and 4.

———. "Mentoring Our Youth in Aviation." *Executive Speeches* 16:2 (2001): 27–29.

———. "Facing the Tests of History." *Executive Speeches* 16:3 (December 2001): 33–36.

Miyamoto, S. Frank. "The Career of Intergroup Tensions: A Study of the Collective Adjustments of Evacuees to Crises at the Tule Lake Relocation Center." PhD diss., University of Chicago, 1950.

———. "Dorothy Swaine Thomas as Director of JERS: Some Personal Observa-tions." In Ichioka, ed., *Views from Within*, 31–64.

———. "Immigrants and Citizens of Japanese Origin." *Annals of the American Academy of Political and Social Science* 223 (1942): 107–113.

———. "The Japanese Minority in the Pacific Northwest." *Pacific Northwest Quarterly* 54:4 (1963): 143–149.

Molotsky, Irvin. "The Heat of War Welds a Bond That Endures across Aisles and Years." *New York Times,* April 26, 1988. http://www.nytimes.com/1988/04/26/us/washington-talk-friendships-heat-war-welds-bond-that-endures-across-aisles-years.html.

Morrison, Karl F. *I Am You: The Hermeneutics of Empathy in Western Literature, Theology, and Art.* Princeton, NJ: Princeton University Press, 1988.

Muller, Eric L. "All the Themes But One." *University of Chicago Law Review* 66:4 (1999): 1395–1433.

———. *American Inquisition: The Hunt for Japanese American Disloyalty in World War II.* Chapel Hill: University of North Carolina Press, 2007.

———. "Apologies or Apologists? Remembering the Japanese American Internment in Wyoming." *Wyoming Law Review* 1:2 (2001): 473–95.

———, ed. *Colors of Confinement: Rare Kodachrome Photographs of Japanese American Incarceration in World War II.* Chapel Hill: University of North Carolina Press, 2012.

———. *Free to Die for Their Country: The Story of the Japanese American Draft Resisters in World War II.* Chicago: University of Chicago Press, 2001.

———. "Inference or Impact? Racial Profiling and the Interment's True Legacy." *Ohio State Journal of Criminal Law* 103 (2003): 103–131.

———, ed. "Judgments Judged and Wrongs Remembered: Examining the Japanese American Civil Liberties Cases on Their Sixtieth Anniversary." Special issue of *Law and Contemporary Problems* 68:2 (2005).

———. "A Penny for Their Thoughts: Draft Resistance at the Poston Relocation Center." In Muller, ed., "Judgments Judged and Wrongs Remembered," 119–157.

———. "12/7 and 9/11: War, Liberties, and the Lessons of History." *West Virginia Law Review* 104:3 (2002): 571–592.

Murasky, Donna M. "*James v. Valtierra*: Housing Discrimination by Referendum?" *University of Chicago Law Review* 39:1 (1971): 115–142.

Murray, Stephen O. "The Rights of Research Assistants and the Rhetoric of Political Suppression: Morton Grodzins and the University of California Japanese-American Evacuation and Resettlement Study." *Journal of the History of the Behavioral Sciences* 27:2 (1991): 130–156.

Musof, Gil Richard. "The Chicago School." In Larry J. Reynolds and Nancy Herman-Kinney, eds., *Handbook of Symbolic Interactionism,* 102–106. Walnut Creek, CA: AltaMira Press, 2003.

Nagata, Donna K. *Legacy of Injustice: Exploring the Cross-Generational Impact of the Japanese American Internment.* New York: Plenum, 1993.

Nagata, Donna K., and Yuzuru J. Takeshita. "Coping and Resilience across Generations: Japanese Americans and the World War II Internment." *Psychoanalytic Review* 85 (1998): 587–613.

National Japanese American Student Relocation Council. *From Camp to College: The Story of Japanese American Student Relocation.* Philadelphia: National Japanese American Student Relocation Council, 1945.

———. *How to Help Japanese American Student Relocation.* Philadelphia: National Japanese American Student Relocation Council, 1944.

New Canadian. Vancouver, BC; Kaslo, BC.

Ngai, Mae M. *Impossible Subjects: Illegal Aliens and the Making of Modern America.* Princeton, NJ: Princeton University Press, 2004.

———. "'An Ironic Testimony to the Value of American Democracy': Assimilationism and the World War II Internment of Japanese Americans." In Manisha Sinha and Penny von Eschen, eds., *Contested Democracy: Freedom, Race, and Power in American History,* 237–257. New York: Columbia University Press, 2007.

Ninh, Erin Khuê. "The Model Minority: Asian American Immigrant Families and Intimate Harm." *Kalfou* 1:2 (2014): 168–173.

Norman Mineta Papers. San Jose, CA: San Jose State University Special Collections and Archives.

O'Brien, Robert W. "The Changing Role of the College Nisei during the Crisis Period: 1931–1945." PhD diss., University of Washington, 1945.

Ogburn, William F. "The Folkways of a Scientific Sociology." Presidential address to the American Sociological Society annual meeting in 1929; reprinted in *Publications of the American Sociological Society* 24 (May 1930): 1–11.

Oikawa, Mona. *Cartographies of Violence: Japanese Canadian Women, Memory, and the Subjects of the Internment.* Toronto: University of Toronto Press, 2012.

Okada, John. *No-No Boy.* Rutland, VT: Tuttle, 1957.

Okihiro, Gary Y. *Storied Lives: Japanese American Students and World War II.* Seattle: University of Washington Press, 1999.

Okubo, Miné. *Citizen 13660.* New York: Columbia University Press, 1946.

Omatsu, Maryka. *Bittersweet Passage: Redress and the Japanese Canadian Experience.* Toronto: Between the Lines, 1992.

Osajima, Keith. "Asian Americans as the Model Minority: An Analysis of the Popular Press Image in the 1960s and 1980s." In Gary Y. Okihiro, ed., *Reflections on Shattered Windows: Promises and Prospects for Asian American Studies,* 165–174. Pullman: Washington State University Press, 1988.

Paik, A. Naomi. *Rightlessness: Testimony and Redress in U.S. Prison Camps since World War II*. Chapel Hill: University of North Carolina Press, 2016.

———. "Testifying to Rightlessness: Redressing the Camp in Narratives of U.S. Culture and Law." PhD diss., Yale University, 2009.

Parker, Linda S. *Native American Estate: The Struggle over Indian and Hawaiian Lands*. Honolulu: University of Hawai'i Press, 1989.

Patterson, Orlando. *Slavery and Social Death: A Comparative Study*. Cambridge, MA: Harvard University Press, 1985.

Piper, Karen. *Left in the Dust: How Race and Politics Created a Human and Environmental Tragedy in L.A.* New York: Palgrave Macmillan, 2006.

Price, John. *Orienting Canada: Race, Empire, and the Transpacific*. Vancouver: University of British Columbia Press, 2011.

Provinse, John H. "Relocation of Japanese-American College Students: Acceptance of a Challenge." *Higher Education* 1:8 (April 16, 1945): 1–4.

"Relocating Japanese American Students." *Education for Victory* 1:14 (1942): 24.

Robinson, Greg. *After Camp: Portraits in Midcentury Japanese American Life and Politics*. Berkeley: University of California Press, 2012.

———. *By Order of the President: FDR and the Internment of Japanese Americans*. Cambridge, MA: Harvard University Press, 2003.

———. *A Tragedy of Democracy: Japanese Confinement in North America*. New York: Columbia University Press, 2009.

Robinson, Greg, and Toni Robinson. "*Korematsu* and Beyond: Japanese Americans and the Origins of Strict Scrutiny." In Muller, ed., "Judgments Judged and Wrongs Remembered," 29–55.

Romano, Renee C. *Racial Reckoning: Prosecuting America's Civil Rights Murders*. Cambridge, MA: Harvard University Press, 2014.

Roy, Patricia. "The Re-Creation of Vancouver's Japanese Community, 1945–2008." *Journal of the Canadian Historical Association/Revue de la Société historique du Canada* 19:2 (2008): 127–154.

Saito, Natsu Taylor. "Interning the 'Non-Alien' Other: The Illusory Protections of Citizenship." In Muller, ed., "Judgments Judged and Wrongs Remembered," 173–213.

Sakoda, James. "Reminiscences of a Participant Observer." In Ichioka, ed., *Views from Within*, 219–245.

———. "The 'Residue': The Unresettled Minidokans, 1943–1945." In Ichioka, ed., *Views from Within*, 247–281.

Saxton, Alexander. *The Indispensable Enemy: Labor and the Anti-Chinese Movement in California*. Berkeley: University of California Press, 1971.

Seigel, Micol. *Uneven Encounters: Making Race and Nation in Brazil and the United States*. Durham, NC: Duke University Press, 2009.

Shah, Nayan. *Contagious Divides: Epidemics and Race in San Francisco's Chinatown.* Berkeley: University of California Press, 2001.

Shay, William L. "Reflections on Tamotsu Shibutani: On a Biography and Sociology of America." *Symbolic Interaction* 28:4 (2005): 521–523.

Shibutani, Tamotsu. "The Circulation of Rumors as a Form of Collective Behavior." PhD diss., University of Chicago, 1948.

———. *The Derelicts of Company K: A Sociological Study of Demoralization.* Berkeley: University of California Press, 1978.

———. *Improvised News: A Sociological Study of Rumor.* Indianapolis: Bobbs-Merrill, 1966.

———. "Rumors in a Crisis Situation." MA thesis, University of Chicago, 1944.

———. *Society and Personality: An Interactionist Approach to Social Psychology.* Englewood Cliffs, NJ: Prentice-Hall, 1961.

Simpson, Caroline Chung. *An Absent Presence: Japanese Americans in Postwar American Culture, 1945–1960.* Durham, NC: Duke University Press, 2002.

So, Christine. *Economic Citizens: A Narrative of Asian American Visibility.* Philadelphia: Temple University Press, 2007.

Spickard, Paul R. "Injustice Compounded: Amerasians and Non-Japanese Americans in World War II Concentration Camps." *Journal of American Ethnic History* 5:2 (1986): 5–22.

———. *Japanese Americans: The Formation and Transformations of an Ethnic Group.* New York: Twayne, 1996.

Sunahara, Ann Gomer. *The Politics of Racism: The Uprooting of Japanese Canadians during the Second World War.* Toronto: Lorimer, 1981.

Suzuki, Peter. "Anthropologists in the Wartime Camps for Japanese Americans: A Documentary Study." *Dialectical Anthropology* 6:1 (1981): 23–60.

———. "For the Sake of Inter-University Comity: The Attempted Suppression by the University of California of Morton Grodzins' *Americans Betrayed.*" In Ichioka, ed., *Views from Within,* 95–123.

———. "University of California Japanese Evacuation and Resettlement Study: A Prolegomenon." *Dialectical Anthropology* 10:3 (1986): 189–213.

Takahashi, Jere. *Nisei/Sansei: Shifting Japanese American Identities and Politics.* Philadelphia: Temple University Press, 1997.

Takezawa, Yasuko I. *Breaking the Silence: Redress and Japanese American Ethnicity.* Ithaca, NY: Cornell University Press, 1995.

———. "Children of Inmates: The Effects of the Redress Movement among Third Generation Japanese Americans." *Qualitative Sociology* 14:1 (1991): 39–56.

Tashima, A. Wallace. "Play It Again, Uncle Sam." In Muller, ed., "Judgments Judged and Wrongs Remembered," 7–14.

tenBroek, Jacobus, Edward N. Barnhart, and Floyd W. Matson. *Prejudice, War,* and the Constitution: Causes and Consequences of the Evacuation of the Japanese Americans in World War II. Berkeley: University of California Press, 1954.

Thomas, Dorothy Swaine. *The Salvage*. With Charles Kikuchi and James Sakoda. Berkeley: University of California Press, 1952.

———. "Statistics in Social Research." *American Journal of Sociology* 35:1 (1929): 1–17.

Thomas, Dorothy Swaine, and Richard S. Nishimoto. *The Spoilage*. With Rosalie Hankey et al. Berkeley: University of California Press, 1946.

Thomas, William I., and Florian Znaniecki. *The Polish Peasant in Europe and America*. Chicago: University of Chicago Press, 1918.

Ty, Eleanor, and Donald Goellnicht. "Introduction." In Eleanor Ty and Donald Goellnicht, eds., *Asian North American Identities: Beyond the Hyphen*, 1–14. Bloomington: Indiana University Press, 2004.

Ubyssey staff. *Return: A Commemorative Yearbook in Honour of the Japanese Canadian Students of 1942*. Vancouver: University of British Columbia, 2012.

U.S. Commission on Civil Rights. *Equal Opportunity in Suburbia*. Washington, D.C.: Government Publications Office, 1974.

U.S. Commission on Wartime Relocation and Internment of Civilians. *Personal Justice Denied: Report of the Commission on Wartime Relocation and Internment of Civilians*. Washington, D.C.: Government Publications Office, 1982.

———. *Personal Justice Denied, Part II: Recommendations*. Washington, D.C., 1983.

Wegars, Priscilla. *Imprisoned in Paradise: Japanese Internee Road Workers at the World War II Kooskia Internment Camp*. Moscow, ID: Asian American Comparative Collective/University of Idaho, 2010.

Weglyn, Michi. *Years of Infamy: The Untold Story of America's Concentration Camps*. New York: Morrow, 1976.

Weyergraf-Serra, Clara, and Martha Buskirk, eds. *The Destruction of Tilted Arc*. Cambridge, MA: MIT Press, 1991.

Wood, Alexandra L. "Challenging History: Public Education and Reluctance to Remember the Japanese Canadian Experience in British Columbia." *Historical Studies in Education/Revue d'histoire de l'éducation* 25:2 (2013): 65–85.

Wu, Ellen. *The Color of Success: Asian Americans and the Origins of the Model Minority*. Princeton, NJ: Princeton University Press, 2013.

Wu, Judy Tzu-Chun. *Radicals on the Road: Internationalism, Orientalism, and Feminism during the Vietnam Era*. Ithaca, NY: Cornell University Press, 2013.

Yamamoto, Eric K. "White (House) Lies: Why the Public Must Compel the Courts to Hold the President Accountable for National Security Abuses." In Muller, ed., "Judgments Judged and Wrongs Remembered," 285–339.

Yanagisako, Sylvia J. *Transforming the Past: Tradition and Kinship among Japanese Americans*. Stanford, CA: Stanford University Press, 1985.

Yang Murray, Alice. *Historical Memories of the Japanese American Internment and the Struggle for Redress*. Stanford, CA: Stanford University Press, 2008.

Yu, Henry. *Thinking Orientals: Migration, Contact, and Exoticism in Modern America*. Oxford: Oxford University Press, 2001.

———. "Towards a Pacific History of the Americas." In Yu and Beauregard, eds., "Pacific Canada," xi–xix.

Yu, Henry, and Guy Beauregard, eds. "Pacific Canada: Beyond the 49th Parallel." Special issue of *Amerasia Journal* 33:2 (2007).

Zich, Arthur. "Japanese Americans: Home at Last." *National Geographic* 169:4 (1986): 512–539.

INTERVIEWS

Furutani, Warren. Interviewed by Karen M. Inouye, Sacramento, CA, June 26, 2012.

Kashima, Tetsuden. Interviewed by Karen M. Inouye, Seattle, WA, April 19, 2013.

Kitagawa, Mary. Interviewed by Karen M. Inouye, Vancouver, BC, May 30, 2012.

Korematsu-Haigh, Karen. Interviewed by Neal Conan, January 31, 2012. http://www.npr.org/2012/01/31/146149345/the-legacy-of-civil-rights-leader-fred-korematsu.

Mineta, Norman. Interviewed by Tom Ikeda, July 4, 2008. Denshō Archive, Norman Mineta Collection.

Oshiro, Roy. Interviewed by Karen M. Inouye, Vancouver, BC, May 31, 2012.Uyeno, Teiso Edward. Interviewed by Karen M. Inouye, Vancouver, BC, May 30, 2012.

Index

Page numbers in *italics* indicate illustrations; those followed by "n" refer to endnotes.